ISRAEL'S RELATIONS WITH THE EAST EUROPEAN STATES

From Disruption (1967)
to Resumption (1989–91)

Israel's Relations with the East European States

From Disruption (1967) to Resumption (1989–91)

YOSEF GOVRIN

VALLENTINE MITCHELL
LONDON • PORTLAND, OR

First published in 2011 by Vallentine Mitchell

Middlesex House,	920 NE 58th Avenue, Suite 300
29/45 High Street, Edgware,	Portland, Oregon,
Middlesex HA8 7UU, UK	97213-3786 USA

www.vmbooks.com

Yosef Govrin, *Israel's Relations with the East European States: From Disruption in 1967 to Resumption in 1989-1991*
Copyright © 2009 Yosef Govrin
Hebrew Language Copyright
All Right Reserved
The Hebrew University Magnes Press

British Library Cataloguing in Publication Data

Govrin, Yosef.
Israel's relations with the East European states : from disruption to resumption.
1. Israel—Foreign relations—Europe, Eastern. 2. Europe, Eastern—Foreign relations—Israel. 3. Israel—History—1967-1993. 4. Europe, Eastern—History—1989-
I. Title
327.5′694047-dc22

ISBN 978 0 85303 893 1 (cloth)

Library of Congress Cataloging-in-Publication Data
A catalog record has been applied for

Printed in Great Britain by the MPG Books Group, Bodmin and King's Lynn

Contents

Preface

Dear Reader

In a 'Letter to the Reader' published in my book *Israeli-Soviet Relations 1953–1967. From Confrontation to Disruption* (London and Portland, OR: Frank Cass, 1998), I described the humiliating situation in which Israel's diplomatic staff in Moscow – including myself as first secretary of the Embassy – found themselves on Saturday, 10 June 1967. This was the moment when the deputy foreign minister of the Soviet Union handed over to Israel's ambassador in Moscow the Soviet government's note informing the government of Israel of its decision to sever diplomatic and consular relations with Israel, following the events of the Six Day War. This announcement was the culmination of Soviet political support – in addition to massive military support – for the Arab countries in their fight against Israel.

On that day, at noon, I was walking from our residence to the Embassy through the central streets of Moscow, where I encountered dozens of cars with loudspeakers informing the public of the Soviet Union of its breach of relations with Israel. For a moment it seemed as if the Soviet Union was declaring war against Israel. Upon reaching the street where the Embassy stood, I could hardly make my way through. Hundreds, if not thousands, of workers, brought in from different enterprises in Moscow, were blocking the entrance to the Embassy. They were carrying anti-Israel slogans, and shouting 'Down with Israel' every few minutes. When I finally succeeded, with great effort, in entering the Embassy building and after having joined the rest of the members of our diplomatic staff, we were looking through the window at the outrageous mob outside the gate. It was a frightful scene, as if they were going at any moment to break into the courtyard and then into the building itself. It was hours before they left, and not before we were instructed several times by the Protocol Department of the Soviet Foreign Ministry to pull down our national flag. We did so, at sunset, singing, at the same time, our national anthem *Hatikva* ('The Hope').

A similar experience was encountered by all of Israel's diplomatic missions accredited to the East European communist states (except Romania) that followed closely the path of the Soviet Union in announcing the severance of their diplomatic relations with Israel, on the same or the next day.

From 1976–85 I was director of the East European Department of Israel's Ministry of Foreign Affairs in Jerusalem. Israel's relations were mainly focusing then on Romania, under the leadership of Nicolae Ceauşescu, who rejected the Soviet pressure to sever Romania's diplomatic relations with Israel. As for the rest of the East European communist states, we tried to exploit every possible loophole in order to develop mutual relations, in all possible fields, and work towards the possibility of their renewal, on the diplomatic level, in the near future. And, indeed, we partly and gradually succeeded, as described in this book.

In the years 1985–93, after having concluded my mission as Israel's ambassador to Romania, I became deputy director general of Israel's Ministry of Foreign Affairs, with responsibility for Central and East Europe. In this capacity and against the background of the political upheavals of the East European regimes, we succeeded in conducting the processes – some short, some prolonged – to a satisfactory end, by having renewed Israel's diplomatic relations with the East European states that were disrupted following the Six Day War in 1967, and to the establishment – for the first time – of diplomatic relations with Albania and the fifteen Republics of the Former Soviet Union. Later, the political discussions held between Israel's representatives and the representatives of the German Democratic Republic (GDR) on the possibility of establishing diplomatic relations between the respective states led nowhere and moreover, shortly afterwards, the GDR ceased to exist as an independent state due to the reunification of Germany.

The sources of this book are mainly based on my notes, following my discussions and those of Israel's representatives abroad with our East European counterparts, on the official announcements and declarations of the East European states, on information released by press agencies and on the reports of our colleagues in Israel's Foreign Ministry, in Jerusalem and abroad. It is my pleasant duty to thank all of them, wholeheartedly, and those who have read the relevant chapters of this book, noting their comments, made from their particular perspectives and specialisms. They are the ambassadors Moshe Melamed, Mordechai Palzur, Yoram Shani, Michael Shilo, Yoel Sher and Dr Moshe Yegar, as well as Benjamin Anolik, director general of the Janos Korczak Association, Israel, and the writer and historian, Raoul Teitelbaum.

My profound gratitude goes also to the Magnes Press of the Hebrew University of Jerusalem for publishing the Hebrew edition of this book in 2009; to the Abba Eban Center for Israeli Diplomacy of the Harry S. Truman Research Institute for the Advancement of Peace, and to the Leonid Nevzlin Research Center for Russian and East European Jewry, Hebrew University of Jerusalem, for their kind support; to Vallentine Mitchell of London and Portland, Oregon, for publishing the English edition of the book; to its editor Heather Marchant in London, and to Nigel Wheale for his copy-editing skills; and to Fern Seckbach, in Jerusalem, for her important collaboration in preparing the English text.

Finally, my deep gratitude goes to my wife, Dr Hanna Govrin, who has always assisted me in implementing my diplomatic missions, in Israel and abroad.

Yosef Govrin, PhD

1. Israel's Diplomatic Relations with Eastern Europe: An Overview

Between the years 1989 to 1991 all member states of the East European Communist Bloc – Bulgaria, Czechoslovakia, Hungary, Poland, the Soviet Union and Yugoslavia – which had severed their relations with Israel following the Six Day War in June 1967, renewed diplomatic links gradually in the course of these years. They were joined by Albania which established diplomatic relations with Israel for the first time in August 1991,[1] and by a series of talks (1989/90) also held for the first time, between Israel and East Germany (GDR, the German Democratic Republic) with the aim of establishing diplomatic relations between them. This was a possibility which Israel did not pursue, owing to East Germany's refusal to bear its responsibility in paying restitution (as was the case with West Germany) to the surviving Jewish victims of its former Nazi regime, and in view of the subsequent process of Germany's reunification.[2] After the dismemberment of the Soviet Union into fifteen independent republics (December 1991), Israel established diplomatic relations with each of them.

The historiography of Israel's foreign policy concerning its relations with the East European states has concentrated mainly on Israel's relations with the Soviet Union from disruption to their resumption,[3] and there was almost no research on Israel's relations with the rest of the East European Communist states during the same period. This attitude can be explained by the following factors: First, the

1

East European countries of the Soviet Bloc (except Romania) were considered to be satellites of the Soviet Union in all matters that concerned foreign policy, so that the decisive factor seemed to be, not the policies of the individual countries themselves, but the Soviet Union's dominating foreign policy. Second, as the Soviet Union conducted the confrontation with the Western Bloc, and while its Middle East policy influenced – sometimes decisively – the Arab-Israeli conflict, during the cold war period, between both blocs, East and West, it seemed somehow natural that the East European Soviet Bloc states were actually implementing the Soviet policy and not their own. Third, on account of the worldwide struggle that Israel led for the right of Soviet Jewish citizens to emigrate to Israel, and to enable those who chose not to emigrate to develop their national Jewish heritage, in the same way that the Soviet Union enabled its national minorities to do.

Thus, since the East European states strictly adhered to the harsh Soviet anti-Israel policy, both in the Middle East and in the international arena (except Romania), no research has been conducted, thus far, in Israel concerning any of these states or their separate relations with Israel during this period, from the collective disruption (June 1967) of diplomatic relations with Israel until their separate resumption (1989/91), though bilateral relations with Israel did continue, on a small scale, in the tourist, trade and cultural spheres. The same is true for their policies towards the local Jewish communities, which differed from one state to another, as well as between each state and the Soviet Union.

This book deals, consequently, for the first time in the historiography of Israel's foreign policy, with the separate stages and landmarks during the prolonged process which led the East European communist states from the disruption of their diplomatic relations with Israel to their resumption. The book also examines the process of the establishment of diplomatic relations with Albania for the first time, and the negotiations held between official representatives of Israel

2

and the GDR, which were conducted in the last years of the GDR's existence as an independent state, but especially during the last years of its existence (before it was united with the Federal Republic of Germany), with the aim of establishing diplomatic relations between their respective states. These political contacts aimed at the renewal of diplomatic relations and their establishment with Albania and the GDR may be regarded as the result of a combined process: on one hand, the gradual liberation of the East European states from their political dependence upon the Soviet Union, in transition to planning an independent foreign policy; on the other, the upheaval that took place in the regimes of each of the East European states, during their gradual transition from a communist regime to a liberal democratic one. This combined process might not have occurred if it had not been preceded by the reforms initiated in the Soviet Union by its leader, Mikhail Gorbachev,[4] in the social, economic and political fields,[5] and, if he had not outlined a foreign policy striving, most energetically, to put an end to the cold war between the Eastern and Western Blocs. This resulted in the shaping of a new era of cooperation between the Soviet Union and the West, aimed at reducing political and military tensions in the world and broadening the scope of mutual economic, scientific and technological relations. This policy had a decisive influence on the East European communist states by weakening their political dependence on the Soviet Union and by strengthening their ambition for an independent status. They were encouraged to introduce in their own states reforms similar to those of Gorbachev: the implementation of an internal liberal and democratic policy and an external policy suited to their national interests, drawing the right conclusions from their past mistakes. In this respect, one may distinguish three major motives characteristic to each of the East European states that had disrupted their diplomatic relations with Israel more than twenty years earlier, as follows.

3

First, they concluded that the severance of diplomatic relations with Israel was the result of an impetuous decision that did not contribute anything to a solution of the Arab-Israeli conflict. Nor did they reject the Israeli representatives' arguments that the severance of diplomatic relations between their respective countries, and the massive military, political and economic assistance that the Soviet Union and the East European states were giving to the PLO and to some of Israel's neighbours, in their struggle against the Jewish State, not only did not contribute to the settlement of the Arab-Israeli conflict but, on the contrary, helped to prolong it. Moreover, the severance of their diplomatic relations with Israel, followed by a malicious anti-Semitic and anti-Israel campaign similar to that of the Soviet Union caused them to be considered in the international arena, not only part and parcel of the Soviet Bloc, but also as states that adhered to the Soviet Union in its confrontation with the West, even if Israel and the Jewish world did not form part of the Western alliance during the cold war.

In this regard Romania – a member of the Soviet Bloc as well as a member of the Warsaw Pact that did not break its relations with Israel after the Six Day War – served as an exemplary resource. Romania could liaise between Israel and the Arab countries, since it maintained diplomatic relations with both protagonists in the conflict. Hence its prestige in the Arab world and the West was considerably higher than that of any other East European state. Israel well remembers its contribution, as the single country from the Soviet Bloc, to the peacemaking process between Egypt and Israel, through the encouragement of Egypt's President Anwar Sadat to visit Israel and by supporting the Israel-Egypt Peace Agreement. Romania was also the only member of the East European countries not to have voted in favour of the UN resolution that equated Zionism with racism; consequently, Romania enjoyed the appreciation of Israel, world Jewry and the West. In addition, Romania

4

cultivated its bilateral relations with the West and with Israel in all possible domains, thus serving its own national interests, once again, more than any of its neighbours. Contrary to the hostile attitude of the East European Bloc towards Israel in the Middle Eastern and international arena, the relations between Israel and Romania were constantly developing. The level of Romanian diplomatic representation was raised from the status of legation to that of embassy approximately one year after the severance of diplomatic relations between the East European states and Israel. Israel and Romania also established direct flight routes and shipping links between them. From time to time, Romania offered hospitality to prominent Israeli figures, including prime ministers, ministers of foreign affairs, ministers of trade and industry, tourism, communications, members of the Knesset (the Israeli parliament), heads of parties, writers and poets and other Israeli personalities. Israeli visitors to Romania topped the list of Western tourists to the country (relative to the size of its population). Romania permitted its Jewish citizens to emigrate to Israel, and during the Gorbachev era, Romania served as a conduit between the Soviet Union and Israel for Soviet Jewish citizens who were permitted to migrate to Israel. Romania was often praised by Israeli, world Jewish and Western leaders for all these contributions. The Jewish community of Romania was given the right to foster its national and traditional values in the religious, educational, cultural and social fields as well as the possibility of freely developing its relations with Israel and with Jewish communities and organizations in the world. The status of the Jewish communities in the rest of the Soviet Bloc countries, however, was by comparison poor and humiliating, as they were under permanent suspicion of maintaining contacts with the enemy. But here too the situation differed from state to state. The attitude towards the Jewish communities in Hungary, Bulgaria and Yugoslavia was more liberal than in Poland, Czechoslovakia, the Soviet

5

Union and the GDR. Often these communities were compelled by the local authorities to publish harsh anti-Israeli and anti-Zionist declarations.

Romania's deviation from Soviet policy towards Israel, China and West Germany, its open criticism of the Warsaw Pact armies' invasion of Czechoslovakia and Afghanistan, encouraged the image of a state that conducted an autonomous foreign policy within the Soviet Bloc, and for that Romania gained economic and political dividends in the USA and the West.[6]

The second motive was the conclusion reached by the East European states that by being cut off from Israel, they were prevented from developing economic ties and cooperation in the fields of technology and agriculture for the advancement of their own economies, bearing in mind Israel's positive image in the world, particularly in the USA and the West, due to its achievements in the fields of economics, science, education, culture, technology, medicine and security – despite its being in a war situation with some of its neighbours. Also, the existence of an influential Jewish community, strongly supporting Israel in the USA and the West, strengthened Israel's importance in their minds, fostering the idea that 'the road to the developed West, especially the road to Washington, leads through Israel'. As we shall see in the following chapters devoted to each of the states that renewed its relations with Israel, they all had expectations of receiving economic, scientific and technological assistance from Israel as well as from world Jewry.

The third motive was the awareness that by breaking off their relations with Israel they had removed themselves from the peacemaking process in the Middle East. This was especially true of the Soviet Union as a superpower when compared with the USA, which maintained relations with both sides of the Arab-Israeli conflict. The harsh anti-Israeli policy of the Communist Bloc countries – with the exception of Romania – especially after the Six Day War, and the intensive military support they gave to some Arab states and the PLO, which openly strived for the destruction of Israel, prevented the Soviet Union, its satellites and Yugoslavia from playing an objective role in resolving the Arab-Israel conflict, although they declared more than once that they had never denied Israel's right to existence.

All East European states (including Romania) sided with the Soviet threefold formula during the 1970s and 1980s for resolving the conflict, which called for the following:

1. Israel's withdrawal from all territories occupied in 1967.
2. The right of self-determination for the Palestinian people, including their right to establish their own independent state.
3. Security guarantees maintained by the UN Security Council for the states in the area.

Israel rejected this formula, claiming that two members of the Security Council – the Soviet Union and China – did not maintain diplomatic relations with Israel, and that it did not regard the PLO as an equal counter-partner for political talks as long as the PLO held fast to its Palestinian Covenant, which denied Israel's right to existence.

In July 1987 the Soviet Union presented a slightly different six-principle formula, with the full support of the East European states, calling this time for peace between Israel and the Palestinians, but Israel rejected this too on the same grounds.

From 1989 the Soviet Union, under Gorbachev's leadership – with the full support of the East European states – focused its position on calling for recognition of the principle of 'balanced interests' between, on the one hand, security for Israel, and on the other, rights for Palestinians, without repeating its previous formulas. The key element of this proposal – and that of the East European states – was the call to convene an international conference to settle the Arab-Israeli conflict under the auspices of the permanent members of the Security Council, without forcing the participants, Israel and the PLO 'as the legitimate representative of the Palestinian people' and Arab states, to accept its resolutions.

Mikhail Gorbachev initiated the policies of 'glasnost' (maximal publicity, openness and transparency in the activities of all government institutions, together with freedom of information) and 'perestroika' (political and economic reforms) in 1987. He had introduced, for the first time in the history of the Soviet Union, reforms in political and economic management (agricultural and industrial enterprises) throughout the Soviet Union, for the efficient improvement of the central planning systems, aimed at accelerating economic and industrial development, and increasing their production by combining private and cooperative economic activity in agriculture. Gorbachev also introduced freedom of expression in newspapers and other communications media, free competitive elections throughout the Soviet Union to choose regional representatives of the (ruling) Communist Party of the Soviet Union and the 'Congress of People' (considered to be the new parliamentary body, that was intended to elect the members of the 'Supreme Soviet').

At a later stage (1990), a resolution was adopted by the representatives of the Congress to enable additional parties to be elected to the Supreme Soviet, removing the domination of the Party, and introducing multi-party parliamentary representation. At the same time, Gorbachev outlined a policy of reducing the inter-bloc tension by initiating intensive negotiations with the USA and the West, striving to improve the Soviet Union's relations with the USA and other world powers, including China, together with the establishment of diplomatic relations with South Korea and South Africa and of closer relations with Israel.

The policies which Gorbachev initiated made a powerful impact on the East European states, which were also striving to lead an independent foreign policy according to national and economic interests, such as developing their relations with the West and with Israel. In this respect, not only did they encounter no objection from the Soviet Union, but on the contrary, the Soviet Union welcomed this initiative. Gorbachev's new internal and foreign policies had, consequently, a decisive influence on the process of democratization in each of the East European states (including Albania and the GDR), according to the political circumstances dominant in each of them, following the ideological confrontation between the conservatives – followers of the communist regime – on one hand, who lost their parliamentary power and their influence within their own nations, and on the other hand, the liberal forces professing the ideas of glasnost and perestroika. These liberal tendencies, widely supported by the majority of the people within their nations, were striving for a broad development of their states' relations with the West and with Israel. These new processes were the factors that accelerated, sometimes at a short range (Hungary, Czechoslovakia, Poland) and sometimes at a longer range (Bulgaria, Yugoslavia, the GDR), after the free elections held in each of these states and, consequently, after the removal of the previous (communist) leadership from the respective governments. The rhythm of the renewal of their diplomatic relations with Israel was thus dictated by the change of regime in each of the East European states, as well as by the fear of some states (Bulgaria, the Soviet Union, Yugoslavia) of a damaging Arab reaction. For these reasons the process of the renewal of diplomatic relations with Israel lasted about two years.

Some of the East European states had received the consent of the Soviet Union before they started the rapprochement process with Israel. Since there were also others who feared that their relations with some Arab states would be badly affected if relations with Israel were renewed, a formula was invented, after a long process of negotiations to renew relations in three stages: first, by exchanging mutual representations under the auspices of the states who were representing their interests (Poland, Hungary, the Soviet Union); second, the establishment of independent missions at consular level (Poland, the Soviet Union); third, renewal of full diplomatic relations. Hungary was the first to complete the process in September 1989; they were followed by Czechoslovakia and Poland in February 1990; Bulgaria in May 1990; Yugoslavia and the Soviet Union in October 1991 – all of them at ambassadorial level. It should be noted, however, that during the years of the severance of diplomatic relations, and particularly from the mid-1970s onwards, bilateral relations were cultivated in the commercial, economic, cultural and tourism fields, between Israel and the majority of the East European states. This had taken place, however, on a limited scale, which did not correspond to the large potential that remained unexploited. Israel, for its part, took advantage of every opportunity that presented itself in this process. However, bilateral relations were largely extended in due course, constituting an important basis towards the renewal of diplomatic relations between the East European states and Israel. But whereas Hungary, Czechoslovakia and Poland were the first to renew their diplomatic relations with Israel, soon followed by Bulgaria, Yugoslavia and the Soviet Union were remarkably the last states to renew them.

YUGOSLAVIA

Yugoslavia was not a member of the Warsaw Treaty and did not belong to the Soviet East European Bloc. It was, however, part of the Communist Bloc, under the leadership of Broz Tito, who had initiated the severance of diplomatic relations with Israel as a result of his friendship with the Egyptian president, Gamal Abdel Nasser, out of solidarity with him in his fight against Israel, following the Six Day War. Another reason for Tito's position, in this regard, was his ambitious striving to lead the Non-Aligned Movement that conducted a clear-cut pro-Arab and anti-Israeli policy in every aspect of the Arab-Israel conflict.

After Tito's death in 1980, the rotating Yugoslavian leadership surprisingly was not inclined to deviate from his policy towards Israel, or perhaps it did not have the appropriate authority to do so, in the absence of a strong leader such as Tito. The paradox was, however, that both Nasser and Tito were no longer alive when Egypt established diplomatic relations with Israel, whereas Yugoslavia's diplomatic relations with Israel continued to be disrupted. Two additional aspects might also be taken in consideration: Yugoslavia's fear that resumption of diplomatic relations with Israel might endanger its economic interests in the Arab states as well as its status within the Non-Aligned Movement. Its orientation towards this movement remained incomprehensible, even when the movement's importance lessened with the rapprochement between the Eastern and Western Blocs. It may well be that when Yugoslavia finally decided to resume diplomatic relations with Israel, it became clear that its fears were unfounded and that the severance of its diplomatic relations with Israel prevented it from enjoying a fruitful cooperation with Israel that would clearly be in its own interests. It was also apparent that relations with the Arab states were not impaired for the rest of the East European states, which had renewed their diplomatic relations with Israel, including the Soviet Union, at consular level: so it was that Yugoslavia remained the single state among the East European countries that had not yet decided to renew its diplomatic relations with Israel. Yugoslavia's final decision to do so in 1991 was taken at a time when it needed the support of the international community in order to ensure its continued existence as a federal republic, and as a result of Croatia and Slovenia's declarations of independence. However, the renewal of diplomatic relations with Israel did not prevent its subsequent dismemberment as a federal republic.

THE SOVIET UNION

The two main factors that characterized Israeli-Soviet relations from the mid-1950s onwards were (a) the Soviet involvement in the Middle East, and (b) Israel's worldwide struggle for the rights of Soviet Jewry. Both factors lost their specific importance during Gorbachev's rule.

a) There was evidence at the time that the Soviet Union was attempting to influence the PLO to moderate its extreme position towards Israel. The Soviet Union also had some influence on Syria's president, Hafez al-Assad, in restraining his ambitions to reach a strategic military balance with Israel. From this point of view, there was a positive attitude on the part of Israel to the Soviet Union's policy in the Middle East. From the mid-1950s, the Soviet Union had gradually inflamed the Arab-Israeli conflict, believing that a tense situation might ensure its strategic foothold in the Middle East more than a peace arrangement that might have strengthened security and stability in the region. Moreover, the process of rapprochement between the Soviet Union and the USA, by putting an end to the cold war between the Eastern and Western Blocs, diminished tensions in the Middle East to a considerable degree. The hope that closer cooperation between the superpowers would ease territorial and political conflict throughout the world was making some progress. This development led to the Madrid Peace Conference, for the settlement of the Arab-Israeli conflict (1991) under the auspices of the Soviet Union and the USA and with Israel's full agreement, in view of the positive changes that marked the Soviet Union's policy towards Israel.[7]

b) During Gorbachev's rule a radical change seemed to have occurred concerning the national and judicial status of the Jewish minority in the Soviet Union. Permission was given to Jews to emigrate to Israel and Soviet Jews were allowed to organize themselves within the frameworks of national and cultural associations and to revive Jewish religious and secular institutions; these new freedoms brought an end to the need to struggle for their rights.

The process of normalizing Soviet-Israeli relations was carried out in three stages: first, the exchange of missions at consular level, under the auspices of those embassies that represented their interests – Israel, at the Dutch Embassy in Moscow, and the Soviet Union via the Finnish Embassy in Tel Aviv (1987/88); second, official mutual representations at the level of General Consulates (1990); third, renewal of diplomatic relations (October 1991). This occurred simultaneously with Israel's consent to participate in the Madrid Peace Conference, given to Boris Pankin, Soviet Foreign Minister, in the course of his visit in Jerusalem.

Israel was very interested in re-establishing its representation in Moscow, particularly in view of the need to deal with the great wave of Soviet Jews who were applying for immigration visas to Israel. This is why Israel accepted the three stages as the best available alternative. Yet, in view of the radical changes that took place in the internal and external policies of the Soviet Union, the question arose as to why the Soviet Union would require the three stages in order to advance its relations with Israel? The answer lies in the following presumptions: first, the influence of the pro-Arab apparatus in the Soviet administration, including the staff of the Soviet Foreign Ministry, who argued that the full renewal of diplomatic relations with Israel might cause harm to Soviet status in the Arab world, mainly in the economic and political fields. Second, the exaggerated tendency to take into account the negative reaction of the millions of Muslims in the Asian Republics of the Soviet Union (a factor which had not been considered in the past), whose national attachment to the Arab and Muslim states in their geographical vicinity was supposed to be growing. Third, the intention to hold on to the 'ultimate card' to compel Israel, in view of its great interest in the renewal of diplomatic relations with the Soviet Union, to agree to the convening of the Madrid Peace Conference.

The Soviet Union renewed its diplomatic relations with Israel not only as a consequence of the radical political and economic reforms under Gorbachev's leadership, including his positive policy towards Israel, but also and mainly because Israel gave its consent to the convening of the Madrid Peace Conference under the auspices of the two superpowers, and with the participation of Israel, Egypt, Jordan, Syria and the PLO, which was included in the Jordanian delegation. It was not just a coincidence that the two announcements, first on the renewal of diplomatic relations between the Soviet Union and Israel, and second, the convening of the Madrid Peace Conference, were made simultaneously by US Foreign Minister James Baker and Soviet Foreign Minister Boris Pankin, during their visit in Jerusalem. Their declarations in Jerusalem were more than a symbolic act of mutual cooperation between both superpowers, who had together found a common denominator for implementing a central and equal role in the peace conference. In the course of the conference (30 October 1991) the Soviet Union presented a new formula for the solution of the Arab-Israeli conflict, which corresponded, to a large degree, to the policy of dispelling inter-bloc tension by searching for common ways to solve regional conflicts. The new Soviet formula stated:

1. The peacemaking process became possible thanks to the end of the cold war and the cooperation and coordination between the Soviet Union and the USA that would continue by giving advice and auspices, without applying compulsory means on the participants.
2. Security Council Resolution 242 should apply to all sections.
3. The right of the Palestinians (the PLO was not mentioned) for self-determination is based on the UN Charter.
4. The settlement of the conflict would be carried out in stages.
5. The question of Jerusalem, as it is sensitive and complicated, will be discussed at the end of the peacemaking process and not at its beginning.

6. The stopping of the settlements (in the administered territories) will be considered as a gesture of Israel towards the Arabs and will be positively received by them.

Though the Madrid formula was adopted by the rest of the East European states, in fact after the renewal of their diplomatic relations with Israel, they showed diminishing interest in the Arab-Israel conflict, and focused increasingly on advancing their national interests, including the rapid development of their relations with Israel.

Thus ended the era of more than twenty years' disruption of Israel's diplomatic relations with the East European states, following the Six Day War, and their establishment with Albania. This history formed an intrinsic part of the cold war between the Eastern and Western Blocs, which brought more damage to these countries than benefit to the Middle East, in the international arena, or in the field of bilateral relations with Israel. The opening of the new era of the relations between Israel and the East European states was characterized by very friendly and frequent contacts on all possible levels – political, social, cultural, economic, academic and educational – as well as by extensive and fruitful cooperation in all practical domains, including close cooperation and coordination in the European and in the international arenas. The transition in the East European states from communist to liberal, democratic regimes was also followed by granting the Jews, in all these countries, the right of unhindered migration to Israel, as well as the right of the Jewish communities to develop freely Jewish education and Jewish traditions and culture, including the possibility of fostering relations with Jewish communities and organizations throughout the world. Yet, the Jewish populations are gradually declining, mainly because of factors such as intermarriage and emigration. At the same time we are also witnessing a wave of resurgent anti-Semitism, drawing on traditional stereotypes and beliefs from both right and left-wing extremists, that the Jews were responsible for the establishment of the communist regimes, while the left accuses the Jews of causing the fall of the communist regimes. This phenomenon is characteristic mainly of the post-communist states. However, it should be noted that the democratic leadership of all these states sharply condemns these manifestations, although they have not managed to uproot them.[8]

NOTES

1. Y. Govrin, 'Annals of Israeli-Albanian Contacts on Establishing Diplomatic Relations', *Jewish Political Studies Review*, 17, 34 (Fall 2005), pp.67–74.
2. Y. Govrin, 'Paving a Path from Pankow to Jerusalem: GDR-Israel Relations 1989–1990', *The Israel Journal of Foreign Affairs*, 2, 3 (2008), pp.141–57.
3. A. Dagan, *Moscow and Jerusalem* (London: Abelard-Schuman, 1970); A. Yodfat, *The Soviet Union and the Middle East* (Tel Aviv: Misrad Ha'Bitachon, 1973) [Hebrew]; A. Ben-Tzur, *Soviet Factors and the Six Day War* (Tel Aviv: Sifriat Poalim, 1973) [Hebrew]; Y. Ro'i, 'Soviet Policies and Attitudes toward Israel, 1948–1978', *Soviet Jewish Affairs*, 8, 1 (1978), pp. 35–45, and *The Limits of Power, Soviet Policy in the Middle East* (London: Croom Helm, 1979); Y. Govrin, *Israeli-Soviet Relations 1953–1967. From Confrontation to Disruption* (London: Frank Cass, 2002); M. Zak, *Israel and the Soviet Union: Forty Years of Dialogue* (Tel Aviv: Sifriat Hapoalim, 1988) [Hebrew]; A. Levin, *Envoy to Moscow. Memoirs of an Israeli Ambassador 1988–1992* (London: Frank Cass, 1996); M. Oren, *Six Days of War* (Oxford: Oxford University Press, 2002).
4. Y. Govrin, 'Mikhail Gorbachev', in *Encyclopaedia Hebraica*, Supplement vol.3 (Tel Aviv: Sifriat Poalim, 1995) [Hebrew].
5. M. Gorbachev, *Perestroika* (Tel Aviv: Sifriat Maariv, 1988) [Hebrew].
6. Y. Govrin, *Israeli-Romanian Relations at the End of the Ceausescu Era, as Observed by Israel's Ambassador to Romania 1985–1989* (London: Frank Cass, 2002), pp.299–334.
7. E. Bentzur, *The Road to Peace Leads through Madrid* (Tel Aviv: Sifrei Hemed, Yediot Achronot, 1997) [Hebrew].
8. Y. Govrin, 'Anti-Semitic Trends in the Post-Communist East European States', *Jewish Political Studies Review*, 15 (Fall 2003), pp.141–9.

2. Israeli–Albanian Political Contacts on the Establishment of Diplomatic Relations Between Them[1]

SWIFT RECOGNITION, NO RELATIONS

Albania was the only country in the East European Communist Bloc that declined to establish diplomatic, trade and economic relations with Israel throughout the cold war era, from the time it recognized Israel de jure in 1949 until the collapse of the Albanian Communist regime in 1991. This unwillingness contradicted the friendly tone of a telegram sent on 16 April 1949 from Albania's Prime Minister and Foreign Minister Enver Hoxha to Israel's Foreign Minister Moshe Sharett, which accompanied the granting of official recognition to Israel. The telegram stated,

> The government of the People's Republic of Albania along with the Albanian people have been following with interest the efforts the Jewish people have invested in the restoration of their independence and their sovereignty. They are happy to see that these efforts have been crowned with success with Israel's declaration of its statehood.[2]

Albania's recognition of Israel was given in response to a letter from Sharett to Hoxha dated 13 February 1949.[3] Israel's request to Albania for recognition was sent nine

17

months after Israel declaration of independence, unlike similar approaches that Israel made to other East European countries shortly after that event; no explanation has been found for this.[4] It is possible that Sharett, together with the heads of his ministry, felt that approaching Albania sooner would have been inappropriate as long as Hoxha was waging a struggle to establish his rule there.[5] However, Albania's swift and positive response in April 1949 should be seen in light of three factors:

1. Albania belonged to the Communist Bloc led by the Soviet Union, which supported Israel's establishment, and was the first country to grant it formal recognition.
2. Albania's small Jewish community was saved during the Nazi occupation, thanks to protection offered by the Albanians, the majority of whom were Muslims.[6]
3. Hoxha had led the Albanian underground that fought against the Italian and German occupation (1939–1944) of his country.

Nevertheless, despite recognizing Israel's independence, Albania did not respond to repeated Israeli approaches to establish diplomatic, commercial and economic relations. On the contrary, Albania regarded Israel with great hostility, especially following the Six Day War when the Communist Bloc countries, except Romania, severed diplomatic ties with Israel. Albania did so even though it was then involved in a bitter dispute with the Soviet Union and Yugoslavia. Its attitude only changed in the late 1980s when the democratization process began.

ISRAEL'S REJECTED OVERTURES

What explains the fact that, whereas Albania officially recognized Israel, it refrained from establishing relations with it for forty-two years? The first available evidence on Albania's position regarding relations is found in a memorandum from Shlomo Leibovitch of the Research Department of Israeli's Foreign Ministry, dated 15 December 1954, to the head of the East European Department. Leibovitch reported that the French Foreign Ministry had recently become interested in diplomatic relations between Israel and Albania, but Tirana had informed Paris that 'This possibility has never been discussed.'[7]

Israel's Foreign Ministry documents show that its representatives made several overtures to Albanian officials between 1955 and 1967:

1. Reuven Nal, chargé d'affaires of Israel's legation in Sofia, visited Tirana in July 1955. In a letter to the head of the East European Department dated 9 December 1956, he mentions the visit and says its purpose was 'First to establish the fact of a visit of an official representative of the Israeli Foreign Ministry in Albania, and second, to try to forge contact with the Albanian government to raise the question of Jewish immigration to Israel. Officially, the visit was to explore the possibility of opening commercial relations.'[8]

2. In May 1958, the Israeli legation in Prague forwarded an official communication to the Albanian legation there with a proposal to establish Israeli-Albanian commercial relations. No response was ever received.[9] In addition, Shmuel Bendor, Israel's ambassador in Prague, spoke with his Albanian counterpart there about commercial ties; again, no reply was forthcoming.[10]

3. On 3 September 1961, Katriel Salmon, Israel's ambassador in Bucharest, was instructed to request Albania's approval to be appointed non-resident ambassador in Tirana. The appeal was delivered to Albania's ambassador in Bucharest, but again there was no response.[11] In a report dated 9 October 1961 to the head of the East European Department, concerning his conversation on this subject with the Albanian ambassador, Salmon says he felt a coolness toward the idea. In

his opinion, there were three reasons: (a) the Albanian ambassador could not react differently until he received instructions; (b) possibly because of Albania's tense relations with other countries in the Eastern Bloc, its hosting a non-resident Israeli ambassador would be resented; and (c) Albania's special relationship with the People's Republic of China and with the United Arab Republic since the 1956 Sinai Campaign made it unwilling to develop ties with Israel.[12]

With hindsight it seems that Ambassador Salmon's evaluation was correct. The Albanian ambassador was apparently aware of the fact that his country was not interested in relations with Israel. Albania was then in conflict with its Eastern Bloc neighbours based on ideological opposition – initially Stalinist, now Maoist – to the domestic policy of Yugoslavia's President Tito, who supported a more liberal economy than that which was customary in the Soviet Bloc, while Hoxha, the ruler of Albania, was concerned that Tito might introduce his own doctrine into Hoxha's country. In addition, Albania strongly opposed the de-Stalinization process taking place in the Soviet Union, and as a result even broke off diplomatic relations with Moscow – an exceptional phenomenon in the socialist camp. For these reasons there was complete justification for Ambassador Salmon's premise that accrediting a non-resident Israeli representative whose permanent service was in this 'camp' would not be agreeable to Albania. Yet we have actual proof that if Israel had accredited its representative in Tirana from his permanent posting in one of the Western countries then Albania might have agreed to Israel's proposal. Albania's relations with the West, as we know, were also in a state of serious political confrontation and whoever supported US policy – such as Israel – was certainly considered unacceptable. Given its isolation from both East and West, Albania forged ties, instead, with the People's Republic of China, which maintained no relations with Israel and headed those opposing the Soviet Union in the communist world.

In addition to all these factors there was the Sinai Campaign involving Israel's joint military operation with France and Britain in their war against Egypt, which was condemned by the Arab world, the Communist Bloc, and the non-aligned nations, while Israel was presented in its propaganda as the spearhead of Western imperialism. In light of all this, it seems that Israel's proposal to establish relations with Albania did not coincide with Albania's policy. Yet as memories of the Sinai Campaign receded and Israel withdrew to its pre-war borders, it was thought in the Foreign Ministry in Jerusalem that it was worthwhile continuing with the initiative towards establishing connections with Albania.

ADDITIONAL ATTEMPTS

There were subsequently three additional Israeli initiatives, apparently influenced by a statement in the official newspaper of Albania's Communist Party, *Zeri i Poppulitt*, on 9 January 1962. Albania, the paper said, wanted to establish diplomatic, economic and trade relations with all the capitalist countries, especially with its neighbours, on the basis of peaceful coexistence. This avowal, accompanied by moves to open commercial ties with Italy, France, West Germany, the Middle East and Africa – but excluding the United States – seems to have led the Israeli Foreign Ministry to renew its – albeit futile – efforts to forge relations with Albania:

1. In October 1962, the head of the East European Department toured the areas under his jurisdiction. The Albanian government refused to grant him a permit to enter the country.[13]
2. In 1964, Israel's ambassador to Romania, Eliezer Doron, was instructed to discuss diplomatic ties with his Albanian counterpart in Bucharest. However, after the Albanian ambassador reported on the talk to his foreign minister, no reply was received.[14]

21

3. In February 1967, Doron renewed his contacts with the Albanian ambassador. Albania did not respond to this approach either.[15]

This was Israel's last initiative to establish diplomatic and economic ties with Albania. In the wake of the Six Day War in 1967, Albania joined the other Eastern Bloc countries – except Romania – together with the Arab states in their stridently anti-Israel policy, both at home and abroad.

On 19 August 2002, I asked Bashkim Dino, formerly Albania's ambassador to Israel and head of its Foreign Ministry's Middle East Department toward the end of communist rule – who had also been present with me at the ceremony of the signing of the memorandum on the establishment of diplomatic relations between Israel and Albania, at the Foreign Ministry in Jerusalem in 1991 – why he thought Albania had ignored Israel's overtures in the 1950s and 1960s. In a personal letter dated 25 December 2002, he responded at great length, stressing that Albania and the Albanian people 'have always assumed a friendly attitude towards the State of Israel and its people', and that

> The friendly relations between the Albanians and the Jews are deeply rooted in history, but they know the [reached their] apogee [*sic*] during the Second World War, when Albania and all the Albanian people harboured, protected and saved all the Jews in Albania from the Nazi Holocaust … The Jews who lived in Albania considered it as a second mother country and side by side with the Albanian people gave their valuable contribution for the development and prosperity of Albania.

He added, however:

> The former dictatorial socialist regime of Albania following a prejudiced foreign policy against the USA and some of its western partners, Israel included, it is understandable and clear that the Albanian former regime

would not have the will to establish diplomatic relations with the State of Israel … Albania under the Marxist-Leninist dictatorial regime was in full solidarity with the revolutionary movements in general and with the PLO in particular. Furthermore, at the time the State of Israel was considered in Albania as a 'lackey' of the United States, while Israeli foreign policy was condemned as a policy in the service of the 'imperialistic powers'. Israel was called 'pistol of the USA' in the Middle East.

Dino's words clearly show us the contradiction that typified the attitude of communist Albania to Israel during the forty-two years that had passed from the time of its full recognition of Israel and its hostility towards the nation – until the start, on its own initiative, of the process for the establishment of diplomatic relations with Israel, at the close of the communist era and at the beginning of its democratic period (1990/91). If not for the change of regime in Albania and the radical revision of its domestic and foreign policy, it is doubtful that relations would have been established with Israel. The Muslim majority among the Albanian people, however, had no role in determining Albania's policy towards Israel, neither in the communist era nor in the liberal period.

A CHANGING ATTITUDE

The first indication of a change in Albania's policy toward Israel was a conversation initiated by its ambassador in Rome, Dashnor Darvishi, with his Israeli counterpart, Mordechai Drori, in mid-May 1990. The Albanian ambassador told his Israeli counterpart that his country was slowly emerging from its isolation and was interested in developing its links with the countries of the world. The regime in his country, he said, was striving for democratization and would continue on this path, taking reasonable steps. Economic problems, he added, were the major concern and gradually his country would be open to international economic cooperation, by encouraging foreign investments in Albania and the development of commercial ties with foreign countries. In this context, he expressed great hope that it would not be too long before his country would have ties with Israel. Attributing the lack of relations to the 'blackmail of the Arab states', Darvishi said it was becoming absurd that Arab states such as Egypt maintained full diplomatic relations with Israel while Albania avoided all contact.[16] The Albanian ambassador to Egypt expressed the same view to his Israeli counterpart. Drori was advised to inform Darvishi that any Albanian diplomatic initiative 'would be given the appropriate attention by us'.[17]

The second indication was heard – this time openly – from an Albanian diplomat in Paris, probably the ambassador, who gave an interview to Gideon Kutz, the correspondent of the Israeli newspaper *Davar*, that was published on 14 October 1990. It was the first such interview granted by an Albanian official to an Israeli journalist, and the former stated:

Albania is interested in commercial, cultural, tourism, and sport ties with Israel as preparation for the establishment of diplomatic relations between them … There is absolutely no reason why diplomatic relations between the two countries will not be established in the future, even if the present international situation does not permit their immediate renewal.[18] In addition, Albania would be pleased to receive proposals from Israeli businessmen to invest in Albania, which is rich in natural resources and is interested in developing its technological infrastructure. These connections between the two countries must be prepared through the two peoples becoming acquainted with each other, and Albania is now more open to making acquaintances … Albania holds the achievements of Israel and the talents of the Israelis and the Jews in esteem. Albania has always related to Israel and the Israeli nation in a friendly manner, even if it opposed the policy of the Israel government …

24

Albania has always supported the State of Israel's right to exist, but it opposes the denial of this right from other nations. Albania also has traditional friendship with the Arab Muslim states. Yet, there is a sense of identification, since Israel, like Albania, is a small country facing difficult problems and hostile forces. The Jewish people suffered more than any other nation in the Second World War and Albania was the first country to suffer from a fascist invasion by Mussolini's forces, even before Hitler invaded Poland. The Jews of Albania were few at that time, but all of them were saved because the Albanians protected them ...

To this he added,

Albanian sources say that the legal side of the renewal of relations with Israel, when a decision will be made about that, will be easy, since in the 1950s Albania had taken a decision about establishing relations with it. This decision was never put into effect owing to the circumstances, but it was never annulled. Thus, establishing relations will simply be the implementation of this decision.[19]

This was the first Albanian public statement in this vein, and was made within the framework of Albania's plan to develop its relations with the West. Perhaps there were some among the Albanian leadership who felt that ties with Israel would advance Albania's standing in the West, in light of the influence attributed to Israel in Eastern Europe and to the influence of the United States' Jews on the policy of the American administration. Soon after, on 14 March 1991, Albania renewed ties with the United States following a fifty-two-year break.[20] On that very day, Albania's foreign minister, Muhamet Kapllani, stated at a press conference in Rome that his country 'would shortly establish diplomatic relations with Israel'.[21] And again, this was the first such declaration of its kind by an Albanian foreign minister in favour of establishing relations between his country and Israel, aimed at preparing the way for realizing this goal. On the instructions of the deputy director general, East and Central European Department in the Foreign Ministry in Jerusalem, the Israeli ambassador to Rome met with the Albanian ambassador in Rome to examine practical possibilities for the advancement of the Albanian declarations on the intention to establish diplomatic relations with Israel.[22]

On 16 March 1991, the Israeli and Albanian ambassadors in Rome met for a friendly discussion during which the Albanian ambassador referred to the free Albanian elections (under international supervision and in the presence of 300 foreign reporters) to be held on 31 March, and their expected outcome, which he anticipated (as in fact transpired) would see the Labour Party (the former Communist Party) gaining the majority of votes. He also mentioned the opposition parties that were being organized; the popularity of the president, Ramiz Alia; the anticipated reforms in the Albanian constitution, and his hope that after the installation of the new government, relations would be established with Israel. In this context, he added that 'economic activity of Israeli and Jewish businessmen would greatly encourage the president to establish diplomatic relations'. Ambassador Drori responded to him, saying, 'Israeli businessmen will receive encouragement and a feeling of confidence for such activity, if there will be relations between the two countries, and not the opposite'. When he went on to say 'that Albania was the last country in Europe that did not maintain relations with Israel, and that establishment of relations would be a welcome symbolic entrance of Albania into international activity, after a long period of isolation', the Albanian ambassador reiterated his hope that his government would indeed take such a decision soon.

Darvishi further stated that an Albania-Israel Friendship Society had been formed in Tirana, and invited Drori to be guest of honour at its inaugural ceremony in April. Its founders would inform the Israeli foreign minister about this and invite him to take part. Drori participated, and Kutz reported that the organization numbered 150 members, including journalists, scientists, teachers, government officials, physicians and other professionals.[23] The event took place about three weeks after the Albanian general elections, during which both the ruling party and the opposition party declared, 'We will establish relations with Israel.'[24] President Alia, who was defeated, said on the day of the elections:

> We always believed that no problems existed between Albania and Israel. On the contrary, our relationship with the Jewish people has always been positive. No Jew in Albania was ever handed over to the Nazis during the Second World War. Israel has a problem with the Arabs and we hope that this conflict can be solved peacefully and as quickly as possible in accordance with the wishes of the two peoples – Israeli and Arab.

As Kutz noted:

> These words, stated during a press conference in the Palace of Congresses in Tirana, were broadcast in their entirety on official Albanian television. In Tirana and other cities, which I visited yesterday, all my interlocutors told me excitedly about the president's statement. They see in his stating this, the president's blessing for the government to establish diplomatic ties with Israel. The same opinion was held by members of the Albania-Israel Friendship Society, recently established in Tirana.[25]

THE FORGING OF TIES

On 19 July 1991, Ambassador Drori visited Tirana with the aim of conducting talks on the establishment of diplomatic relations between Israel and Albania. During his visit, he met with Foreign Minister Kapllani and gave him an invitation from Israel's foreign minister, David Levy, to make an official visit to Israel during which the protocol on the establishment of diplomatic relations between the two countries would be signed. David Levy added the following section to the letter of invitation: 'Our sincere hope is that the establishment of relations between our two countries and your visit to Israel will constitute not only an important milestone, actually the first, in our interrelations, but will lay a solid foundation for the continued development and expansion of these relations in every sphere possible.'[26]

Kapllani expressed satisfaction at receiving the invitation and said that he would visit Israel as soon as possible. He came to Israel on 18 August, and the next day the two foreign ministers signed a Memorandum of Understanding establishing diplomatic ties. Paragraph 2 of the memorandum stated, 'The two governments will promote relations between them in the sphere of economics, science, technology, culture and other areas of joint interest.'

In an initial working session between the two ministers in Jerusalem (before the signing of the Memorandum of Understanding), Israel expressed its readiness to develop its relations with Albania in all the spheres mentioned in the Memorandum and to share information regarding Israeli technological and other achievements. It was suggested that an Albanian delegation first visit Israel to receive such information, and subsequently that an Israeli delegation go to Albania to explore ways in which Israel could lend assistance. As a first step in this direction, Levyproposed to the Albanian foreign minister the establishing of twenty-five scholarships for Albanians to participate in courses organized by Israel's Foreign Ministry's Department of International Cooperation, setting up two mobile Israeli courses in Albania in areas of interest to the Albanians, and encouraging Israeli businessmen to become active in Albania.

This was an expression of goodwill towards post-communist Albania, which had initiated the establishment of diplomatic relations with Israel after a break of forty-two years between the two countries. These proposals, which the Albanian foreign minister received quite favourably, were presented to Albania as part of the extensive technical aid that Israel extended to developing countries in Africa, Asia and South America. Levy also expressed appreciation for the Albanian people's attitude towards the Jews of Albania – and to the Jews who had taken refuge there during the Holocaust – and admiration for those Albanians who had rescued Jews at that time.[27] Israel's appreciation was also expressed for Albania's allowing Jewish immigration to Israel over the past year.[28]

And so ended the chapter of the establishment of diplomatic relations between Israel and Albania, thus laying the basis for cooperation in the fields of agriculture, economy, trade, culture and science. Since their establishment Israel has been represented in Albania by its ambassador in Rome, while Albania is represented in Israel by its ambassador in Tel Aviv.

NOTES

1. An abridged version of this chapter appeared in *Jewish Political Studies Review*, 17, 3/4 (Fall 2005), pp.67–74, translated from Hebrew by Shalom Bronstein.
2. File on Albania's Recognition of Israel, 2391/10 HZ, Israel State Archive (ISA).
3. Ibid. (Translation by author.)
4. Ibid.
5. For details about Hoxha, who ruled from 1949 to 1985, see *Encyclopaedia Hebraica*, Supplement vol.3 (Tel Aviv: Sifriat Poalim, 1995), pp.87–8 [Hebrew].
6. The 1930 census counted 204 Jews in Albania. In 1939 refugees from Germany and Austria added to their number and additional refugees from Croatia and Serbia followed them. During the Nazi occupation, the Germans deported some 400 Jews to the Bergen-Belsen death camp, about half of whom were still alive when the camp was liberated. *Hebrew Encyclopaedia*, vol. 3, p.336.
7. Albania File, 103.1 HZ, ISA.
8. Ibid.
9. Ibid.
10. Ibid.
11. Ibid.
12. Ibid.
13. Ibid.
14. Ibid.
15. Ibid. See also Eliezer Doron, *Be-Tazpit U-ve-Imut: Mi-Yomano shel Shagrir Yisrael*

[Observing and Confronting: From the Diary of an Israeli Ambassador] (Jerusalem: Keter, 1978), pp.136–7.

16. Albania File, 103.1 HZ, ISA.
17. Ibid.
18. Albania renewed diplomatic relations with the United States on 15 March 1991. See *Jerusalem Post*, 14 March 1991, which also reports Albania's intention to establish ties with the European Union.
19. Although confirmation that this was Albania's attitude could not be found, it is unlikely that the diplomat would have used this rationale if there was no basis for it.
20. Reported on 14 March 1991 in *Haaretz*, the *Jerusalem Post*, *Maariv*, *Yediot Achronot*, and *Davar* [Hebrew].
21. Ibid.
22. Albania File, 103.01 HZ, ISA.
23. *Davar*, 31 March 1991 [Hebrew].
24. *Davar*, *Yediot Achronot*, 31 March 1991 [Hebrew].
25. Albania File, 103.01 HZ, ISA.
26. Ibid.
27. Yad Vashem, The Holocaust Martyrs' and Heroes' Remembrance Authority, Jerusalem, has awarded medals of Righteous among the Nations, to sixty-three Albanians, in deep gratitude for having saved the lives of Jews during the Nazi occupation of Albania.
28. Between 1990 and 1991, some 300 Albanian Jews arrived in Israel. Very few remained in the country after 1991. Between 1948 and 1991, 356 Albanian Jews settled in Israel. See *Jewish Communities in the World* (Jerusalem: World Jewish Congress, 1996), p.132.

3. The Process of Renewal of Diplomatic Relations between Israel and Bulgaria, 1985–1990

HISTORICAL BACKGROUND

In the historical Memorandum of the Jewish people, the Bulgarian nation is marked as one that acted bravely and successfully during the Second World War to thwart the Nazi plan to send 49,000 Jews of Bulgaria – then an ally of Nazi Germany – to extermination camps in Poland. This act of salvation, in which fifty-nine members of the Bulgarian parliament and dozens of clergymen took part, under Bulgaria's royalist-fascistic regime, did not apply to 11,343 Jews of Thracia, Macedonia and the Serbian city of Pirot, who were expelled by soldiers of the Bulgarian army to the Treblinka extermination camp, on the authority of King Boris III of the Popular Republic of Bulgaria. Only twelve Jews survived; all others perished.[1]

The long-term sympathy and warmth that the Bulgarian nation felt for the Jewish minority in its country was inherited from one generation to the next, even after Bulgaria had become a 'popular democracy' (1946) and an integral part of the East European Communist Bloc. In the main, this was expressed in granting permission to the Bulgarian Jews for mass emigration to Israel (1948/49)[2] – and for this, honourable mention goes to the communist prime minister of Bulgaria, Georgi Dimitrov, who considered the emigration of the Jews of Bulgaria to Israel as the return to their historical homeland – and which warranted the integration of those who remained in Bulgaria in parliamentary, political, scientific, cultural, economic and social activity.[3] At the same time, Bulgaria recognized Israel de jure on 7 February 1949 and began to develop mutual trade, economic and tourism relations.

In the wake of the USSR's decision to sever diplomatic relations with Israel on 11 February 1953 (towards the end of the Stalinist regime),[4] the USSR was represented in Israel by Bulgaria, in whose capital, Sofia, negotiations were conducted between the chargé d'affaires of Israel's legation in Sofia and the Soviet ambassador towards renewal of diplomatic relations between the two countries, some three months after Stalin's death, on 1 June 1953. Yet, casting a pall over the mutual relations for a lengthy period was the incident of the downing of an El Al passenger plane, in July 1955, in Bulgarian skies, by two Bulgarian fighter planes, on the suspicion that it was a NATO spy plane. The plane crashed on the Greek border and all its passengers were killed.[5]

Israeli-Bulgarian relations from their inception to their severance, on 11 June 1967, had their difficulties, mainly in the political sphere, while commercial relations and the flow of tourists continued normally. Bulgaria, as a member of the East European Communist Bloc, toed the political and ideological line of the USSR and broke diplomatic relations with Israel in the wake of the Six Day War, along with the other countries of the East European Bloc (except for Romania). It supported the anti-Israel line of the USSR in the international arena; in the Middle East, it recognized the 'new State of Palestine', and it allowed the PLO to open an embassy in Sofia. Likewise, Bulgaria adopted the USSR positions on the Arab-Israeli conflict and the way to resolve it, calling for (a) Israel's withdrawal from all Arab land conquered in June 1967; (b) a guarantee for the legal and national rights of the Palestinian people, including the right to establish their own independent state on its national land; (c) a guarantee for the independence and sovereignty of all countries in the region, and recognition of the PLO as the sole national representative of the Palestinian people.[6] The way to implement this formula, as Bulgaria saw it, was the adoption of the Soviet proposal to convene an international conference for the solution of the conflict under the auspices of the UN and with the participation of the permanent members of the Security Council and the parties to the dispute. This included the PLO, with which Bulgaria had developed close relations, allowing its members to take advantage of training bases on its soil and providing the organization with weapons. Similarly, Bulgaria nurtured close ties with Arab countries, especially Syria.

Yet Bulgaria's contacts with Israel during the period of severed diplomatic relations were characterized by some exceptions which did not always mesh with the policy of the other countries in the East European Communist Bloc that had broken relations with Israel. In particular, the continued existence – albeit on a limited scale – of commercial and tourism ties (Israelis had no difficulty in obtaining entrance visas to Bulgaria, in contrast to the attitude of the USSR, Poland and Czechoslovakia from the 1970s through the mid-1980s); the granting of permission for Israeli delegations and representatives to take part in international conferences meeting on Bulgarian territory. Talks were initiated at government level (from the end of the 1970s onward), and cordial relations were maintained via political discussion between the Israeli foreign minister and his Bulgarian counterpart when they came to participate in the opening of the UN General Assembly.

So, for example, a delegation from Israel, headed by Eliezer Shmueli, director general of the Ministry of Education and Culture, participated in the third UNESCO Conference of Ministers of Education which took place on 12–21 June 1980, where it was received warmly by official Bulgarian representatives. Haim Klein, responsible for international connections in the Ministry of Commerce,

Industry and Tourism, took part in April 1981 in the European Regional Congress of the World Tourism Organization that met in Sofia. During the course of the Congress he held conversations with, among others, the deputy prime minister, the president of the National Tourism Authority and his second in command, and with the head of the Department for International Cooperation. Professor Raphael Meshulam, rector of the Hebrew University of Jerusalem, participated in October 1981 in an international conference on the chemistry of natural materials at Varna, at the invitation of the Bulgarian National Academy of Sciences. His Bulgarian colleagues' attitude towards him was most warm and cordial. The Bulgarian scientists expressed great interest in strengthening relations with Israeli scientists and proposed cooperation in the production of medicines; Yoel Zur, head of the patent unit in the Ministry of Justice, went on an official mission to Bulgaria in April 1980 to take part in a conference of the International Organization for Intellectual Properties.[7]

From the mid-1980s the Bulgarian diplomatic mission to the UN began to absent itself and later to abstain from voting on the Arab proposition to discuss revoking Israel's accreditation to the UN (which actually meant negating Israel's right to participate in General Assembly discussions), while the USSR and its satellites (except Romania) voted for it. At a later stage Bulgaria was joined in this approach by Yugoslavia, Poland and Hungary.

Bulgaria was also among the first countries in the Eastern Bloc to initiate political contacts with Israel for the establishment of 'quasi-official' relations (at the level of chambers of commerce), but it was also among the last to re-establish diplomatic relations. Relative to the other countries of the East European Bloc (except for the USSR and Yugoslavia), Bulgaria took cautious (apparently for fear lest it damage its relations with the Arab countries) and slow but gradual steps in the direction of renewing diplomatic relations with Israel.

MILESTONES TOWARD RENEWAL OF
DIPLOMATIC RELATIONS

Stage One: Visit of the Wife of the President of Israel, Ofira Navon, to Bulgaria

The wife of Israel's president, Ofira Navon, met for a discussion with Lyudmila Zhivkova, a member of the Politburo of the Bulgarian Communist Party, and the Bulgarian minister of culture when they took part in the Conference on the International Year of the Child held in Mexico in November 1979. (Zhivkova is the daughter of Todor Zhivkov, secretary general of the Bulgarian Communist Party and president of Bulgaria, who led the Communist Party and the Bulgarian people for thirty-five years.) At their meeting, Zhivkova told Ofira Navon about the rescue of the Bulgarian Jews during the time of the Nazi occupation, thanks to the intervention of the Bulgarian people to prevent their deportation, and she indicated that it would be possible to begin cultural exchanges between Bulgaria and Israel, even before reinstitution of diplomatic relations between them.

And indeed during 1980 a number of cultural exchange activities took place between the two countries. In an exceptional move, Ms Zhivkova invited Ms Navon to visit Bulgaria to discuss the progress in implementing the programmes devised at the Mexican conference. Ms Navon accepted the invitation and attended this discussion, which took place in Bulgaria in 1981.

Stage Two: Contacts between Israeli and Bulgarian Diplomats

In the early 1980s the Bulgarians initiated a number of milestones that were then considered exceptional in the Eastern Bloc:

1. Holding political discussions between ambassadors of the two countries in Athens. Initially, these were conducted between Ambassador Nissim Yaish and then Ambassador Yeheskel Barnea of Israel, and

their Bulgarian counterpart Nikolai Todorov, a professor of history specializing in the history of the Jews of Bulgaria in the middle ages at the Bulgarian Academy of Sciences in Sofia.

2. The invitation of Israel's ambassador in Bucharest, Aba Gefen, to a reception hosted by the Bulgarian ambassador in his home in honour of the conclusion of his period of service in Romania. Ambassador Gefen was received with demonstrable warmth by his Bulgarian host. The two used to exchange opinions publicly whenever the opportunity presented itself.[8]

3. The press officer in the Israeli Embassy in Brussels met on 1 December 1980 with the secretary for press and cultural affairs of the Bulgarian Embassy where he was invited to attend two memorial ceremonies organized by the Bulgarian Embassy in Belgium in memory of Angelov Todor, aBulgarian fighter who had fought in the Spanish Civil War and who, during the period of German occupation of Belgium, had led a Resistance groupconsisting entirely of aliens. Among the actions thegroup carried out was gaining access to the Gestapo lists of the names of Jews intended for expulsion toextermination camps. At this meeting, the Bulgarian diplomat discussed with his Israeli colleague that the fact of lack of diplomatic relations between their two countries should not prevent their representatives from conversing and exchanging ideas.

4. Conversation between Moshe Melamed, director of the Department of International Organizations in the Foreign Ministry in Jerusalem with the director of the Middle East Department in the Bulgarian Foreign Ministry. This took place during the visit of the Israeli delegation led by Eliezer Shmueli, director general of the Ministry of Education, on the occasion of his participation in the Third UNESCO Conference of Ministers of Education, convened in Sofia in June 1980.

5. The Bulgarian UN delegation sent an official letter to the

Israeli UN delegation asking for Israel's support for its candidate to the UN International Law Commission. The Israeli representative informed the Bulgarian candidate, Bulgaria's deputy foreign minister, that following instructions received from the Foreign Ministry in Jerusalem Israel would support his candidacy.[9]

Stage Three: Discussions between the Foreign Ministers of Israel and Bulgaria

For the first time in the period of severed diplomatic relations between Israel and Bulgaria, Israeli Foreign Minister Yitzhak Shamir met with Bulgarian Foreign Minister Peter Mladenov at Israel's initiative, within the framework of the openings of the UN General Assembly in 1985 and 1986.

During the first conversation, on 4 October 1985, when Foreign Minister Shamir pointed out, inter alia, that Israel had no conflict with Bulgaria so there was no basis for the break in relations, Foreign Minister Mladenov responded that 'when the reasons behind our severing relations with Israel will disappear, we will renew them'. In reference to the Arab-Israeli conflict the Bulgarian foreign minister noted that only negotiations would lead to peace, 'and not wars that bear no solution', adding that a resolution to the situation must be found at an international conference under UN auspices and with the participation of the USSR, the United States, and the parties to the conflict, including the PLO. Shamir stated that 'We want peace and we believe that we will achieve peace, but only through direct talks'. As for Shamir's comment that 'We must construct instruments for discussions between us, for exchange of opinions, to maintain economic relations, to sell and buy and develop cultural ties, to be pragmatic in our approach', his Bulgarian colleague replied, 'We will hold consultations and meet with you again at the UN.'[10] One gains the impression that the Bulgarian foreign minister was not interested in deviating from the political line then accepted by the USSR and the authorities in his country. Yet, it could also be seen that he tended to listen more than voice his opinions and that he left an opening for continued contact at the next UN General Assembly, but not before then.

In the second conversation between them, on 24 September 1986, Foreign Minister Shamir reiterated his proposal to expand the mutual links between the two countries – in light of the non-utilized potential existing on both sides – which would solve the petty issues before resolving the serious problems. He asked his Bulgarian counterpart, 'Why isn't public expression given to this, as for example Poland has done?' (In 1985 Poland initiated official talks with Israeli representatives, as a result of which it was agreed to open interests offices, in Warsaw – under the patronage of the Dutch Embassy that represented Israel in Poland during the period of severed relations – and in Tel Aviv, under the auspices of the Polish PKO bank. These offices helped in the establishment of a new foundation for mutual relations until they became embassies.) Mladenov responded that 'he had listened attentively' to Shamir, and asked him to see to it that Israel would use its influence in the United States 'beyond the differences of opinion between us' so that the Bulgarian authorities would not be falsely accused of attempting to assassinate the pope[11] (nor on their cooperation with Libya in carrying out acts of terror, which, for obvious reasons, the Bulgarian foreign minister did not mention even though rumours about this were rife in the West).

From the formulation of the Bulgarian foreign minister's response and his request one discerns an increasing willingness on Bulgaria's part to institutionalize contacts with Israel but in a manner that was not as yet clear to either side. This new attitude derived from the need to improve Bulgaria's standing and image in the Western world so as to promote its economic and political interests. At that time, Israel was apparently perceived by the Bulgarian government as possessing great influence in the US and as such could help the Bulgarian administration attain this goal, just as Israel and the American Jewish organizations helped communist Romania obtain the status of 'Most Favoured Nation' from the American government. The fact that Romania had not severed its relations with Israel, together with its ability to manoeuvre in trying to make peace between the antagonists in the Middle East conflict, had improved Romania's prestige among the western countries as a state conducting an independent foreign policy, despite its being an integral part of the East European Communist Bloc. Undoubtedly, these facts were not overlooked by those formulating Bulgaria's foreign policy.

The need to have recourse to Jewish assistance for improving Bulgaria's image was given actual expression three years later, when the president of the World Jewish Congress (WJC), Edgar Bronfman, paid a visit to Bulgaria, on 14–16 October 1989, at the invitation of the government. Bronfman conducted discussions with Bulgarian ministers and with Peter Mladenov, secretary general of the Communist Party, former foreign minister and future president of Bulgaria. They attempted to describe to him the heart of the administrative and economic reforms that had been instituted in the past few years in Bulgaria, and he was asked how it would be possible to improve Bulgaria's international status and image by means of the WJC? Alan Steinberg, a member of the delegation accompanying Bronfman, responded by saying that first of all they had to renew their diplomatic relations with Israel.[12]

In fact the Bulgarians had already begun to take small steps in this direction, about four years earlier, following the first talks between the the Bulgarian and the Israeli foreign ministers in October 1985, as will be detailed below.

Stage Four: Invitation to Shulamit Shamir, to visit Bulgaria

Even before the foreign ministers of Israel and Bulgaria had met for their second talks, when they were at the UN General Assembly in New York, the wife of Israel's foreign minister, Shulamit Shamir – in a rare move for that time – was invited to visit Bulgaria, her birthplace. This came at the invitation of the chairman of the main organization for education and culture among Bulgarian Jews, Iosif Astrukov, so that Mrs Shamir could see for herself the work of the organization among the Jews of Bulgaria, who then numbered some 5,000 people. The visit took place in the first week of September 1986, and even though it was defined by the government as a 'private visit', it actually had an official character as demonstrated by the escort and resources put at the disposal of Mrs Shamir, and of the external expressions of respect and friendship given to her – as attested by Moshe Melamed, director of the Department for International Organizations in the Foreign Ministry in Jerusalem, who accompanied Mrs Shamir.

Moshe Melamed further adds from his impressions, 'Clearly this visit had reasons and a goal – an attempt to make a friendly gesture towards Israel, without assuming any political obligation towards it, and perhaps to release a trial balloon and then to later examine what the responses of the Arabs and the USSR would be.' Melamed concludes 'Undoubtedly, this visit had political significance.'[13] Within this significance one may also include the Jewish aspect, as a sideways glance to the Jewish organizations in the West, especially the United States, with the aim of acquiring their sympathy for Bulgaria in light of its policy towards the Jewish minority – authorization to organize itself into its own institutions, development within them of cultural-ethnic activity, permission for the immigration of Jews from Bulgaria to Israel, and the maintenance of direct contact between them and their brethren in Israel and all over the Diaspora.

In November 1988, Shulamit Shamir paid a second visit to Bulgaria. She was invited to participate in a round-table discussion on the occasion of the forty-fifth anniversary of the thwarting of the plan to expel the Jews of Bulgaria to Nazi extermination camps. As during Mrs Shamir's first visit to Bulgaria, the Bulgarian goal of stressing Bulgaria's friendship toward the Jewish people was evident.

Stage Five: Visit of Ariel Sharon, Minister of Trade and Industry, to Bulgaria

In the first week of October 1988, Israeli Minister of Industry and Commerce Ariel Sharon made the first visit of its kind to Bulgaria, in response to the invitation from Bulgarian Minister for Foreign Economic Affairs Andrei Lukanov. During his stay, possibilities were discussed about expanding commercial and economic ties between the two countries, and in this context the ministers signed a Memorandum on mutual aid towards the establishment of economic relations between the two countries. In the wake of the visit and the Memorandum, in January 1989 a Bulgarian economic delegation arrived in Israel, headed by the Director General of the Ministry for Foreign Economic Affairs and the director of the Bulgarian chambers of commerce. In the course of discussions with their hosts in Israel, an agreement was signed between the Association of Chambers of Commerce in Israel and the Bulgarian chambers of commerce on the establishment of reciprocal chambers in each country. The Bulgaria chamber of commerce opened in Tel Aviv in April 1989; the two Bulgarian representatives of the chamber were granted Bulgarian diplomatic passports, and even received diplomatic entry visas on arrival in Israel. This step shows us that the Bulgarian government wished to grant their two representatives diplomatic status, even if they could not be considered as such with regard to Israeli consular procedures.

RENEWAL OF DIPLOMATIC RELATIONS

A year passed from the time of the opening of the Bulgarian chamber of commerce in Tel Aviv until the renewal of diplomatic relations between the two countries. In that period great changes took place in Bulgaria. In 1987 President Todor Zhivkov had declared a series of economic reforms – in the spirit of the reforms in the USSR under the leadership of Mikhail Gorbachev – but they were never instituted. Opposition to Zhivkov arose in the Communist Party and among various ethnic groups in the country, which lead to him being deposed on 10 November 1989 and to the collapse of the communist regime. From this point Bulgaria began gradually to shift to a democratic-liberal regime. The economic sphere was also shaken by an extremely serious crisis, either because its economic structure was no longer fit for the demands of world trade or because its financial system collapsed, and Bulgaria was forced to pay its foreign debts that amounted to about ten billion dollars – as estimated by the deputy foreign minister of Bulgaria, Filip Ishpekov, when speaking to the deputy foreign minister of Israel, Benjamin Netanyahu, during his visit to Bulgaria in early April 1990.[14]

At that time Israel was perceived by the new leaders of Bulgaria not only as a state with rich potential for economic, technological and scientific cooperation but – as previously noted – a country with paramount economic and financial importance among western countries. Relations with Israel could therefore become a means by which Bulgaria could derive great benefit both in spreading out its debts over a number of years, in receiving aid towards emerging from the economic crisis and in reinforcing its first steps towards a free economy. Therefore, it is no wonder that the new government proposed, at the end of 1990, through a dialogue between its UN ambassador and his Israeli counterpart, to begin talks about renewing diplomatic relations. To that end, the Bulgarian ambassador to the UN, on instruction from his government, invited the Israeli deputy foreign minister, Benjamin Netanyahu, to visit Bulgaria in the second half of March for discussion during the course of which the two parties would initiate a protocol for the re-establishment of diplomatic relations. The Bulgarian ambassador suggested that the official signing of the document take place in April 1990, 'if possible, as part of the official visit of the foreign minister, Moshe Arens, to Bulgaria'.[15] The Foreign Ministry in Jerusalem responded positively to the proposal and, as stated, Deputy Foreign Minister Netanyahu visited Bulgaria on 2–3 April 1990 and initialled as proposed, along with his Bulgarian counterpart, the protocol for the renewal of diplomatic relations between the two countries. Foreign Minister Arens paid his official visit on 2–3 May 1990 to endorse the signing of the document for the resumption of diplomatic relations at embassy level (until the break in relations in 1967, mutual representation had been at the level of legations).

During the visits to Bulgaria of Deputy Foreign Minister Netanyahu and a month later of Foreign Minister Arens, two historic events took place – not just the actual signing of the document for the renewal of diplomatic relations, but the fact that these were the first visits of their type since diplomatic relations had been established between the two countries. The itinerary of their separate visits included a series of political talks that were conducted in a frank and positive atmosphere between the guests from Israel and their entourage and their hosts. Deputy Foreign Minister Netanyahu met with his counterpart, the Bulgarian deputy foreign minister, Ishpekov, and with the deputy minister for foreign economic relations, Constantin Galvanakov, and their aides. Foreign Minister Arens, however, met with Bulgarian President Mladenov, with Prime Minister Lukanov, and with Foreign Minister Boiko Dimitrov and their aides. In these talks one could discern the expectations each side had of the other; especially noticeable were the expectations which the Bulgarian government leaders had of Israel, which were expressed in their statements on the occasion of the renewal of mutual relations, and in the responses of their Israeli guests.[16]

The Bulgarians, after welcoming the re-establishment of relations, noted the following:

1. The long break in the relations between Bulgaria and Israel 'was an anomaly and a harmful phenomenon forced on Bulgaria by the old regime'. They mentioned the mutual relations that had prevailed between the Jewish and Bulgarian peoples throughout their common history and determined that, in effect, there was no reason to taint the atmosphere of mutuality between Bulgaria and Israel in times to come. In their opinion, these relations must develop and flourish.

2. In the future Bulgaria's foreign policy would be based 'on the principles of justice and international ethics from the Bulgarian point of view'. In light of this, Bulgaria would reconsider its position regarding Zionism and would vote at the UN against the decision equating Zionism with racism, when and if this topic were again to be raised for discussion. Similarly, Bulgaria would oppose international terror and not do anything to encourage or support it.

3. A change in Bulgaria's order of priorities did not mean a worsening of its relations with other countries. Bulgaria would continue to maintain good relations with the USSR and with the Arab countries. In previous years mutual Bulgarian-Arab dependence had been created in the fields of commerce and economics. Israel would certainly understand that (good) relations did not have to be influenced by reference to relations with other countries.

4. Bulgaria was following with great trepidation the developments in the Middle East, mainly because of its geographical proximity to the region. Bulgaria would continue to see in the convening of an international conference for peace in the Middle East an efficient means for settling the Arab-Israeli conflict. Bulgaria hoped that the renewal of its diplomatic relations with Israel would contribute to thawing the freeze in the Middle East.

5. Bulgaria anticipated negative responses to the re-establishment of its relations with Israel on the

part of certain Arab countries and would explain to them that this step by Bulgaria was not taken out of any desire to harm its relations with them.

The Bulgarian assumption proved correct. After publication of the announcement about the re-institution of Israeli-Bulgarian relations, at the time of the visit by Foreign Minister Moshe Arens in Sofia, the new embassy of the State of Palestine in Sofia published a proclamation on 3 May 1990 which, inter alia, stated:

> The PLO considers the renewal of diplomatic relations between Bulgaria and Israel as an internal Bulgarian matter ... We would like to note that the State of Israel ... continues to negate the right of the Palestinian people to self-determination and to the establishment of its own independent state ... and is trying with all its might to crush the uprising of the Palestine people by means of oppression and terror against the Declaration of Human Rights and the Fourth Geneva Convention. The PLO is convinced that the friendly Bulgarian people and its government will always support the just matter of the Arab nation, of Palestine, in its struggle for liberation, democracy, and self-determination on the soil of its homeland.

6. It was proposed that immediately upon the signing of the protocol on the renewal of diplomatic relations, 'the two governments will exploit the political good will that has been created' and open negotiations toward the signing of the following agreements:

   - Agreement for cooperation in economic and commercial activity.
   - Agreement for cooperation in scientific, technological activity.
   - Agreement to prevent double taxation.
   - Agreement for the encouragement and protection of investments.

- Agreement on aviation.
- Agreement on shipping.
- Agreement on tourism.

7. After they described the dire economic and financial straits of Bulgaria, and the courageous striving of Bulgaria toward democratization – through institution of radical changes in the methods of governance and social management – the Bulgarians requested that Israel provide it with direct financial aid to pay off its foreign debt. In this context it was said that Bulgaria had ceased paying the principal on its foreign debt since it was left without resources. Moreover, Israel was asked to make use of its connections in the realm of international banking and world financial organizations so that Bulgaria would be given sympathetic treatment in its attempt to spread out repayment of its debts over a period of many years. Asking for aid from Israel on these two topics was a desperate cry for help.

Deputy Foreign Minister Netanyahu and Foreign Minister Arens (each separately) opened their statements of response by underscoring the rescue of the Jews of Bulgaria from deportation to extermination camps during the Holocaust period as well as with words of appreciation and sympathy for the democratization processes taking place in Bulgaria, and they expressed Israel's willingness to help it to its utmost. As an initial step, they proposed putting into effect, immediately upon the renewal of diplomatic relations, the agreement for cooperation in the areas of economic and commercial activity, culture, tourism and aviation that could be signed by the two sides at the earliest possible moment.

Netanyahu added, on his part, that Israel was unable to provide monetary aid to Bulgaria 'because of the need to absorb immigration, but of course we want to and will be able to help with our connections in the world of finance'. He also offered 'in the long run Israel's help in the development of

Bulgaria's links to American Jewry and with the appropriate American congressmen', and he stressed that the renewal of diplomatic relations 'will open a positive atmosphere toward Bulgaria in the Jewish world'. Finally, he suggested that 'we should move at an accelerated pace toward the signing of the agreements', as specified by the deputy minister for the foreign economic affairs of Bulgaria.

In summing up these talks, it would not be wrong to say that Israel's promises to Bulgaria did not match their expectations – for example, receipt of immediate monetary aid for the payment of its foreign debt. Yet, it certainly reinforced their leaders' opinion that, indeed, through Israel – thanks to its influence on American Jewry and the financial institutions in the United States – Bulgaria would be able to gain assistance in realizing its economic goals and in improving its image in the Western world, since it also expected to reap great benefit from this understanding. Renewal of diplomatic relations with Israel, therefore, meshed with the vital interests of Bulgaria. Moreover, Bulgaria was no longer the first country in the East European Bloc – now standing on the brink of disintegration after its break with Soviet hegemony – to renew its diplomatic relations with Israel. It had been preceded by Hungary, Poland and Czechoslovakia, in addition to the USSR, which already maintained official relations with Israel at consular level. As to relations with Arab countries and the PLO, Bulgaria had already decreed that re-establishing relations with Israel would not occur at the cost of damaging good relations with them.

A short time after the signing of the document on the renewal of diplomatic relations between Israel and Bulgaria, an Israeli Embassy was established in Sofia and a Bulgarian Embassy in Tel Aviv, bringing to a close twenty-three years of diplomatic rupture between the two countries. A new chapter had begun in their mutual relations that was expressed in the strengthening of their connections on the political-economic plane as well as on that of aviation, tourism, sport and culture.

NOTES

1. The districts of Thracia and Macedonia were captured by Nazi Germany from Greece and Yugoslavia, and they were annexed after their occupation (April 1941) to the territory of Bulgaria, which joined the Axis states on 1 March 1941. See Nir Baruch, *Annihilation and Survival in United Bulgaria* (Herzliya: Association for the Study of the Balkan Jewish Communities and Their Comemoration, 2003) [Hebrew].
2. According to A.E. Ben Asher, *Yahasei Hutz* (Tel Aviv: Ayanot, 1957), pp.211–12, the number of emigrants was estimated at 38,000 (Ben Asher is the anonymous name of Katriel Katz, who served during his term as director of the Research Department of the Foreign Ministry, Jerusalem). Another source puts the number of Jews who emigrated from Bulgaria to Israel at 50,000. See Haim Kishles, *History of the Jews of Bulgaria* (Tel Aviv: Davar, 1969) [Hebrew]. The first source apparently refers to the number of Jews who left Bulgaria for Israel after the Second World War, while the second seems to relate to the total number of immigrants from Bulgaria.
3. According to the 1984 *Annual* of the Cultural Committee of the Jews in Sofia, Bulgaria, the community then numbered 5,108 Jews. Of these, 600 were professors, teachers and scientists; ten belonged to the writers' association; three were members of the Central Committee of the Communist Party; three were members of parliament. According to the *American Jewish Year Book* (New York: American Jewish Committee, 2001), the number of Jews was estimated at 2,500.
4. Y. Govrin, *Israeli-Soviet Relations 1953–1967: From Confrontation to Disruption* (London and Portland, OR: Frank Cass, 1998), pp.55–60.
5. Abraham Goldreich, 'The Israeli Plane That Was Identified as American', *Haaretz*, 19 June 2005 [Hebrew].
6. These ideas were expressed by the Bulgarian foreign minister, Peter Mladenov, at the UN General Assembly on 10 October 1977, in Bug 103.1, Israel State Archives, (ISA). All documents mentioned or quoted in this chapter are compiled in this File.
7. Memorandum by Yosef Govrin, director of the East European Department in the Foreign Ministry in Jerusalem, 26 March 1982, in combination with data from Yoav Bar-On, assistant to the department director.
8. Aba Gefen, *A Small Window to the Iron Curtain* (Tel Aviv: Sifriat Maariv, 1985), pp.207–12 [Hebrew].
9. The request was sent in an official letter from the Bulgarian delegation to the UN on 20 November 1982 to the Israeli UN delegation.
10. Report by Aharon Ofri, Israel's Diplomatic Mission to the UN, 4 October 1985.
11. According to a report by the Israel's Diplomatic Mission to the UN, 29 September 1986.
12. Report by Dr Avi Beker, secretary general of the Israel Office of the WJC, which was given to the deputy director general of the Foreign Ministry, Yosef Govrin, 27 November 1989.
13. Memorandum by Moshe Melamed, director of the Department for International Organizations in the Foreign Ministry, 6 September 1986.
14. Memorandum by Moshe Melamed, 18 April 1990.
15. Telegram from Johanan Bein, Israel's Diplomatic Mission to the UN, 27 February 1990.
16. Reports by Moshe Melamed, 18 April 1990, 1 May 1990, and 6 May 1990.

4. The Process of Renewal of Israel's Diplomatic Relations with Czechoslovakia, 1987–1990[1]

HISTORICAL BACKGROUND

In the early 1950s, Israel's relations with Czechoslovakia swung from deeply rooted friendship to open hostility. This was due to the change in that country's government from democratic rule to a totalitarian communist regime subject to the dictates of the Kremlin. The pendulum swung back from hostility to renewed friendship with the establishment of democratic rule in Czechoslovakia following the Velvet Revolution, at the end of 1989, which peacefully overthrew the communist regime.

In the historical consciousness of the revival of the State of Israel, democratic Czechoslovakia, between the two world wars, held a special place. Its president, Tomas Masaryk, fought for the rights of the Jewish minority in his country, supported the Zionist movement, and even visited Palestine in 1927. He was the first European president to publicly demonstrate such support.

After the Second World War, Czechoslovakia, under President Edvard Beneš and Foreign Minister Jan Masaryk, assumed a most cordial attitude towards the *Yishuv* (the Jewish community in Mandatory Palestine). In 1946 the Czech Government helped smuggle Jewish refugees through Czechoslovakia from Poland to Austria and to the displaced persons camps in Germany, and from there to

Italy, and was also supportive when the issue of Palestine was put to a vote at the UN in 1947. At that time, Czechoslovakia was a member of UNSCOP, the UN committee on issues pertaining to Palestine. Czechoslovakia voted in favour of the partition plan for dividing Palestine into two states – one Jewish and one Arab. Jan Masaryk's speech at the UN General Assembly on the Jewish people's right to its own country was one of the most impressive speeches heard there.

In its first year of communist rule (1948/49), Czechoslovakia was one of the first countries after the Soviet Union to recognize the State of Israel de jure, in May 1948. During Israel's War of Independence, when other channels of supply were blocked, Czechoslovakia provided badly needed arms for self-defence, as well as important military services on its own soil by training Israeli soldiers and pilots. There is no doubt that this aid played a major role in determining the outcome of the war in Israel's favour.

The first Israeli envoy to present his credentials anywhere in the world was the Israeli envoy to Prague, Ehud Avriel, on 29 July 1948. In July 1948, the Israeli minister for transportation, David Remez, visited Prague. Then Foreign Minister Moshe Sharett followed in May 1949, and was warmly received. In pursuing a friendly policy toward Israel, Czechoslovakia was toeing the Soviet Union line, but also adhering to its own traditionally supportive attitude towards Zionism since the time of President Tomas Masaryk.

Until the end of 1949, Czechoslovakia was the friendliest Eastern European country towards the fledgling State of Israel. However, beginning in early 1950, with the establishment of the communist regime which closely followed the line laid down by Stalin, Czechoslovakia radically changed its policies toward Israel. In keeping with the anti-Semitic, anti-Zionist and anti-Israeli policies of the Soviet Union, Czechoslovakia moved from one extreme to the other – from friendliness to hostility. The most ominous sign of trouble ahead was an article in the Communist Party's weekly magazine, *Tvorba*, titled 'Cosmopolitanism as an Aggressive Instrument of Imperialism', that stated:

> [R]ecently many cosmopolitan elements have become agents of the Anglo-American aggressors, from the ranks of active Zionists who have not put down roots in our people. The Jewish state, Israel, is currently in the hands of the Jewish nationalist bourgeoisie who have become addicted to American imperialism. They use this country as an agency operating against the nationalist liberation movements in the colonies, and they exploit the Zionist movement as an agency for terror, harassment and hatred against the Soviet Union and the People's Democratic Republics.[2]

In 1951, Czechoslovakia began to conduct Soviet-style purges among veteran members of the Czechoslovak Communist Party, including those of Jewish origin who were accused of treason. One of the purges that severely rocked Israeli-Czechoslovak relations took place during the Prague trials, when Rudolf Slansky, the Jewish-born secretary general of the Czechoslovak Communist Party, was put on trial with veteran Communist Party activists, many of whom were Jews. Slansky was imprisoned in late 1951 on various trumped-up charges, including treason, for his alleged cooperation with Zionist organizations in contravention of Czechoslovakia's interests. He was sentenced to death and executed in November 1952. Eleven of the fourteen defendants in this trial were Jews. Eight of them were executed, and the other three were sentenced to life imprisonment.

Two Israelis, Mordechai Oren – a Mapam (United Workers Party) leader who went on party missions abroad from time to time – and Shimon Orenstein, a member of Hashomer HaTzair (the Mapam 'Young Guards') who was a commercial attaché at Israel's Legation in Prague and subsequently conducted private business affairs, were arrested while visiting Prague in late 1951. They were tortured and sentenced to long prison terms after being forced to give fabricated testimony dictated to them in order to incriminate Slansky, his friends and themselves.[3]

It was alleged that Israel's Legation in Prague was being used as a centre for espionage, and the Israeli envoy to Czechoslovakia, Arye Kubovi, was declared persona non grata in December 1952. Prime Minister David Ben-Gurion and Foreign Minister Moshe Sharett responded with fiery speeches in the Knesset (Israel's parliament) on 24 and 25 November 1952. They vehemently denied all charges against Israel and attacked the government of Czechoslovakia for the anti-Semitic, anti-Zionist and anti-Israeli policies manifested during the trials, while expressing appreciation for Czechoslovakia's friendly relations with Israel prior to the purges.[4]

Although Stalin's death in March 1953 ended the show trials and eventually the purges as well, in the post-Stalinist era Czechoslovak-Israeli relations did not return to their former cordiality. Although the two countries maintained diplomatic relations until the Six Day War, there was an element of tension between the parties due to Czechoslovakia's hostile policy towards Israel, Zionism and Jewish organizations. Relations deteriorated further following the Egyptian-Czechoslovak arms deal in 1955 and the Sinai Campaign in 1956.

Following the Six Day War, on 10 June 1967, Czechoslovakia severed diplomatic ties with Israel together with the rest of the East European Communist Bloc, excluding Romania. It was decided that Austria would represent Czechoslovak interests in Israel, and Sweden would represent Israeli interests in Czechoslovakia.

Explanations for the severance of relations in the Czechoslovak press were even more hostile than the Soviet propaganda prevalent at the time. For example, an article published on 15 June 1967, in the Czechoslovak

Communist Party daily *Rude Pravo* was titled 'The Illicit Activities of Israeli Diplomats in the CSSR' (Socialist Republic of Czechoslovakia).[5] The article levelled serious accusations against the diplomats of Israel's Legation in Prague, who in various ways tried, it claimed, 'to interfere grossly in Czechoslovakia's internal affairs ... to arouse pro-Israel nationalistic sentiments among some of Czechoslovakia's citizens ... and to obtain important information on its internal affairs from members of the religious Jewish community – whether during visits to their homes or during gatherings on religious holidays – about the CSSR and its relations with the Arab countries', in addition to their 'efforts to convince them, especially the youth, the technical cadres, and specialists to emigrate to Israel'.

With regard to the Arab-Israeli conflict, the article contained elements of admonishment and slander, denouncing 'the aggressive nature of the *Jewish State*' (emphasis mine – Y.G.). The denunciation of Israel included wording identical to that of the Soviet media, except for its references to the Jewish character of Israel. The authors of the article apparently wanted to create the impression that diplomatic ties with Israel had been severed due to 'acts of espionage' by the Israeli Legation in Prague. This was evidently more important than the fact that Czechoslovakia had joined the East European Communist Bloc (excluding Romania) in the decision to sever diplomatic relations with Israel in the aftermath of the Six Day War. This decision was made in order to demonstrate the Bloc's collective solidarity with Arab countries after the military defeats of Egypt, Syria and Jordan in the war. The motif of spying and labelling Israel as a Jewish state was indicative of the anti-Semitism that typified Czechoslovakia's official propaganda at that time.

From the time of severance of diplomatic ties with Israel until the late 1980s, Czechoslovakia continued, parallel to the Soviet Union, to maintain a fierce anti-Israel policy. This was manifested in Prague's extensive political and military aid to the Arab countries and the PLO (including training its members to commit terrorist acts) and its virulent anti-Zionist and anti-Israeli propaganda, both internally and internationally. This also included its UN votes in favour of resolutions proposed by the Arabs to revoke Israel's UN credentials and equating Zionism with racism.

Unlike Yugoslavia, Hungary and Bulgaria (the latter two having been, alongside Czechoslovakia, members of the Warsaw Pact), Czechoslovakia completely severed its commercial and cultural relations with Israel and even refused to have any contact with Israel in the realm of sports or tourism. Czechoslovakia also refrained from conducting any political discussions, official or unofficial, with Israel. Even at diplomatic receptions around the world, Czechoslovak representatives avoided any social or casual contact with Israeli representatives.

Czechoslovakia made it very difficult for Israelis to enter the country, whether for family visits or for participation at international conferences. Similarly, the Jewish community (numbering 14,000) was not allowed to maintain ties with Israel or with Jewish organizations in the West. Emigration to Israel (or other Western countries) was also forbidden. The incitement against Israel even went so far as to recruit the Jewish community leadership in Czechoslovakia to wage an anti-Israel propaganda campaign.

During Czechoslovakia's brief liberal regime, dubbed the 'Prague Spring' (January–August 1968), the government's attitude toward Jews changed for the better. Consequently, many were able to emigrate to Israel and other Western countries. Additionally, many voices were heard – especially among the Czechoslovak intelligentsia – calling for the renewal of diplomatic relations with Israel. These voices were not silenced even after the invasion, led by the Soviet Union, of the Warsaw Pact armies (excluding Romania) into Czechoslovak territory to reinstate communist rule in the country.

TURNING POINTS LEADING UP TO RENEWED
DIPLOMATIC TIES

1. First Sparks

The first signs of change with regard to Czech policy toward Israel became evident in April 1987 when – for the first time since severing ties with Israel – the Czechoslovaks hosted the Israeli tennis team, accompanied by the chairman of the Knesset Sports Committee, MK Goldstein, as well as a few dozen Israeli fans. They also allowed scientists from Israel to participate at international conferences held in Prague, although their stay was only permitted for the duration of the conferences. Later the same year, Israeli tourists were allowed into the country.

At the same time, in April 1987, Soviet President Mikhail Gorbachev paid an official visit to Czechoslovakia, during which he expressed his explicit reservations abut the Soviet invasion of Czechoslovakia in 1968 (that is, reservations about the 'Brezhnev Doctrine' of interfering in the affairs of every Warsaw Pact member whose communist regime was endangered). He was also very well received by the Czechoslovak population because of his policies of perestroika and glasnost in the Soviet Union, which he compared to the programmes of social and economic reform which Czechoslovakia had begun to adopt during the Prague Spring.

Although Gorbachev was not wont to intervene in the internal affairs of Soviet Bloc countries, and chose not to become involved in the differences of opinion that had arisen within Czechoslovakia on the need for reforms, his visit greatly contributed to the strengthening of liberal circles in the country that supported the introduction of changes similar to those that Gorbachev himself advocated. This weakened the opposition espoused by the conservative leadership of the Czechoslovak Communist Party.

To implement economic reforms, Czechoslovakia needed to broaden its cooperation with Western countries and, in this context, the Czechoslovaks did not encounter Soviet opposition. Israel was perceived as part of the West. The Czechoslovaks understood that conducting business with Israel could advance Czechoslovakia's economy. There is no doubt that Czechoslovak leaders were aware of the informal ties that had begun to be established between Israel and the Soviet Union, Poland and Hungary. It was obvious that the hesitation over whether to draw closer to Israel was not based on fears of what the Soviet Union would say, but rather on what the Arab countries, with which Czechoslovakia conducted widespread commercial, military, economic and industrial activity, would say.

An important milestone, the first of its kind since the severance of diplomatic relations between the two countries, occurred during a meeting between then Deputy Prime Minister and Foreign Minister Shimon Peres and Czechoslovak Foreign Minister Bohuslav Chnoupek, initiated by Israel during the UN General Assembly on 27 September 1988. Since their conversation established a basis for continued political contact between the representatives of both countries and reflected the turning point in Czechoslovakia's position regarding Israel, we will present its main points here.

2. Israel's Deputy Prime Minister and Foreign Minister Shimon Peres' conversation with Czechoslovak Foreign Minister Bohuslav Chnoupek

Foreign Minister Chnoupek began by noting that this was the first meeting to take place since the severance of diplomatic relations between the two countries in 1967. He emphasized that due to the general improvement in the situation (apparently referring to the end of the cold war and the establishment of diplomatic contact between Israel and the rest of the Soviet Bloc countries), it was logical that Czechoslovakia had responded positively to Israel's proposal to hold this meeting in the framework of the UN General Assembly. He opened with a survey of the history of Israeli-Czechoslovak relations and noted that in the Second World War, Czechoslovak soldiers had fought and fallen on the soil of Palestine. (It is true that Czechoslovak soldiers had been in Palestine as a unit of the British army on their way to the Western Desert and from there to Italy, but they certainly did not fight or die in Palestine – Y.G.)

Czechoslovakia had played a role in the decision to establish the State of Israel, being a founding member of the UN in San Francisco in 1945 and a member of the special committee that recommended ending the British Mandate in Palestine. It was also a member of the UNSCOP committee that recommended the Plan of Partition of Palestine in 1947. In his estimation, this explained Czechoslovakia's special attitude towards Israel and the speed with which it established diplomatic relations with Israel immediately after its establishment. He further explained that Czechoslovakia had never taken a negative stance towards Israel until the difficult years of 1967 and after, when relations were frozen between the two countries. Even after that time, Czechoslovakia never supported extremist positions, despite its friendly relations with the Arab world, from Rabat to Baghdad and Riyadh.

Chnoupec stated that throughout the years, Czechoslovakia had respected Israel as an independent state and a member of the UN. He maintained that at every opportunity, his country had presented this position to Arabs in Tripoli, Baghdad and Algiers and added, without being specific, that 'Israel, however, must adopt a realistic position'. He said, 'recently we have seen positive signs pointing to the rehabilitation of our relations with Israel in the fields of economics and industry, and even in the polit-ical arena'. He mentioned the visit to Israel of a member of the Central Committee of Czechoslovakia's Communist Party, whom he said had held (without specifying details) beneficial talks in Israel.

'Now', he continued, 'we intend to send a group of two or three consular officials to Tel Aviv' to take care of consular problems that had arisen following the liberalization process that Czechoslovakia had introduced regarding the issuing of entry permits to tourists and individuals arriving from Israel to participate at international conferences. This had generated quite a lot of traffic from Israel to his country, and it was not convenient, he said, 'to resolve problems of entry permits via the Austrians in Vienna'. The staff was committed to stay in Israel for a period of four to six weeks. He also said, 'We intend to send two to three people to Tel Aviv from the Conextrade Company to handle economic issues.' This was all done 'to improve bilateral relations between Czechoslovakia and Israel'. He also related that there were plans to send additional delegations consisting of parliamentarians, Communist Party members and representatives of cities twinned with Israeli counterparts.

He summarized the topic of bilateral relations between his country and Israel by saying:

> The signs pointing to our intentions to improve relations between us are a cause of concern and anger in Arab countries. For example, the Libyan press protested the 'socialist countries'' betrayal with regard to the Arab issue, but we must continue on this logical path. To be sure, Czechoslovakia does not have the same constraints that motivated Hungary and Poland [from which tens of thousands of Jews emigrated to Israel, while from Czechoslovakia 35,000 emigrated], but the economic interest prompts us to follow the path we have determined for ourselves. The Czechoslovak economy is undergoing a process of decentralization and economic reform in the direction of broad economic cooperation with foreign companies.

As for the Middle East, he announced that Czechoslovakia intended to convene an exemplary non-governmental international conference. The intention was to hold the conference from 6–8 December 1988. He noted that US

Attorney General Ramsey Clark had promised to participate, that a delegation from the Soviet Union was expected
to attend, and that most Arab countries intended to send
delegations. The director of the Czechoslovak Institute for
International Relations, he said, had visited Israel to
examine the possibility of Israel's participation. The press
had reported that Abba Eban might attend, but he thought
this might be 'journalistic speculation'.

The best way to settle the Arab-Israeli conflict seemed to
him to be through an international conference. He noted
that he had suggested this to Anwar Sadat in 1963, at which
time, he emphasized, there was no Soviet proposal. He
further noted that he had raised the idea in Algiers and
Damascus and that, in October 1987, he had discussed it
with Hafez al-Assad for four hours. He concluded by
saying, 'there is no better way than an international conference', and that the Intifada would continue and that Israel
would not be able to stop it. 'It is only a pity for the victims.
It is important, therefore, to convene an international
conference with the participation of all relevant parties.'

In his response, Israel's then Deputy Prime Minister and
Foreign Minister Shimon Peres praised his Czechoslovak
colleague's desire to improve bilateral relations. He noted
that the people of Israel had fond memories of their
relationship with Czechoslovakia during the early days of
the State's independence. He mentioned in particular their
appreciation of the fact that Czechoslovakia sold badly
needed munitions to Israel in the critical period 1948/49. He
added that 'although there was not a massive
Czechoslovak immigration to Israel, the significant contribution of Czechoslovak Jewry towards building the Land
of Israel is recorded in the annals of Israel's history'.

Peres also noted that good relations with Israel did not
have to come at the expense of good relations with the
Arabs. He added that the Czechoslovaks should not pay
too much attention to the Arabs' protests and reasoned that
if there was an Israeli Embassy in Egypt and an Egyptian

Embassy in Israel, there was no reason why there should not be an Israeli Embassy in Prague and a Czechoslovak Embassy in Jerusalem. The Russians also admitted they had erred when they decided to sever relations with Israel, and they now understood that 'it is not possible to include them in the (Middle East) political process as long as they do not have full diplomatic relations with Israel'. As for the international conference, Peres noted, 'this is a difficult and complicated matter'. Even Sadat understood that this plan should be abandoned: 'Israel does not need an international conference.'

Peres said Israel was closely monitoring the changes occurring in the East European Bloc. It was aware that Czechoslovakia was the most developed East European country and 'hoped that Glasnost and Perestroika would succeed'. As for the Middle East, Peres noted that three Middle Eastern ills needed to be eradicated: fundamentalism, war and poverty. Regarding the Palestinians, he stated, 'We do not want to rule over them. In Israel's 4,000 year history we have never ruled over any other nation, because that is contrary to our moral values, and those that ruled over us have disappeared from the annals of history.' Peres advised his Czechoslovak colleague not to draw out the process of re-establishing relations with Israel. He told him about the conversation he had held with the prime minister of Spain, Felipe Gonzales, in which he explained that the establishment of diplomatic relations with Israel would not damage Spanish-Arab relations, as indeed it had not. That was also the case with Egypt. However, he added that if Czechoslovakia wanted to establish only economic ties, 'then a lot of matters would be limited just to that domain'.

Regarding the idea of holding a non-governmental international conference in Prague, he said he would not encourage Israeli participation 'as long as we have not established official relations'. He concluded by saying, 'We see this meeting as a first step toward the strengthening of relations between Czechoslovakia and Israel', and that he hoped that 'the long road ahead would not be hindered by slow steps'.

The Czechoslovak foreign minister thanked Peres for his remarks and expressed his confidence that 'indeed, it seems likely that the two countries will re-establish diplomatic relations. The question is only when this will take place, and I hope that time will not be measured by Chinese standards but, rather, by European ones.' He estimated that Hungary and Poland would renew relations with Israel 'in the coming year' (1989), and that he 'assumes and hopes that Czechoslovakia will follow suit'.
Three other topics were raised in the conversation: Israeli-Soviet relations, Syria and the international conference to settle the Arab-Israeli conflict, and the issue of Arab refugees from 1948.

1. Israeli-Soviet relations: Peres noted that despite differences of opinion between the Israelis and the Soviets (differences he did not specify but called 'an issue that is crucial to us'), the Soviets had increased tenfold the number of exit visas for Soviet Jews; thousands of Soviet tourists visited Israel; and, from time to time, the two countries held talks because Israel's relations with the Soviets 'are more significant in practical terms than theoretical ones'.
2. Syria: The Czechoslovak minister asked what Israel's position was regarding Syria's participation in an international conference. Peres rejected the idea and described Assad's extremism on the strategic level. He re-emphasized his belief that an agreement between Israel and Syria could be reached by direct negotiations, not by coercion.
3. Arab refugees: The Czechoslovak minister described his experiences as a refugee during the Second World War, when he was expelled from his village at the age of 13. He compared his experience to that of Arab refugees and emphasized the emotional aspect of the refugee

61

situation. Peres absolutely rejected the comparison, noting that the Israelis were in Palestine before the Palestinians. The Mufti, not the Israelis, had encouraged them to leave Israel in 1948. 'We did not declare war on the Palestinians; on the contrary, they declared war on us. We agreed to the Partition Plan of Palestine, but they rejected it. Today they are paying for their mistakes, and we hope they will not continue to make mistakes.'

Finally, the Czechoslovak minister praised Israel as a 'bastion of democracy in a sea of Arab reactionism', and wished Peres success in the forthcoming Israeli elections. Peres commended his Czechoslovak colleague for taking the first step 'towards the renewal of relations between us' and invited him to visit Israel whenever he wished 'before, during, and after the [forthcoming] elections [in Israel]'.

Raphael Gvir, a member of Israel's Diplomatic Mission to the UN present during the conversation, added that 'it took place in a friendly and businesslike atmosphere. It was obvious that the Czechoslovaks were interested in starting a new chapter in Israeli-Czechoslovak relations and that they were looking for a way to do so without any unnecessary tumult.'[6]

It could be added that one of the ways to 'start a new chapter', as will be shown, was the Czechoslovak leaders' idea to convene a non-governmental international convention in Prague on the subject of the Arab-Israeli conflict. Implementing this idea would grant the hosts the status of mediator, pave the way for establishing relations with Israel, and neutralize the anger of Arab countries, as well as the PLO (which the Czechoslovaks feared), over Czechoslovakia's policy change regarding Israel.

3. Knesset Member Abba Eban's visit to Czechoslovakia, 23–25 October 1988

As agreed upon by then Foreign Minister Shimon Peres and his Czechoslovak counterpart, at their meeting during the UN General Assembly, Knesset Member Abba Eban was dispatched by Israel's Labour Party, (accompanied by his parliamentary assistant Itai Bartov) for further discussions in Czechoslovakia and in Yugoslavia at the invitation of Bahomiel Kuiera, chairman of Czechoslovakia's Socialist Party. (This party numbered 17,000 members in 1984 and operated under the patronage of Czechoslovakia's Communist Party to establish ties with socialist parties in the West.) Kuiera also served as deputy speaker of the Czechoslovak parliament and head of the Czechoslovak Institute for International Relations. This was the first political meeting of its kind between representatives of the ruling parties of both Israel and Czechoslovakia. However, its significance transcended partisan politics, and the meeting actually assumed an official, state character.

The discussions held at the Czechoslovak Institute for International Relations focused primarily on the Czechoslovak proposal for an international 'model conference' with all parties in the Arab-Israeli conflict participating, and on the possibility of MK Abba Eban's participation in the conference as a representative of the Labour Party. The chairman of the Socialist Party of Czechoslovakia presented to Abba Eban his country's position concerning the need to hold the proposed conference, for the following reasons.[7]

Czechoslovakia, said Bahomiel Kuiera, had proper relations with all the Arab parties and from this derived its ability to assist in the solution of the conflict. It persistently supported Israel's right to exist in security. Yet, Czechoslovakia had expressed its reservations about Israel's policy in the Occupied Territories and apprehension concerning the situation prevailing in the Middle East, as well as the possibility that a flare-up might spread and radiate to the entire world. From his talks with Arab politicians, he received the impression that a new readiness for progress towards a settlement of the conflict could be discerned. In Czechoslovakia there was absolute abhorrence of an imposed solution. It was impossible today to ignore the legitimate rights of the Palestinians. Czechoslovakia expected and hoped for the establishment of a Palestinian government and state. The possibility for a settlement to the conflict had become stronger in light of the general atmosphere of reconciliation in the world during the past two years.

From this, in his estimation, derived the importance of the 'model' conference that Czechoslovakia intended to help arrange for the solution of conflict in the Middle East. This would be a meeting of senior representatives from all parties, but with non-governmental status; they would attempt to agree upon a formula for convening the fully international conference that would then be able to resolve all the substantive issues involved in the Arab-Israeli conflict.

Eban surveyed Israeli-Czechoslovak relations since 1948. He stressed, 'it is particularly important to maintain diplomatic ties and engage in continual dialogue when differences of opinion exist between two countries'. He also reviewed Israel's relations with the East European countries, remarking that in the USSR voices were also being heard claiming that the break in relations with Israel had been a mistake. He cited the example of Romania, which had not severed its diplomatic relations with Israel and despite that remained 'influential', and he proposed 'reaching an arrangement (between Israel and Czechoslovakia) that would enable a continual dialogue similar to that being conducted with the USSR, Poland, and so on'. As for the situation in Israel, Abba Eban presented the positions of the two main (party) blocks in Israel and stressed that 'those striving to conclude domination of 1.5 million Arabs aspire to do so out of personal interest, since continuation of the status quo was causing great damage to the State of Israel, to its security, economy, values, relations in the world, and the peace treaty with Egypt'. He presented to his interlocutor the political platform of the Labour Party and its perception of the role of an international conference 'and the importance of the third party that would bridge between positions and be a guarantor to agreements'.

In referring to the PLO, he explained that

[T]he necessary change had not yet occurred, that is accepting Security Council Resolution 242, abandoning terror, and recognizing Israel's existence. Thus, the PLO cannot take part in a political process when it refuses to accept the rules of the game. To be sure, there are moderate elements demonstrating willingness to become more moderate, but it did not seem that Arafat had placed himself in support of such stances. It may be that these changes are 'frozen' until after the elections in Israel with the aim of first verifying the profitability of the change.

On the topic of the 'model conference', Eban clarified the legal situation in Israel that prevented participation in such a conference alongside PLO members, such that it was not possible to pledge at this stage that he would be able to take part in their conference. Similarly, it would be fitting for his participation to be agreeable to the Labour Party, since there was no interest in participation that was not representative.

Kuiera, when responding to MK Eban's explanations, added the following statements: First, that he was impressed by the common elements in the opinions that Abba Eban had presented. He did not believe in the chances for bilateral talks between Israeli and Arab representatives without guarantees. He expressed hope for the success of the Labour Party in the elections and the importance of the election results from the perspective of the step Czechoslovakia was initiating. Second, he sought to differentiate between carrying on a dialogue between Israel and Czechoslovakia and instituting full diplomatic relations. He explained that diplomatic relations were conditional upon a significant political turning point. Likewise, he noted that events in the past year in the territories occupied by Israel had negatively influenced the dialogue that had taken place to date. The current meeting, he added, would be part of the new page being opened in Czechoslovak-Israeli relations. And they should continue along the trail that had been blazed. Third, he voiced deep appreciation to Abba Eban and said that 'the meeting with him verifies the great esteem he receives the world over. Therefore, his participation in the conference is very important, both for its success and for the improvement in Israel's image in the world and in Czechoslovakia.' And finally, the Palestinian representatives invited to the conference were not chosen for their links with the PLO 'but because they are suitable to represent the Palestinian people'. At the same time, he said, it was possible to be flexible as to the final list of invitees, adding that special note should be given to 'the great interest the Palestinian representatives had shown in holding the conference, and deriving from this is the great importance in the continuation of the Israeli dialogue with them'. Also, the list of previous Egyptian foreign ministers expected to participate in it 'indicates the importance of the conference for the Egyptians'.

The two representatives agreed between them that the recommendation of the Labour Party would be transmitted to Czechoslovakia and that an effort would be made to assemble representation that would enable participation from all sides, since participation that was not on the agreed terms was liable only to be deleterious to the success of the 'model conference'. Kuiera concluded by saying 'that fitting representation at the conference is likely to open a new chapter in Israel-Czechoslovakia relations'.

During his visit, Eban was received by members of the Jewish community in Prague. He was given an informative overview of their activities in the areas of religion and culture, and a description of the Hebrew-language classes given to the community's youth. He was also told that community representatives were recently permitted to participate in World Jewish Congress conferences and were now able to welcome tourists from Israel, something which had previously been forbidden. In addition, he visited the Jewish Museum, the Alt-Neu Shul (Old-New Synagogue), the old Jewish cemetery in Prague and Theresienstadt (the Terezin concentration camp). These visits were included in Eban's itinerary at the initiative of his Czech hosts, even before the beginning of talks. This, too, was one of the political turning points in Czechoslovakia's attitude towards the local Jewish population and Israel.

The talks between the foreign ministers and the two party representatives – held a month apart – attest to the fundamental differences of approach between diplomatic and party echelons which existed in Czechoslovak policy toward Israel. In both cases, however, joint conclusions were apparently reached that relations must be advanced for Czechoslovakia's own benefit. The diplomatic echelons referred to the 'honeymoon period' of Czechoslovak-Israeli relations (deliberately omitting the hostile years) and hoped that diplomatic relations would soon be renewed, given the new political détente between the Eastern and Western blocs, with the USSR no longer an obstacle.

However, the Czech politicians made progress on the renewal of diplomatic relations conditional upon Israel's agreement to participate in the proposed non-governmental conference in Prague. The conference was to include Israel's Middle East adversaries in order 'to create a dynamic to promote relations with Israel', according to the Czech Socialist Party chairman. At the same time, he scolded Israel (albeit moderately) for its policy in the Occupied Territories. Since in that period, until late December 1989, Czechoslovakia was under communist rule, it seems that the political class dictated Czechoslovak policy to a greater degree than did the diplomatic corps.

On the other hand, Abba Eban and Shimon Peres also presented different approaches to the Czechoslovaks, as reflected in their talks with them. Peres rejected the idea of

Israel's participation in the proposed model conference, while Abba Eban tended to favour the idea, conditional upon the Labour Party's decision. Since the Labour Party did not agree to participate in such a conference, the Czechoslovak leadership's motivation to promote relations with Israel at that time also dissipated, which was in any case what the Czech politicians wanted.

It was a year before discussions were held again. The Velvet Revolution had taken place in Czechoslovakia, following a series of mass protests (17–28 November 1989) in which hundreds of thousands demonstrated for a democratic government to replace communist rule. These events were influenced by the political and social upheavals that took place throughout Eastern Europe, after the fall of the Berlin Wall, as a result of its disengagement from the Soviet Union. In the first days of the mass protests, the Citizens' Forum, established and led by Vaclav Havel,[8] espoused the ideas of democracy and Western liberalism for Czechoslovakia and was widely supported.

Due to pressure from the Forum, the communist government under Mils Jakes was forced to disband and, a few days later, on 10 December 1989, President Gustav Husak also resigned. Havel, chairman of the Citizens' Forum, began to conduct negotiations with the various political movements in order to put together a new government. On 29 December 1989, he was temporarily elected Czechoslovakia's new president by the federal parliament until the free general elections, which were scheduled to take place in July 1990 (when Havel was elected president for two years, by an overwhelming majority). In this way, the Communist regime came to an end in Czechoslovakia.

In his first speech as president of the Republic, on 1 January 1990, Havel said:

> Masaryk based his politics on morality. Let us try, in a new time, and in a new way to restore this concept of politics. Let us teach ourselves and others that politics should be an expression of a desire to contribute to the

happiness of the community rather than of a need to cheat or rape the community. Let us teach ourselves and others that politics can be not simply the art of the possible, especially if this means the art of speculation, calculation, intrigue, secret deals, and pragmatic manoeuvring, but it can be also the art of the impossible, that is the art of improving ourselves and the world ... My honourable task is to strengthen the authority of our country in the world. I would be glad if other states respected us for showing understanding, tolerance and love of peace ... I would be happy if we succeeded before the elections in establishing diplomatic relations with the Vatican and with Israel.[9]

President of Israel Chaim Herzog sent a congratulatory telegram to President Havel on 2 January 1990, in which it was said, 'I am sure that your country will enjoy liberty and democracy and will become again a centre of freedom and mediation as it had been during the unforgettable days of the prominent leaders Masaryk and Beneš. I also believe that the relations between both our nations will develop for the mutual benefit of our states.'[10]

Speaker of the Knesset Dov Shilansky also sent a congratulatory telegram on 3 January 1990 to Alexander Dubček, who was elected speaker of the Czechoslovak parliament and who had previously served as secretary general of the Communist Party during the Prague Spring. A short while after the establishment of the new government in December 1989, preliminary contacts were made with Israeli representatives in preparation for the renewal of diplomatic ties between the two countries.

4. Talks in Prague Held by Ambassador Mordechai Palzur, Head of Israel's Interests Office in Warsaw, 11–14 December 1989
Ambassador Palzur's discussions in Prague were arranged by Czechoslovakia's Foreign Ministry after hearing from the Czechoslovak ambassador in Warsaw of Palzur's intention to tour Prague 'if he could only receive an entry visa to

Czechoslovakia'. When he was informed that he would, indeed, be granted the visa, he asked if, while there, he might be able to discuss issues of common interest at the Czechoslovak Foreign Ministry. His initiative was backed by the Foreign Ministry in Jerusalem.

Palzur's hosts made every effort to treat his visit as an official one, and even published a formal statement at its close. During his stay, he met with heads of the Middle East Department of the Czechoslovak Foreign Ministry and with Deputy Foreign Minister Jaromir Nehera. This was the first visit of an Israeli ambassador to the Czechoslovak Foreign Ministry since the severance of relations between Israel and Czechoslovakia.

On his return to Warsaw on 14 December 1989, Palzur reported to the Foreign Ministry in Jerusalem that he had met with the Director of the Fifth Department of Asian, African and Middle Eastern Affairs, Dr Vaclav Jizdni, and with his deputy and head of the Israeli Affairs division, Jaroslav Cesar. In his report,[11] Palzur pointed out that his interlocutors considered his visit to Prague a 'historic event'. The Czechoslovaks noted that this was the first meeting at a professional diplomatic level to take place in many years. They then explained at length that in early 1989, they had proposed to the Directorate of the Czechoslovak Foreign Ministry 'to take steps towards normalizing relations with Israel but, in the political echelon, the idea was run aground'.

Later on, in private conversations, Palzur was told that 'the fossilized [Czechoslovak] government, which was one of the most conservative in Eastern Europe, was against drawing closer to Israel, as it was against the thawing of relations in other spheres'. With regard to the present these sources noted that with the new, more open government, they expected thawing and normalization of relations with Israel. Nevertheless, they praised their close relations with Arab countries and the scope of their trade with them, which in previous years had reached one billion dollars annually. 'However, this year and in other years, that was reduced to $600–$700 million.' Additionally, they mentioned the credit they had given to Arab countries and the money owed to Czechoslovakia, which they had not succeeded in recouping. Palzur's interlocutors were eager to know how Israel would be able to assist Czechoslovakia. Ambassador Palzur told them, in detail, about the development of Israel's relations with Poland, as an example of similar possibilities regarding Czechoslovakia. He pointed to cooperation in the fields of tourism, agriculture, health, technology and trade, as well as other fields of interest.

Similarly, they said that they intended to send to Israel a representative from the Czech Foreign Ministry to examine the condition of the Czechoslovakian Embassy in Tel Aviv that had been locked since the break in diplomatic relations between the two countries, and that within this context their representative might require the advice of the Foreign Ministry in Jerusalem. The ambassador replied to them that he saw no problem with that. They also expressed interest in establishing direct air links between Czechoslovakia and Israel.

The Czechoslovak foreign minister, who hosted Ambassador Palzur for lunch, sounded optimistic on that occasion as to the future of the relations of his country with Israel. He admitted that it had been a mistake to sever them, and he proposed to discuss, not the past, but rather the future. He added that he assumed that the new foreign minister, Jiri Dienstbier, 'would certainly affirm the proposals of the professional level' but they needed some time 'so that he could become familiar with the issues', and he said further 'that the intention is to proceed swiftly as things move at great speed in Czechoslovakia'.

Ambassador Palzur distributed to his interlocutors information about Israel, which they were very happy to receive, and they pointed out that until then they had been supplied explanatory material about what was going on in our region only from Arab sources. Moreover, he explained

71

the issues with which Israel's foreign policy was concerned, as well as within the Middle East region. At the request of his interlocutors it was agreed to supply them continuously with material about Israel through the Czechoslovak embassy in Warsaw. In response to their question as to what was the most desirable way in which to create a permanent connection between them and representatives of Israel, the ambassador advised them that they would do well to resume diplomatic relations with Israel all at once, and not follow the Polish example (in which an Israel Interests Office operated on the way to establishing an embassy) but rather that of Hungary and of the African states that had renewed their diplomatic relations with Israel that had also been severed as a result of the Six Day War.

At the end of the visit, the Czechoslovak Foreign Ministry published an official announcement about working talks that representatives of the Czechoslovak Foreign Ministry had conducted with Ambassador Palzur on 'topics of bilateral interest, and in addition there was an exchange of opinions on the world situation'. The ambassador's visit received wide coverage in the Israeli media and in a number of other countries.

The day after his talks in the Foreign Ministry, Ambassador Palzur met with the president of the Jewish community in Prague, Dr Desider Galsky, who told him that he had held this position in the past but had been ousted by communists involved in [Jewish] community leadership who had close government ties to the communist regime and 'were hostile towards Israel'. Upon the establishment of the liberal regime in Czechoslovakia, he said, these people were removed from senior positions in the Jewish community, and he had been re-elected, a week earlier, president of the community. This was a short and accurate account of the Jewish community leadership's cooperation with the communist authorities of Czechoslovakia, especially after the Six Day War, and its replacement in the post-communist era.

In December 1989, in my capacity as deputy director general for Eastern European Affairs, I wrote a memo to the director general of the Foreign Ministry in Jerusalem, summarizing Ambassador Palzur's talks in Prague:

> The talks were constructive and should be viewed as a successful first step. One can conclude that Czechoslovakia will move towards normalizing relations with Israel, perhaps to a greater extent than what the professional echelons of the Czechoslovak Foreign Ministry recommended at the beginning of the year, restrained as they were by the previous regime. They exhibited: (a) a desire to secure aid from Israel in developing their country and to forge economic cooperation; (b) a desire to strengthen their position in the West by emphasizing their detachment from the policies of the previous regime; (c) disappointment in Arab countries and a tendency to separate the issue of the Israeli-Arab conflict from the issue of the re-establishment of diplomatic relations with Israel.
>
> It seems that at this stage, we will have to wait for the Czechoslovaks' proposals on the way how to advance further.[12]

So it was that in the first week of January 1990, the head of the Fifth Section in the Czechoslovak Foreign Ministry called me to inform us of his intention to come to Jerusalem with his colleague, the director general of the Czechoslovak Ministry of Foreign Trade, on 8–11 January 1990, for preliminary talks towards the resumption of diplomatic relations between Czechoslovakia and Israel, 'even this month or next month'. He received a positive reply.

5. Visit to Israel by Dr Vaclav Jizdni, Head of the Fifth Department of the Czechoslovak Foreign Ministry, and Engineer Ladislav Dobrovolny, Director General of the Czechoslovak Ministry for Foreign Trade, 8–11 January 1990

This visit of a two-member delegation from Czechoslovakia

for talks in Jerusalem was also considered a first. It was the first time in the history of Israeli-Czech relations that a delegation such as this had invited itself to come to Israel for 'advance talks'. These would take place in the Foreign Ministry and the Ministry of Industry, Trade and Labour in Jerusalem, and their purpose was to discuss the development of political and economic relations between the two countries, leading to the renewal of diplomatic relations. The talks were held with me, in my capacity as deputy director general for Eastern Europe of Israel's Ministry for Foreign Affairs,[13] with Foreign Minister Moshe Arens,[14] Deputy Director General for Economic Affairs Yaacov Cohen of the Ministry of Foreign Affairs, and Zohar Perry[15] of the Ministry of Industry and Trade. The Czechoslovaks' main purpose in these talks was to focus on the clarification of the following three issues:

1. The renewal of diplomatic relations with Israel, and Czechoslovakia's position with regard to the Arab-Israeli conflict.
2. The expected ramifications of the renewal of diplomatic relations with Israel on Czechoslovakia's relations with Arab countries.
3. A definition of the expected economic cooperation between Czechoslovakia and Israel after the renewal of diplomatic relations between them.

Below is the essence of these three topics as discussed among the members of the Czechoslovakian delegation and their Israeli interlocutors.

a) Renewal of Relations

Dr Jizdni at the working session with me – with the participation of the director of the Eastern European Department, Moshe Melamed, and his deputy, Shmuel Meirom – referred to the talks of Ambassador Palzur in Prague and to his proposals to continue with the political dialogue begun by Deputy Prime Minister and Foreign

Minister Peres with (former) Foreign Minister Chnoupek. We discussed the aspiration of Czechoslovakia to develop new diplomatic initiatives, among them official resumption of relations with Israel, following statements to this effect from the new president, Vaclav Havel. In this context Dr Jizdni described two principles of his country's new foreign policy: the first, to act in favour of the national interest of Czechoslovakia and no longer in the interests of the East European Bloc; second, to respect human rights, in general, and not simply to grant freedom of movement and organization.

In this context, he mentioned the statements by Foreign Minister Dienstbier at his first press conference that 'we shall not change our attitude towards the Palestinian problem since this is within the framework of human rights, and we will support the right of the Palestinians to self-determination. At the same time we will support the right of Israel to peace and security.' (In the version of the remarks by Dienstbier made at this press conference that were distributed by the Czechoslovak Mission to the UN in a press release in New York on 15 December 1989, the 'Palestinian problem' was not mentioned at all. It did state: 'As for the situation in the Middle East, Czechoslovakia will act according to the principle that the problems in this part of the world should be solved through dialogue and as far as possible without violence.') On the whole, Jizdni said, Czechoslovakia will be ready to mediate between the opponents in the Arab-Israeli conflict for the sake of finding a solution to the problem.

As for renewing relations with Israel, he noted that a decision in principle had been accepted on 1 January 1990, while the directive that Foreign Minister Dienstbier should go for talks to Israel had been received on 3 January 1990. The time for resuming relations with Israel, however, had not yet been determined. They must prepare the ground-work for that at home (in the government and parliament) and abroad, and to make this decision known to the Arab countries with which Czechoslovakia had ramified economic links, without asking for their authorization. Thus he felt that the renewal of relations would take place 'in another two or three months'. In the meantime, he expressed the wish of Foreign Minister Dienstbier to meet with Foreign Minister Arens to continue the political dialogue towards resumption of diplomatic relations.

In my reply I welcomed the arrival of the two members of the delegation to Israel. I pointed out that their visit could be considered historic and that accorded well with the delineation of the new foreign policy of their country towards us, as this had been expressed in the statement by Foreign Minister Dienstbier at his first press conference on 14 December 1989 in which he had announced that relations between the two states would soon be rehabilitated. I mentioned that Foreign Minister Arens welcomed this declaration by his Czechoslovak counterpart, and noted that it had received widespread media coverage. As to the proper time for renewing relations, I said that the issue would be determined by a decision of the Czechoslovak government. Whatever it decided would be acceptable, provided that resumption was at the ambassadorial level. I added that our diplomatic relations with Poland would be renewed at the end of February 1990, and I asked whether Czechoslovakia would perhaps want to precede it.

As for a meeting between Foreign Minister Dienstbier and Foreign Minister Arens, I suggested that Dr Jizdni raise the issue in his anticipated talk with Foreign Minister Arens. I proposed that the meeting between the two foreign ministers take place in one of our capitals, and not necessarily within the framework of an international conference (as he had previously suggested[16]). And indeed, at his meeting with Foreign Minister Arens – with my participation and Director General Dobrovolny in attendance – Dr Jizdni stated that he had been authorized by Foreign Minister Dienstbier to invite him for an official visit to Prague on 12 or 14 February 1990.

Dr Jizdni reiterated to the foreign minister the positive decision to renew his country's relations with Israel and the need for time to prepare the paper work, and to explain to Arab countries – to which Czechoslovakia exported merchandise to the value of a billion dollars a year – its motives for resuming relations with Israel. He further noted that they were sensitive to the Palestinian issue; they recognized the right of Palestinians to self-determination. Yet, they also understood that it was not his country's role to make decisions about this situation, since Israel must be allowed to decide on this question for itself. At the same time, they would be ready to help, as far as they could, to promote the peace process. To that Foreign Minister Arens replied:

> Undoubtedly Czechoslovakia has a function in the peace process and that it wants to promote it. I am happy to hear that they want to contribute its share in that. We have not spoken to each other for twenty-two years. Now, when we will have relations between us, we will have the opportunity to speak and to explain our positions. I assume that you will recognize the fact that from among all the states of our region, we have a greater drive for peace than any other.

Beyond that, the foreign minister expressed his pleasure at receiving the delegation members. He pointed out that in Israel people were following with great admiration the changes in Czechoslovakia, which was joining the community of democratic nations. And in this context, he added that 'We are happy, but not entirely surprised, about the decision to change Czechoslovakia's foreign policy and to establish relations with Israel.' Finally, Foreign Minister Arens asked to send his greeting to Foreign Minister Dienstbier and to tell him 'that we would like to host him in Israel', and when he took his leave from Dr Jizdni the foreign minister told him 'and we expect to see you again'.

b) Ramifications of the Renewal of Relations

The anticipated ramifications, in their estimation, of the resumption of their relations with Israel on Czechoslovakia's connections with the Arab countries.

Director General Dobrovolny, in our conversation with him, noted that in his ministry, too, 'a relatively long time ago' the idea of renewing relations with Israel had been raised, on the assumption that it was capable of offering many possibilities for industrial, agricultural and techno-logical cooperation. Yet they had felt that they were not prepared for negative economic responses by Arab countries such as a trade boycott and the like. To be sure, they did not sense significant stress in that direction, but there already were Czechoslovak companies who had been pressured by Syria and Libya. Syria and Iraq had heavy debts that required to be repaid gradually to Czechoslovakia. And this was the crux of the problem: they were liable to evade payment of their debts to Czechoslovakia because of the renewal of its relations with Israel.

In response to my question, 'If it is not secret, what size of debts are you talking about?' Dobrovolny replied:

The Syrians owe us a billion dollars and we have to take into consideration the manner of their reaction after resumption of relations with you. First, the question is posed, whether the Syrians and the Iraqis will continue to repay their debt gradually? Second, many of our companies find a good market in these countries for their products and they want to continue commercial links with them. It is difficult for us to know what their reaction will be in this area. In general, Tunisia and Algeria are interested in our products that we cannot market in other countries. So, as we said, we do not fear those countries. On the part of the Egyptians, too, there will be no problem. Syria receives money from Saudia Arabia, and it repays its debt to us with this money. This means that this chain is definitely liable to be harmed. We do not believe that there is a great chance for repayment of debts in money but rather in merchandise, and therefore the process will be very slow.

I remarked that I did not think that any of the Arab countries would fail to honour their obligations to Czechoslovakia because of resumption of relations with us. If they did so, it meant that from the outset they had not intended to pay their debt.

Dobrovolny added that these countries, which owed Czechoslovakia a great deal of money, were liable to create difficulties since huge amounts were under discussion, 'and we must consider how we will be able to withstand this'. In this context, he asked our advice 'on the topic of economic cooperation between Czechoslovakia and Israel'. I suggested discussing this issue at the meeting arranged between the economic deputy directors (of the Foreign Ministry, Ministry of Finance, Ministry of Commerce and Industry, and the Ministry of Agriculture) on the development of economic and trade links between the two states. I noted that Israel traded with a large number of countries and it was up to them, whether any country was willing – or unwilling – to confront the Arab boycott. 'This, of course, is also a consideration of yours.'

I added that in different countries questions were asked about how the Arab nations would react to the restoration of relations with us. I mentioned to them that we maintained relations with Egypt, that relations were established with Spain, and that we had renewed our relations with Hungary, and were resuming them in the near future with Poland; our relations with Romania – where I had served as ambassador until recently – had never been severed, and no action had been taken on the part of the Arab countries. We knew from these states that Arab countries owed them a tremendous amount of money, and they had no problems because of their connections with Israel. In general, I concluded, one might say that the opportunities for cooperation between Czechoslovakia and

Israel were numerous, considering the as yet untapped potential that was waiting to be realized. Obviously, for the purpose of studying this topic more thoroughly, it was imperative to have trade and economic representatives from both sides meet and conduct professional discussions on the topic. On our part, we were ready for that. I asked both of them whether they had any concrete proposals; Dr Jizdni replied, 'We do not want financial aid at all from you. Our economy is in reasonable shape. Direct official relations would be of assistance, as well as close economic ties.'

c) Anticipated Cooperation

What economic cooperation could the Czechoslovak government expect after renewal of its diplomatic relations with Israel? At a meeting of the Czech delegation with the team of the economic deputy general directors, it was decided upon a visit by an inter-ministerial team to Prague to discuss forms of cooperation between Czechoslovakia and Israel and increasing mutual trade. To make the preliminary arrangements for this meeting, the sides decided that the two parties – Czechoslovakia and Israel – would prepare during the visit a proposal of intentions according to which they would open negotiations on a series of bilateral agreements, including, among others, an agreement to increase mutual trade, encourage investments, prevent double taxation, and promote scientific and agricultural cooperation and the like.[17]

The delegation's visit thus laid the groundwork for the formulation of a joint plan for cooperation between Czechoslovakia and Israel at the same time as the imminent renewal of diplomatic relations between the two countries.

6. Israeli Deputy Prime Minister and Finance Minister Shimon Peres' Visit to Prague, 21–23 January 1990, for Talks on Economic Cooperation between Israel and Czechoslovakia

Ten days after the Czechoslovak delegation's visit to Israel, Shimon Peres made an official visit to Prague, at the invitation of Czechoslovak Finance Minister Vaclav Klaus. This was 'a historic visit', as it was described in the memorandum of agreement signed by both ministers on 22 January 1990, which heralded a new chapter in relations between the two countries, following President Havel's decision to renew full diplomatic relations with Israel. This was also the first visit of its kind by a high-ranking Israeli official. During the visit, the two ministers decided 'to take steps to encourage, to as great an extent as possible, the advancement of economic ties between the two countries, and to facilitate free trade'.

The memorandum of agreement also stated that 'the two sides declare their intent to sign mutual agreements regarding the encouragement and protection of investments, preventing double taxation on income, finance, import taxes and tariffs on goods and services' and that 'delegations from both sides will meet as soon as possible to prepare the documents for signing'. With the declared intent of normalizing trade relations, both sides decided to appoint mutual trade delegations.[18]

During this visit to Prague, Peres was warmly received by President Havel and Prime Minister Calfa. Both revealed to him that the renewal of diplomatic relations between Czechoslovakia and Israel would occur in the very near future.[19]

7. Israeli Foreign Minister Moshe Arens' Visit to Prague, 8–10 February 1990, for the Signing of the Protocol on the Renewal of Relations between Czechoslovakia and Israel

Talks were held on this occasion with Foreign Minister Jiri Dienstbier, Prime Minister Marian Calfa, Speaker of the Parliament Alexander Dubček, and President Vaclav Havel. The festive signing ceremony for the renewal of diplomatic relations between the two countries was held on 9 February 1990. In attendance were Czechoslovak and foreign media and representatives of both countries' Foreign Ministries. Representatives of the Israeli Foreign

Ministry as well as the governor of the Bank of Israel had accompanied Arens on the visit. Greetings were exchanged and memoranda of understanding were signed by the two foreign ministers for cooperation in the fields of education, culture and science. These events and the talks that followed were widely covered in the local media.[20]

During the visit, the Czechoslovaks organized tours for the Israeli foreign minister and his entourage within Prague, as well as to the memorial site for the Terezin concentration camp, the Jewish community centre, the Alt-Neu Synagogue, the Jewish Museum and the old Jewish cemetery nearby. Arens also placed a wreath on Masaryk's grave. The atmosphere surrounding the talks held with Dienstbier, Calfa, Dubček, and Havel was friendly, as if twenty-three years of severed relations had not separated the two countries. The following were the main issues discussed.

Foreign Minister Dienstbier opened by saying that Czechoslovakia's relations with Israel over the past forty years had 'not been the best'. However, he noted that when the State of Israel was established, Czechoslovakia did provide assistance, and then the relations between the two countries were 'very good'. Discussing the present situation, he noted that with the resumption of diplomatic relations between the two countries, 'the basis upon which normal relations can be built is also being renewed'. He did not foresee any obstacles along the way. Czechoslovakia, for its part, could now return to the Middle East as a 'partner of equal status'. Despite the fact, in his opinion, that 'today's Czechoslovakia still does not possess the infrastructure for developing its relations with foreign countries', he suggested establishing mutual relations with Israel based on tourist, youth and student exchanges as well as cultural and economic ties.

On democracy in Czechoslovakia, he noted that 'Stalinism was the root of all evil, and it damaged socio-economic development in Eastern Europe'. After the revolutionary events that had taken place in this area, he felt there was no turning back. 'Without democracy, there is no creativity, and therefore no progress.' Additionally, he said, 'The severance of relations between Czechoslovakia and Israel in 1967 led to the events of 1968 [the Prague Spring]. Many intellectuals refused to join in the criticism of Israel. Society knew what was evil and what was good. Now that Czechoslovak society has lost its fear, it can become involved in its own internal affairs, and will not want to give that up.'

Regarding the Middle East, he noted that Czechoslovakia was having difficulties with Arab countries because of its renewed relations with Israel but, in the end, he said they acquiesced. Furthermore, the PLO Ambassador in Prague even said that renewed relations could help the peace process in the region. To this Dienstbier added, 'We cannot solve the problems of the Middle East, but a solution must be found to the Palestinian problem … Israel's victory in the Six Day War gives it the power to make concessions. However, apparently, internal Israeli issues dictate its position on the Palestinian problem.' He concluded by saying that he was ready to sign documents for mutual cooperation and foresaw very few problems regarding future relations. 'We are part of the same family, and there will be no more ideological problems influencing the relations between the two countries.'[21]

Prime Minister Calfa opened by saying that the renewal of Czechoslovak-Israeli relations was only the beginning of 'much faster paced' developments. He expressed an interest in establishing economic ties with Israel, since at that time mutual trade was almost non-existent. He said there was great potential in mutual cooperation, and that exchanges of teams and experts must commence.

He asked for Israel's help in finding a solution to the problem of air pollution 'that has influence and repercussion not only on the health of the population within the country, but also on the neighbouring countries', as a result of the operation of the power plant located in Czechoslovakia near the Austrian border. They had two options for solving the problem:

1. Would it be possible to establish close cooperation between the authorities in Israel and in Czechoslovakia (dealing with quality of the environment) in finding possible solutions?
2. Since Israel had influence in Austria, would it be able to persuade their government to reduce the pressure it was applying to Czechoslovakia concerning air pollution?

Foreign Minister Arens promised to examine the issue during his visit to Prague and afterwards. (During the course of the visit, I telephoned the director general of the Ministry of the Environment in Jerusalem, Dr Marinov, and I transmitted the information I learned from him to the head of the Middle East Section in the Czech Foreign Ministry, namely, 'Israel does not produce technology for the prevention of air pollution. But we do have good experts who know how to prevent pollution. We export equipment and we have developed our own satisfactory ideas.' It was suggested to the director of the section that the authorities involved in this area in Czechoslovakia turn directly to Dr Marinov so as to specify what they required. As for the second request, to intervene with the Austrian authorities, as far as I know no such action took place on the part of Israel.)

At the end of his remarks Prime Minister Calfa requested that the Israeli ministers 'transmit a message of friendship to the people of Israel, to strike out the unpleasant past and to open a new page of good and friendly relations'.[22]

Speaker of Parliament Alexander Dubček focused primarily on an assessment of Czechoslovakia's situation in this new, post-communist era, with respect to its own region of Eastern Europe as well as to the West. It was a very informative talk, accompanied by frank examination, which elucidated the background to the new Czechoslovak government's decision to renew diplomatic relations with Israel immediately upon the establishment of the democratic regime in his country. His comments reflected the political trends of Czechoslovakia's new leadership – strengthening its position as a democratic country and expressing its expectations that the West would encourage the process of economic and social reform in the Soviet Union under Gorbachev's leadership.

Even if he did not say so explicitly, it was evident that the reforms in the Soviet Union would not only ease the similar process of reform in countries that had belonged to the Soviet Bloc, but also ensure that the Soviets would not interfere in Czechoslovakia's internal affairs (a possible new version of the Soviet invasion of 1968). Therefore, the West's aid was vital to Gorbachev's success, and Israel was perceived as part of the West.

Regarding Czechoslovakia, he said:

Changes in Czechoslovakia are taking place without tensions. Enterprises continued to operate during the revolution, and there were no strikes. The revolutionary movement started in 1988/89. Social pressure started to surface in October 1988. Peaceful demonstrations took place in November 1989, although confrontations took place between the government and students. Now, with the end of the revolution, new people have come onto the scene [including himself]. Many think that the important work has already been done, but the important work is actually ahead of us. We cannot change over twenty years [that is, since the Prague Spring] or paralysis in only a few days. Hundreds and thousands of reformers were persecuted and oppressed. They were kept out of leadership roles and intellectual society was harmed as a result. The difference between twenty years ago and today is that then the reformers were in leadership positions; today the pressure for change comes from the outside. Today, we need to deal with ideas and plans that could not be implemented then because of military intervention [Dubček was careful not to call the intervention a Soviet invasion]. Then the reformers [such as himself] espoused the following policies: (a) Society must be based on pluralism, and censorship should be abolished. (b) Trade should be renewed as in Western Europe, with the orientation of the socialist countries in Western Europe. Punishment was grave under the neo-Stalinist rule in Czechoslovakia. Now we are not threatened from without [meaning the Soviet Union] but we have great difficulties; Czechoslovak society was morally damaged. The economic gap between us and modern society widened. There is great pressure for advancement and society has no time to lose.[23]

President Havel began by mentioning the statement he had made at his first press conference after having been appointed president, supporting the renewal of diplomatic relations with Israel. There were two reasons for this: first, the special affinity of the Jews of Czechoslovakia with its culture and their contribution to the creation of the unique atmosphere in Prague (together with the German minority). Secondly, there were many who had protested against the 1967 severance of relations with Israel when it was at war. Now everything would be rectified, 'The relations between us should be better than before, since we are now both democratic countries.'

President Havel offered his services as a mediator between Arafat (who was shortly to visit Prague) and Israel, even though he was not experienced in this type of mediation. To this, Foreign Minister Arens replied that it was not worthwhile for the president to take this risk. Dienstbier, who was also in attendance, commented that for a long time, the Czechoslovaks had maintained no presence in Israel. 'First let us get there and, afterwards, we will see if it would be possible.'[24]

Foreign Minister Moshe Arens responded to the three talks. His remarks included the following:

> Israel is carefully following the events of Eastern Europe and the transition from totalitarian regimes to democratic ones. We are pleased that Czechoslovakia is joining the ranks of the democratic regimes ...
>
> In 1948 Czechoslovakia was the only country which rushed to our aid; now we are returning to the situation in which good relations prevail between us, as if nothing had happened. We will erase from our memories the twenty-two years in which there were no diplomatic relations between us. The memory of the Jews who perished during the Holocaust in Czechoslovakia and those Jews of Czechoslovak origin living in Israel can serve as a bridge between us ...
>
> Czechoslovakia preceded Poland in renewing its relations with Israel. We are now receiving indications from East Germany and Yugoslavia of their intentions to renew their diplomatic relations with Israel ...
>
> Our relations with the Soviet Union are developing slowly. Of course, we are interested in broadening them. The rate of the Jewish emigration from the Soviet Union to Israel has risen considerably in the past year. Now there are thousands of people with exit permits to Israel who cannot get a seat on a plane because there is no direct flight between the Soviet Union and Israel.

Here he posed the question, 'Could we transport the new immigrants via Prague? This would be in addition to the two way stations we now have Bucharest and Budapest.'

At the end of his presentation, Arens said to his interlocutors,

> You are making history – not just here, but throughout the entire world. Now the cold war is no more, and the world supports Czechoslovakia. We are a small country, but are willing to put at Czechoslovakia's disposal whatever we can. I hope that from this point on,

relations between our two countries will not just be polite, but meaningful and warm.

After discussions Arens invited all of his hosts to visit Israel. He invited Foreign Minister Dienstbier as his guest; he invited Prime Minister Calfa in the name of Prime Minister Yitzhak Shamir, and presented President Havel with two invitations, one from President Chaim Herzog and the other from the Hebrew University of Jerusalem, so that it could bestow an honorary doctorate upon him. All three were accepted with appreciation.[25]

Parallel to these talks, the governor of the Bank of Israel, Professor Michael Bruno, and deputy director general for Economic Affairs at the Israeli Ministry of Foreign Affairs, Yaacov Cohen, conducted discussions with Czechoslovak ministers of economics, finance, science and technology to consider cooperation between the two countries. They agreed,[26]

1. The cancellation of the custom of conducting trade between the two countries through one company.
2. The signing of trade agreements, encouragement of investments, prevention of double taxation, and an aviation agreement.
3. Mutual visits: a delegation on behalf of the Ministry of Foreign Trade would visit Israel in April 1990.
4. Exchange visits of economic ministers: the visit to Israel by the Czech minister of finance in April 1990.

At the end of the visit, a joint statement was released regarding the talks, including a summary of the main issues discussed. Shortly thereafter the Embassy of Israel in Prague was opened by Ambassador Ephraim Tari, who served as chargé d'affaires for approximately two months. Eli Lopez was then appointed chargé d'affaires, and he occupied that role for seven months. Following Lopez, Yoel Sher was accredited as the first Israeli ambassador to Czechoslovakia in twenty-three years. The ceremony of presenting his credentials to President Havel took place on

27 November 1990. After he inspected the presidential honour guard, the military band played the national anthems of both countries.

In his telegram report to the Ministry of Foreign affairs in Jerusalem, Ambassador Sher summarized the symbolism of coming full circle by saying: '"Hatikva" has returned to the banks of the Vltava'. (Naftali Herz Imber, who wrote the lyrics of the Israeli national anthem 'Hatikva', had borrowed the melody from the Czechoslovak composer Bedich [Frederik] Smetana.) Parallel to this, the Embassy of Czechoslovakia was opened in Tel Aviv, headed by Ambassador Milos Pojar.

EPILOGUE

The Velvet Revolution paved the way for the rapid development of warm mutual relations between Israel and Czechoslovakia in all domains, including the political. Agreements were signed for cooperation in the fields of trade, economics, aviation, culture, health and science. Czechoslovakia was the first post-communist country to join the initiative to abolish the UN resolution which equated Zionism with racism. In 1990 and 1991, reciprocal visits were held by the presidents of the two countries, together with high-ranking personalities. Joint conferences were also held to research the history of the local Jewish population. With the disintegration of Czechoslovakia in 1992, Israel officially recognized the Czech and Slovak Republics, and was one of the countries which sponsored their membership of the United Nations. Shortly afterwards the Slovak Embassy was established in Tel Aviv, while Israel was represented in Slovakia by its Embassy in Vienna. At a later stage a non-resident ambassador was accredited to Slovakia, whose seat was in Jerusalem. As from 2006, an Israeli Embassy was established in Bratislava, the capital of Slovakia.

THE JEWISH POPULATION

The Velvet Revolution enabled the Federation of the Czechoslovak Jewish communities, in each of the two states, to develop freely their activities in the domains of religion, education, culture and social assistance (with the help of the JDC [Joint Distribution Committee], a world-wide American Jewish relief organization, headquartered in New York, active in more than several countries by offering aid to Jewish communities through a network of social and community assistance programmes). They were also able to establish memorials to the victims of the Holocaust and those fighters (particularly in Slovakia) who fell during their revolt against the Nazis. In Bratislava, a Museum of the History of the Jews in Slovakia was set up with the aid of the Slovak government. (In Prague a Museum of the History of the Jews in the Czech Republic was established during the communist regime.) The Federation was also free to cultivate its ties with the Jewish communities in Israel and throughout the world. The Jewish population in Czechoslovakia, before the Velvet Revolution, numbered 12,000 people.[27] Yet their number in both states has declined considerably, due to ageing and emigration. In 2001 the Jewish population in the Czech Republic numbered 2,800, and in Slovakia 3,300.[28]

NOTES

1. An abridged version of this chapter appeared in *The Jerusalem Review*, 1, 1 (2006–7), pp. 67–74, translated from Hebrew by Yvette Shumacher.
2. A.A. Ben-Asher, *Yahasei Hutz 1948–1953* [Foreign Relations 1948–1953] (Tel Aviv: Ayanot, 1957), pp.206–9.
3. Haim Yahil, 'Czechoslovakia', in Ya'akov Tsur (ed.), *Tefutsa: Mizrah Europa* (Jerusalem: Keter, 1976), p.234 [Hebrew]. Several articles and books have been published in Hebrew on the 'Prague Trials': Mordechai Oren, *The Story of a Political Prisoner in Prague* (Merhavya: Sifriat Hapoalim, 1958); Shimon Orenstein, *Prague Libels* (Tel Aviv: Am Hasefer, 1968); the research work by Meir Cotic, *Prague Trials* (Tel Aviv: Milo, 1964); A. Yehoshua Gilboa, 'Prague Nightmares', *Gesher* (September 1967), pp.65–82; Avigdor Dagan, 'The First Anti-Zionist Trial', *Gesher*,

114 (Summer 1986), pp.146–9 [Hebrew]; Moshe Yegar, *Czechoslovakia, Zionism and Israel* (Jerusalem: Hasifria Hazionit, 1997), pp.119–51.

4. *Knesset Minutes*, vol. 13, Second Session, Part A. The day after Moshe Sharett's speech (11 November 1951), pp.130–2, a comprehensive debate was held in which David Ben-Gurion and Knesset Members from Mapai (the Israel Labour Party) participated. They joined Sharett in condemning the Israeli government spokespersons for siding with the Czechoslovak government's smear campaign against Israel, Zionism and Jewish organizations, pp.151–78.

5. Radio Free Europe, Research Department, Czechoslovak Press Survey 134 (146, 148), 23 June 1967.

6. Report of Raphael Gvir to the deputy director general of the Foreign Ministry, 27 September 1988. File CSR 103.01, Israel State Archives (ISA).

7. Report of Abba Eban's visit to Czechoslovakia and Yugoslavia (23–29 October 1988) by Itai Bartov, Abba Eban's parliamentary assistant, File Yugo 103.01, ISA.

8. 'Czechoslovakia, History', in *Encyclopaedia Hebraica*, Supplement, vol.3 (Tel Aviv: Sifriat Poalim, 1995), pp.902–3 [Hebrew].

9. Moshe Yegar, *Czechoslovakia, Hatzionut Veyisrael, Gilgulei Yahasim Murkavim* (Jerusalem: Hasifria Hazionit, 1997), p.169.

10. File CSR 103.01, ISA.

11. Report of Ambassador Palzur to the deputy director of the Foreign Ministry, Y. Govrin, and to the Department for Eastern Europe, 2 April 1990, File CSR 103.01, ISA.

12. Report of Y. Govrin, deputy director general of the Foreign Ministry, 17 December 1989, File CSR 103.01, ISA.

13. Report of Shmuel Meirom, deputy director of the Eastern European Department, 4 February 1990, File CSR 103.01, ISA.

14. Report of Tova Herzl, Foreign Minister's Bureau, 11 January 1990, File CSR 103.10, ISA.

15. Memorandum of Yaacov Cohen, deputy director general, to the director general of the Foreign Ministry, File CSR 103.01, ISA.

16. See n.12.

17. Ibid.

18. The memorandum of agreement was signed on 2 January 1990, and attached to the letter of Hemda Golan, deputy legal advisor of the Foreign Ministry, to the legal adviser of the Finance Ministry, 13 February 1990, File CSR 103.01, ISA.

19. This was announced by Shimon Peres to Israeli journalists at a press conference held in Prague following the signing of the memorandum of agreement and was quoted in the Israeli press the next day (23 January 1990).

20. Joint statement published at the end of the visit of Moshe Arens and entourage to Prague. A photograph of the signing ceremony was published in *Israel Magazine*, June 1990.

21. Report of Y. Govrin of the visit, 25 February 1990, File CSR 103.01, ISA.

22. Ibid.

23. Ibid.

24. Ibid.

25. Ibid. President Havel did, indeed, pay a state visit to Israel, on 24–27 April 1990, accompanied by Foreign Minister Dienstbier. This was the first official visit of its kind to Israel after the resumption of diplomatic ties with East European countries that had severed ties in June 1967. On 25 April 1990 he was granted an honorary doctorate from the Hebrew University of Jerusalem. Report on the visit by Y. Govrin, 1 May 1990, File CSR 103.01, ISA. On 13 October 1991, President Chaim Herzog paid a reciprocal visit to Czechoslovakia. Both visits were the first

of their kind in the history of the relations between the two countries.

26. Report of Yaacov Cohen, 13 February 1990, File CSR 103.01, ISA.
27. *Jewish Communities in the World* (Jerusalem: Institute of World Jewish Congress, 1996).
28. *American Jewish Yearbook* (New York: The American Jewish Committee, 2001).

5. Negotiations between Israel and the German Democratic Republic on the possibility of establishing Diplomatic Relations, 1989–1990[1]

HISTORICAL BACKGROUND

East Germany – or the German Democratic Republic (GDR) as it was officially known – was the only Soviet Bloc country with which Israel did not establish diplomatic relations throughout its entire existence, from 1949–90. Both sides abstained from establishing relations with one another for their own reasons. The turning point came at the end of the 1980s. Gorbachev's economic and social reforms in the Soviet Union, along with the abatement of inter-bloc tensions, brought about a change of government in East Germany in October 1989. However, in the mid-1980s, a gradual change in the policy of East Germany toward Israel was already becoming apparent. This ultimately led its new leaders to seek diplomatic relations with Israel. Israel, which never officially recognized the GDR during the entire forty years of its existence, agreed to the proposal of the new GDR leadership to conduct talks leading in that direction (January–July 1990). Although significant progress was achieved and the gaps between the two sides narrowed, diplomatic relations were not established. This was approximately two months before the reunification of East and West Germany (31 August 1990). Was the era of an absence of diplomatic relations between the two countries, and the talks conducted towards their establishment, a passing episode or an important chapter in the history of the two states? And if this was a significant phase, what were its consequences?

For its part, Israel refrained from establishing diplomatic relations with East Germany, first and foremost, due to East Germany's unremitting denial of its moral and material obligation to the victims of the Holocaust, which contrasted with the policies of West Germany. From the early 1950s until the late 1980s, no East German leader – in contrast to the West German leaders – ever denounced the Nazi regime's crimes against the Jews as a people. The education system was ambiguous in its treatment of the Jewish victims of the Nazi regime, who were stripped of their Jewish identity. The East Germans rejected Israel's requests to engage in discussion on reparations, the return of Jewish property to its owners, and compensation for victims of the Nazis living outside their borders, as East Germany did not see itself as a successor of Nazi Germany, since the GDR was established as an entirely new state in accordance with the Potsdam agreement.[2] The East Germans claimed that most of their citizens had actively fought against the Nazis and many others were, themselves, victims of the Nazi regime, and that the victims of fascism among its residents had already received government assistance. As such, they claimed that the GDR had already fulfilled its obligations. They further maintained that the State of Israel, which did not exist before 1948, was not eligible to demand reparations. In January 1951, through the deputy foreign minister of the USSR, Israel's demands were conveyed to East Germany via the Soviets. (Concomitantly, the US, the UK and France transmitted Israel's claims against West Germany.) Israel's demands were conveyed again in September 1952, this time also through the USSR, when East Germany had become an independent country as part of the Soviet Bloc. Israel's demands were also raised in direct contacts between Israeli and East German ambassadors in Moscow during the mid-1950s. All of the petitions submitted by Israel to East Germany to discuss the GDR's part in paying reparations to Holocaust victims in Israel were solidly rebuffed by the East Germans.[3]

Another factor, although not a decisive one, that influenced Israel's decision not to seek diplomatic relations was the GDR's hostile attitude toward the Jewish State, which was among the most pronounced in the Soviet Bloc. This was so, despite the fact that the central committee of the Sozialistische Einheitspartei Deutschlands (SED), which later became the country's ruling party, welcomed the UN partition plan of November 1947 calling for the partition of Palestine into two states, one Jewish and one Arab, and even declared at the beginning of February 1948 'that the establishment of a Jewish state is a positive contribution that will enable thousands of people who gravely suffered under the fascism of Hitler to build new lives'.[4] Also, a member of the Central Committee, Paul Merker, in an article published on 24 February 1948, in the journal *Neues Deutschland*, wrote, inter alia,

> The joy of the Jewish Yishuv in Palestine over the new state was dampened in light of the great sorrow over the [falling] of fresh victims and then in light of the threat to widening the gap between it and the Arab population. The situation seems critical. Many more hard battles will be necessary to impose calm and security [there], which [the Jewish Yishuv] sorely needs urgently in order to build its state and to develop it to such a level that it will have space and possibilities to ensure the safe existence of thousands of homeless Jews ...
>
> The Jewish Yishuv has received the sympathy and vigorous support of all progressive forces. And in particular the democratic forces of Germany must openly demonstrate their sympathy and willingness to help.

The establishment of a Jewish state in part of Palestine with the progressive ideas and socialist strivings of its labour movement will not remain without influence on the feudal response of the Arab kings, princes, and muftis.

Nevertheless from the beginning of the GDR's existence in 1949 until the mid-1980s, it refused to recognize Israel's right to exist. A joint announcement that its leader, Walter Ulbricht, the general secretary of the Socialist Unity Party (1950–71) and the prime minister of the GDR (1960–73), signed with his host, Gamal Abdel Nasser, at the end of his state visit to Cairo, on 1 March 1965, stated, 'Both sides vilify the aggressive, imperialistic plans as a result of which Israel was created to serve the aims of imperialism by its being the threatening warhead against the rights of the Arab countries and against their struggle for liberation and progress.'[5]

No leader in the Soviet Bloc – which as we know supported the establishment of the State of Israel – had expressed such a hostile position towards Israel. Over the years, East Germany supported the antagonistic attitudes of the Arab countries regarding Israel, proffered military aid to terrorists who acted against Israel, and trained them on its soil, in addition to political and material aid that it gave to the PLO. The PLO legation in East Berlin was the first established in the Soviet Bloc, and the authorities considered it a diplomatic legation in every way, granting it the entire complex of practical functions which that status entailed. Even Walter Ulbricht's successor, Erich Honecker, secretary of the Socialist Unity Party (1971–89) and prime minister of East Germany (1976–89), in his appearance before the attendees of the Tenth Convention of his party on 11 April 1981, followed a similar line to that of his predecessor by declaring,

On everything concerning the Middle East, the GDR has not changed her position that the peace and security of this region are contingent upon the withdrawal of Israel from all the Palestinian Arab territories, the guarantee of their inalienable right to return to their homeland, to self-determination, and to the establishment of an independent Palestinian state. The key to a stable solution of the Middle East conflict was and remains the Palestinian question. Therefore, we are calling upon those who until now have negated any recognition of the PLO and the rights of the Palestinian people to once and forever accept reality. We unconditionally support the new and constructive proposal of the USSR to convene an international conference to solve the Middle East problem.[6]

The reparations agreement signed between Israel and the Federal Republic of Germany on 10 September 1952 was based on Israel's claims for $1.5 billion from Germany (West and East). According to the agreement, West Germany agreed to pay two thirds of that amount and, although this was not explicitly stated, Israel expected East Germany to fulfil its part by paying the other third.[7] As noted, all of Israel's appeals to it with this demand were in vain. East Germany's official spokespersons and its media strongly denounced the reparations agreement, claiming that the payments would strengthen Israel and encourage it to embark on a war of aggression against Arab countries. Following the 1956 Sinai Campaign, the East German government suggested that West Germany start sending Egypt the reparation funds hitherto sent to Israel as compensation for the damage inflicted on Cairo during the war.[8]

East Germany's actions in the UN, including its support of the resolutions equating Zionism with racism and calling for the invalidation of Israel's accreditation in the UN, were in keeping with Soviet foreign policy. The same is true regarding the malicious anti-Semitic and anti-Zionist propaganda it began spreading in the early 1950s, toward the end of Stalin's rule, and which continued during the infamous Prague trials, the Sinai Campaign, the Six Day War, and the Lebanon War. However, in contrast to the anti-Israel and anti-Zionist propaganda of the USSR and Soviet satellites, the East German propaganda seemed more hateful, spread as it was on German soil, among a population which a few years earlier had been involved in persecuting and murdering European Jews during the Holocaust.

For its part, East Germany refrained from establishing ties with Israel owing to the fear that it would lose recognition from Arab states, which was essential, especially against the backdrop of the Hallstein Doctrine of 1955 (according to which West Germany refused to maintain diplomatic relations with countries that recognized East Germany). Arab states ignored this doctrine and were among the first, after the Soviet Bloc countries, to recognize East Germany, which at that time aspired to receive international recognition. The doctrine, however, became less important once an agreement had been signed to establish diplomatic relations between the Soviet Union and West Germany (1958). Even after the two Germanys agreed (1972) on mutual recognition of sovereignty, independence and territorial integrity, the exchange of permanent delegations (which functioned like diplomatic legations), and the development of normal relations between them, the GDR's hostile attitude toward Israel did not abate. This was partly due to its close ties with the PLO and Arab states on the economic, political and military fronts. The fact that all Soviet Bloc countries (except Romania) severed diplomatic ties with Israel after the Six Day War reinforced East Berlin's hostile policy toward Israel.

In 1988 – a year before the change in leadership – a surprising turning point was becoming apparent in East Germany's policy toward Israel, which was manifested in a series of initiatives that gradually revealed a willingness to establish diplomatic relations. The first stage consisted of establishing preliminary contacts and laying the groundwork to correct its image as a hotbed of anti-Semitism and anti-Israeli propaganda. The second stage consisted of direct contact with Israeli representatives. The third stage consisted of three rounds of talks between representatives of both countries about the conditions that would lead to the establishment of diplomatic relations between them. What motivated Erich Honecker in 1988 to initiate contact with Israeli representatives and representatives of the World Jewish Congress for the purpose of normalizing relations with Israel?

From my conversations as deputy director general of the Israel Ministry of Foreign Affairs with Dr Gregor Gysi, chairman of the SED in Germany (who served a short time before unification as the secretary general of the party) during his visit to Israel in March 1991, the following became apparent:[9]

- In 1988 there was a change of direction in the political thinking of the East German leadership. It signified, according to Gysi, the need to move from an ideologically based foreign policy to one with a more economic orientation, which would, through ties with the West, promote expeditious economic development in order to raise the standard of living. East Germany took into account the central role of Jews in the Western economic system, and realized it would be impossible to develop the sought-after ties with Jewish circles without establishing ties with Israel.
- Despite the fact that the East German regime promoted itself as anti-fascist, actually it was West Germany that was perceived by the free world as the state committed to combating anti-Semitism and fascism, demonstrating contrition in the name of the German people for Nazi crimes against Jews. East Germany was seen as denying its role in the Holocaust. This image dictated the impression that East Germany was the continuation of Nazi Germany while claiming to be an anti-fascist regime. This was a

tangible obstacle in the GDR's efforts to be accepted in the West. This prompted the regime to organize an official ceremony with a large number of attendees marking fifty years since *Kristallnacht*, which included, among others, the presence of the president of the World Jewish Congress, Edgar Bronfman, chairman of the Yad Vashem Council, Yosef Burg, and chairman of the Yad Vashem Directorate, Yitzhak Arad.

- Arab states were the first to recognize the independence of East Germany; therefore, the GDR tended to maintain a pro-Arab foreign policy. Once the Arab bloc had become divided on the issue of the Israeli-Palestinian conflict and Egypt had established full diplomatic relations with Israel, East Germany found itself torn between its relations with Egypt and the rest of the Arab states, which opposed Egypt on this issue. In 1988, the time was ripe for East Germany to take a more balanced stand on the Israeli-Palestinian conflict in order to bolster its position in the West, as had Romania, for example, that had been following such a course for years.
- The USSR advised the GDR to move toward normalizing relations with Israel so that it would be easier for the USSR, itself, to do so. Underlying this proposal was the supposition that the more the countries of the Soviet Bloc would normalize their relations with Israel, the easier it would be for the USSR to also act in that direction, towards accommodating the country's public opinion.

I therefore asked Gysi what had caused him to call for the establishment of diplomatic relations between East Germany and Israel in his interviews with the Israeli press,[10] at the time when the disappearance of East Germany through its unification with West Germany seemed to be just around the corner. He replied that when he had given those interviews to the press, he had not sensed that the unification process between East and West Germany would proceed so swiftly. In any event, it was important to him that East Germany did not disappear from the map of the world before fulfilling its obligation to the Jewish people on all aspects related to complying with its role in the payment of reparations. He thought that all the obligations on the part of East Germany in this direction would later make West Germany actually responsible for meeting this obligation, since it was clear that West Germany would bear all the economic responsibilities of East Germany after unification.

That covers the gist of his remarks. We can assume that at the heart of this turnabout in political thinking lay a few additional motives:

- The GDR's economic crisis and its yearning to receive Most Favoured Nation (MFN) status from the US as well as other economic benefits. (The Claims Conference representing the Jewish organizations in the US asked that the State Department not grant that status as long as compensation had not been paid to victims of the Nazis. The US State Department added yet another condition: the allowance of free passage between both sides of Berlin and respect for human rights.)
- Israel's economic, political and scientific status in the US and Western Europe and the recognition that Israel had economic and technological potential that could be useful for raising the standard of living for East Germans.
- The thawing of relations between Soviet Bloc countries and Israel. The GDR certainly did not want to remain the only country in the Bloc that did not have relations with Israel.
- The conclusion that Soviet Bloc countries' unilateral economic, political and military support of Arab states, and particularly the PLO, not only cost them a

great deal (at the expense of their people's standard of living) but also did not advance a solution to the Israeli-Palestinian conflict. In fact, it may have prolonged, rather than hastened, its end. The GDR's negative image in the West was in no small measure due to the massive aid it extended to the PLO, which caused, among other things, an increase in terrorism in Israel and throughout the world.

• The GDR's quest for legitimization as an independent state, especially in light of the rumours grounded in the West German desire to unite the two Germanys into one democratic state. In Israel there was some public and governmental opposition to the unification of Germany; therefore the GDR considered Israel an important political partner that could serve its interests in ensuring its long-term political independence.

THE STAGES THAT LED TO NEGOTIATIONS ON THE
ESTABLISHMENT OF DIPLOMATIC RELATIONS BETWEEN
EAST GERMANY AND ISRAEL

Stage One: Organization of a State Memorial Ceremony, in Berlin, on 9 November 1998, Marking 50 Years since Kristallnacht, With the Official Participation of Israeli Representatives and Representatives of World and Regional Jewish Organizations

Aside from a single event in 1948, on the tenth anniversary of *Kristallnacht*, until 1988, the East German government had never initiated any formal commemoration of this event, in which it is estimated that hundreds of Jews were killed, hundreds of synagogues torched and shops ransacked throughout Germany and Austria. At the end of the pogrom, the Gestapo arrested about 30,000 German Jews and incarcerated them in the Buchenwald and Sachsenhausen concentration camps.[11] The anniversary of *Kristallnacht* was only commemorated by the association of Jewish communities, sometimes in the presence of a representative of the ruling party or the local municipality. Some

600 Jews were registered in the main Jewish communities of East Germany (East Berlin, Leipzig and Dresden) in 1985. Each of them had its own synagogue. But most of the Jews – for whom no estimated number is available – were not registered in communities.[12]

The preparations for the ceremony commemorating the fiftieth anniversary of *Kristallnacht* began in early 1987. The leaders of the GDR believed that they had to correct their country's image in the West and among Jewish organizations throughout the world. They decided to hold the ceremony in the presence of 152 official guests from seventeen countries, including representatives of Jewish communities from East and West Germany, Eastern and Western Europe, the US, and, for the first time, Israel. It sought to gain prestige and especially to lend the impression that it was not only an anti-fascist country, but one in which there was awareness of the persecution suffered by the Jews in Nazi Germany. This began to be expressed in the guided communications media with the mention of the Holocaust of the Jews of Occupied Europe under Nazi rule, with the elucidation of episodes in Jewish history. The media campaign also focussed on the cultural links that had been formed over the generations between the German people and the Jews, with the ensuring of the religious and cultural rights of the eight Jewish communities in East Germany, while stressing the danger of anti-Semitism to every society and state.

This 'information campaign' that the East German authorities began, in the run up to the memorial ceremony, became evident for the first time since the establishment of their state. It included three talks – the first of their kind in the history of the GDR – initiated by the secretary general of the party and the prime minister, Honecker, namely, with Sigmund Rotstein, chairman of the Federation of Jewish Communities in East Germany on 2 June 1988; with the chairman of the Central Council of German Jewry and the chairman of the West Berlin Jewish community, Heinz

Galinski, on 6 June 1988; and with the president of the WJC, Edgar Bronfman, on 17 October 1988. These three talks took place towards the ceremonial events in commemoration of fifty years since *Kristallnacht*. In an interview with East German media, Galinski defined his discussion with Honecker as a 'historic moment'.[13] Undoubtedly, this definition can be applied to the other two talks as well, not only for their being the first of this type to occur, but for their being able to attest to a change in tactics that had taken place among the leaders of East Germany towards Israel and the Jewish organizations in the Jewish diaspora. Its main points were the following:

1. Honecker's Talks with Rotstein and Galinski

The two discussions with the Jewish leaders, each held separately, centred on the whole on three main topics:[14]

First, Honecker told his interlocutors about the preparations being made in anticipation of the fiftieth anniversary of *Kristallnacht*, in the public and educational areas and at party and state levels, adding 'that citizens of the German Democratic Republic will always remember the victims of Hitler's fascism – the six million Jews who had been exterminated, and that the great attention of the state and the social authorities given to the lives and activities of the eight Jewish communities are simply an expression of that'. The leaders of the Jewish communities expressed their appreciation for this attitude to Honecker and told him of the need for closer cooperation between the Jewish communities in East Germany and the state authorities in the areas of religion and culture. Honecker proposed the formation of an international (that is, Jewish) fund, under the direction of Rotstein, for the restoration of the great synagogue in East Berlin. Rotstein and Galinski welcomed the idea and also stressed the need for refurbishing Berlin's Jewish cemetery, which was considered, in their estimation, to be the largest in Europe. Honecker promised to help.

Second, on the question of relations with Israel, Rotstein

and Galinski – each in his own way – emphasized the link between the Jewish people in the Diaspora, including the Jews of East Germany and Israel, and expressed the need for more balanced reporting in the GDR media in their descriptions of Israel and in their one-sided attitude to the Arab-Israeli conflict, in light of the declarations by Arab leaders about their aspiration to destroy Israel. For his part, Honecker promised 'that he would apply his influence on the media, so that they should improve their position in relation to Israel'. At the same time, he noted that the PLO leader, Arafat, had complained to him 'about the horrible behaviour of the Israeli authorities towards the Arabs in the Occupied Territories, and that one must act against the oppression of the Palestinian people'. Galinski replied that one could expect a change in the relations with the PLO, 'if and when the PLO declared that terror was not a tool for conducting negotiations and when the PLO recognized the existence of a Jewish state'. Galinski further argued that East Germany had responsibility towards the existence of the State of Israel since the 'second Germany' also had a part in the horrible past; and as for the remark regarding the aspiration to destroy Israel, Honecker told Rotstein that from the outset he had remarked to Arafat 'that the Jews should not be thrown in the sea'. To sum up, in their talk on this issue it was stated that they agreed that the Arab-Israeli conflict should be solved through negotiations, and as for Honecker, by means of an international conference (as proposed by the USSR).

Third, on the question of reparations, in response to Galinski's raising the subject that East Germany had to pay reparations to the victims of the Nazis, Honecker replied (according to Galinski's version) that he was interested that the negotiations currently under way in the US with the Claims Conference would lead to a payment of one hundred million dollars (according to the minutes of the meeting: between 10 and 100 million dollars), but 'that one must take into consideration that his country did not have an overabundance of foreign currency and therefore it would be necessary to carry out the payments in merchandise, depending on the benefits the US would be willing to grant to its trade with East Germany' (a hint on the granting of the status of Most Favored Nation). This was the first time that an East German leader had expressed himself in such a manner to a Jewish leader. The spokesman for the East German Foreign Ministry, who reported on Galinski's talk with Honecker on this topic at a press conference for foreign journalists on 8 June 1988, said, among other things, that East Germany had met all of its obligations in reparations and damages to its citizens. 'Yet, beyond that East Germany has declared its willingness, upon the request of Jewish organizations, to extend humanitarian aid to needy Jewish victims of the Nazi regime, in other countries, and that negotiations are currently being conducted on the form and extent of this aid'.[15]

In fact, from 1973 the Claims Conference, led by the president of the WJC, Nahum Goldmann, had been conducting negotiations with the Anti-Fascist Committee – non-governmental, as it were – of East Germany to obtain reparations from it for heirless Jewish property to the extent of 100 million dollars. After three years of futile discussions, the Anti-Fascist Committee had presented a cheque for one million dollars to the Claims Conference. Nahum Goldmann saw this an insult and ordered the immediate return of the cheque, and so it was. Yet, the fact that the government of the GDR was willing to enter negotiations on this issue – that had been going on for upwards of fifteen years – was considered at the time as progress, considering its past refusal in principle to conduct any negotiations at all on the payment of reparations. However, from the start of the negotiations between the Claims Conference and representatives of the East German government until the unification of Germany (1990), no agreement was reached between them on this issue.[16]

2. Honecker's Talk with Edgar Bronfman

Bronfman was welcomed regally in East Berlin. The East German government awarded him, at a well-attended official ceremony, the Grand Star of People's Friendship, which the GDR customarily gave to individuals of exceptional merit from abroad as a sign of appreciation of their activity towards friendship between nations. The (spoon-fed) media reported on that extensively and prominently. Bronfman himself defined the event as 'historic', and in his talk with Honecker – the first of its kind – he focused mainly on the need for East Germany to act towards establishing relations with Israel. In his reply, Honecker referred to 'the complex situation in the Middle East' and to the need for convening an international conference for 'the solution of the conflict' and for 'the recognition of a Palestinian state as well as of the State of Israel'. Even if he did not say it specifically, one could discern from his words that the establishment of relations between East Germany and Israel would only be possible when a solution was found to the Israeli-Palestinian conflict, and as a result of which a Palestinian state could be founded. Thus one may conclude that no radical change had occurred in Honecker's position towards Israel.

In contrast to Honecker's reply to Bronfman's proposal to act towards the establishment of relations with Israel, the response to Bronfman's idea on this issue, which came from the minister of religious affairs in the East German government, Kurt Löffler, was much more amenable. The minister detailed to Bronfman the ties that had been formed between his country and Israel in the field of literature and in exchange visits in the academic sphere.[17] Accompanying Bronfman on his visit to Berlin was Dr Israel Singer, general secretary of the WJC, and during the talk with the minister of religious affairs, both of them suggested that he visit Israel so as to gain an impression of the state and its institutions for commemoration, especially Yad Vashem and the Diaspora Museum, with the aim of examining what might be done in this area in East Germany. The minister responded positively to this idea.

3. Invitation of the Israeli Delegation to the Events Marking the Fiftieth Anniversary of *Kristallnacht*

The Israeli delegation was comprised of eight members, including Dresden-born Dr Yosef Burg, former interior minister and minister of religion, in his capacity as chairman of the council of Yad Vashem, Dr Yitzhak Arad, chairman of the executive of Yad Vashem, and Dr Shmuel Krakowski, Holocaust researcher at Yad Vashem.[18] One can assume that since representatives from other countries also came, and since the event, itself, was connected to *Kristallnacht*, the invitation extended to the Israelis could not be interpreted by the PLO and Arab states as signifying any real change in the GDR's official policy toward Israel. Indeed, Israeli representatives were not even invited to talk with Honecker, but only to attend the reception he held for all the guests. Nevertheless, the Israeli delegation was invited to meetings with Minister for Religious Affairs Löffler and with the administrators of the official archives in Potsdam. At those meetings, Drs Arad and Krakowski raised the possibility of cooperation in Holocaust research and requested some archive documents for that purpose. Dr Arad's prior requests to obtain archival material from East Germany on Holocaust-related issues, in general, and on German Jews, in particular, had gone unanswered. However, this time, he and Dr Krakowski were told that their hosts were willing to help with these matters. Another goodwill gesture toward the Israeli delegation was the simultaneous translation into Hebrew of Honecker's speech, delivered in German, at the official reception that he hosted for the guests.

If the East German leadership thought that by nurturing its relationship with the president of the World Jewish Congress (who was known as being influential in the American government) and with the heads of Jewish communities in East and West Germany, its image in the West would be improved and it would thus merit economic benefits (such as MFN status), it quickly realized that as long as the issue of relations with Israel went unresolved, it could not expect to achieve its political and economic goals. Consequently, the GDR tried, in fits and starts, to establish contacts with Israel both in the public and official sectors, by taking slow, cautious steps so as not to endanger its ties with Arab states and the PLO.

Stage Two: Direct Contacts between Representatives of the GDR and Representatives of Israel

1. First Visit of the East German Minister of Religious Affairs to Israel

Following the contact established during the events marking the fiftieth anniversary of *Kristallnacht*, the East German minister of religious affairs, Kurt Löffler, was invited by Yad Vashem and the WJC to visit Israel on 28 January–4 February 1988. During Löffler's visit – the first East German ministerial visit to Israel – he met with his Israeli counterpart, Zevulun Hammer, in Jerusalem and with the mayor of Jerusalem, Teddy Kollek, and the mayor of Tel Aviv, Shlomo Lahat. In addition, he visited the Diaspora Museum, kibbutz Zora, and the Dead Sea shore. He conducted meetings with Dr Burg, Dr Arad, Reuven Dafni, deputy chairman of the Yad Vashem directorate, and with Yad Vashem department heads during which it was agreed – for the first time – that cooperation would take place between Yad Vashem and relevant academic institutions in East Germany and that archive materials on the Holocaust would be exchanged.[19] Yad Vashem researchers saw this as a significant achievement, which ultimately led to the signing of an official agreement between Yad Vashem and the administration of the official archives of East Germany on 4 December 1989, in the wake of a reciprocal visit by the minister of religion, Zevulun Hammer, and the chairman of the Yad Vashem Directorate, Dr Yitzhak Arad, to East Germany as the guests of the minister of religious affairs, Kurt Löffler.[20]

At a press conference held at Yad Vashem during Löffler's visit, on 2 February 1989, he praised the well-conceived schedule of his 'heartfelt' visit to Israel as well as the 'exceptional hospitality' he received. He stressed that this visit had given his delegation 'an opportunity to become familiar with the work and life of the Jewish people in Israel'. He refused to answer a question as to when diplomatic relations between his country and Israel would be established, since the topic was not included, so he said, in his mandate, adding that 'this should be discussed when the time is ripe. The governments will be those to determine when that moment has come.'[21]

Minister Löffler was accompanied by two members of the East German Foreign Ministry and a translator. The three of them were received for a talk, at their request, with the deputy director general of the Foreign Ministry, Yeshayahu Anug, on 30 January 1989. They were Joachim Babba of the Middle East Department; Dr Norbert Reemer of the United States Department, and Dr Angelica Timm of Humboldt University in East Berlin, a Hebrew speaker. (She visited Israel both before and afterwards, as a guest lecturer at the Hebrew University of Jerusalem and Bar-Ilan University. She took part in talks that representatives of the Israel Foreign Ministry conducted with representatives of the East German Foreign Ministry in Copenhagen in 1990, and is the author of books about Israel and Israeli relations with East Germany.)

The two members of the Foreign Ministry, Babba and Reemer, defined the purpose of their meeting as 'an informal opportunity to hear the Israeli approach to East Germany'. To that Anug replied:

Our mutual perceptions are based on a deep rift, our image in East Germany is based on almost never-changing cliches that are passé. In that, they are not even marching with East European time, while on our side

110

there exists, as the main brake, the non-acceptance of their version that no moral obligation rests on them deriving from inheritance of the Third Reich, while their western sister has taken this legacy upon herself and acts accordingly. Yet, we were favourably impressed by the events marking fifty years since *Kristallnacht* and in their interest in ties with Jewish public opinion in the West [and] from their initiatives towards the small Jewish community in their country.[22]

According to Anug's testimony, his guests refrained from responding directly to the content of his remarks.

In the second part of their talk and in response to their statements about 'the great changes in the world and in the Middle East', whereby they meant the aim of solving the conflict through negotiations, and 'to the dramatic change that has occurred within the PLO, which is very close to us and which now accepts our persistent advice that they become moderate', Anug spoke of East Germany's one-sided policy on this topic as expressed in its press, 'which sweepingly accuses us of all the ills of the region, but in which only minuscule changes have taken place lately', and he also mentioned their close links to the extremists among the Arabs. In Anug's estimation, they were not prepared for a real discussion, and in contrast to other East European diplomats at the time, they clung fast to their pre-conceived doctrines. Moreover, one could understand that they had been ordered to clarify Israel's positions regarding the proposal for an international conference for the solution of the Arab-Israeli conflict and towards the PLO, and to begin to conduct a dialogue between the two countries. Anug welcomed this, but 'without demonstrating excessive enthusiasm'.[23]

Thus one may conclude that the first visit to Israel of an official delegation from East Germany had the aim of examining the degree to which Jerusalem would be willing to begin political dialogue and under what

111

conditions. The attempt to persuade Israel of the PLO's moderation and of the need for Israel to agree to the convening of an international conference to solve the Arab-Israeli conflict was apparently meant to demonstrate to the PLO that East Germany was acting in its interest, while at the same time laying the groundwork for the establishment of future ties with Israel. The dialogue was meant to arouse the sympathies of the Jewish organizations in the West, particularly those in the US, for East Germany. Perhaps in these attempts the East German leadership was also trying to strengthen its position internationally, especially among Western states.

2. A Talk between the East German Ambassador and the Israeli Ambassador in Bucharest

On 9 March 1989, in my capacity as Israel's ambassador to Romania, I was invited to a meeting with the East German ambassador, Herbert Plaschke, between him and myself at his residence in Bucharest. This was the result of the discussion between the members of the East Germany Foreign Ministry with the deputy director general of the Foreign Ministry in Jerusalem, and in light of our acquaintanceship and our informal discussions at diplomatic events in Bucharest. At that time, Romania was the only country in the Soviet Bloc that maintained diplomatic relations with Israel. According to Plaschke, the purpose of the meeting was to inform me that his ministry had instructed him to propose to us to continue the political dialogue in Bucharest in order to familiarize ourselves with the positions of both sides. This would lead to the normalization of relations between the two countries. In this context, he said, they would welcome a meeting between his country's foreign minister, Oskar Fischer, and his Israeli counterpart, Moshe Arens, at the UN General Assembly in New York in the fall. I commented that the GDR's failure to accept any moral responsibility with regard to its Nazi past and its unequivocal backing of our enemies cast a shadow over the potential development of mutual relations. The ambassador commented that the PLO had toned down its position regarding Israel and that the convening of an international conference was the only way to solve the Arab-Israeli conflict.

I contradicted the assumption that the PLO had moderated its stance towards Israel as long as its charter still espoused the destruction of the State of Israel. I also noted that the convening of an international conference headed by the Soviet Union, which had severed diplomatic ties with Israel, maintained a hostile foreign policy toward Israel, and supported its enemies politically and militarily, was far from objective, and therefore would not be beneficial.

Ambassador Plaschke's response, which was identical to that of the minister of religious affairs, Löffler, was in keeping with the official line of the USSR and the Soviet Bloc countries. He said that a conference would serve as a convenient rationale for their renewal of diplomatic relations with Israel that had been severed in the wake of the Six Day War, and for their establishment with East Germany. During that conversation, the ambassador expressed his concern over the rejuvenation of the neo-Nazi movement in West Germany. It was evident from his comment that the East Germans wanted Israeli support in condemning them, since Israel and East Germany shared a common interest in combating the neo-Nazi movement, which espoused the unification of the two Germanys. I mentioned that he was surely aware of our firm stance against the renewal of Nazism and fascism in Germany and Europe and that unfortunately, in certain countries anti-Zionism was a guise for anti-Semitism. The ambassador mentioned the events marking the fiftieth anniversary of *Kristallnacht* that had been held in his country, and it seemed that he wished to stress the identification of the authorities in his country with the Jewish people in vilifying that act, half a century earlier, and to underscore the marking of the events in his country as an expression of its desire to establish a bridge between itself and world Jewry and Israel. I asked his (young) secretary, who was present at our talk, if East German schools treated *Kristallnacht* as the beginning of the Holocaust of European Jewry under Nazi occupation. He assured me that the topic of Nazi German war crimes against the Jews was addressed in the curriculum of educational institutions in his country.[24]

On the whole, the conversation between us was conducted in a relaxed atmosphere. I promised to convey Arens' response to the ambassador; however, the response never came. Officials in Israel's Ministry of Foreign Affairs maintained that the time was not ripe because as long as there was no proof of a change in East Germany's position regarding its share of the responsibility for the Holocaust, it would not be fitting to conduct the proposed meeting. In the absence of a response from Israel's foreign minister, the GDR foreign minister concluded that the Israelis were not interested.

Thus ended the second stage whereby representatives of East Germany put out feelers and made contacts with representatives of Israel. On 18 October 1989, following angry protests throughout East Germany, Honecker resigned and was replaced by Egon Krenz. However, after a million-strong rally demanding reform, the fall of the Berlin wall, and the freedom to travel to the West, the members of the Politburo and government resigned. That night, the Berlin Wall was finally breached. The East German parliament elected a new government (13 November 1989) headed by Hans Modrow. Despite his membership of the Communist Party, Modrow supported political, economic and social reform in the spirit of Gorbachev's perestroika and glasnost. Thus, the new leaders of East Germany began taking intensive steps towards promoting ties with Israel with the aim of establishing diplomatic relations.

Stage Three: The Initiative of the East German Government to begin Talks with Representatives of Israel on the Establishment of Diplomatic Relations between the Two Countries

One of the first steps taken by the new East German leaders, in the absence of political dialogue with Israel, was the granting of interviews to the Israeli press. Concomitantly, they expressed their desire to establish diplomatic relations with Israel and their willingness to discuss the issue of 'humanitarian aid' to Holocaust victims with the Claims Conference. Below are a few of the initiatives:

1. The foreign minister in the new government of East Germany, Oskar Fischer (who had also served in this capacity in the previous government headed by Honecker), said, among other things, in an interview with Daniel Dagan, a correspondent of *Haaretz* (19 November 1989), 'The Israelis do not have to be worried. The unification of Germany will never occur ... the two German states are likely to become closer, and we certainly would like that. But relations between them will develop as if between two sovereign states. East Germany remains a sovereign country and there can be no debate about it.' This was in response to the fears that the prime minister of Israel, Yitzhak Shamir, had voiced – which had great repercussions in the East German press – about the reunification of the two Germanys. Professor Michael Wolfson, in his article in *Rhein-Merkur* on 22 December 1989, attributed to Yitzhak Shamir the sentence, 'A strong, reunified Germany will, perhaps, again try to destroy the Jewish people.' Wolfson also quotes from the statements by Minister of Industry and Commerce Ariel Sharon that 'a united Germany constitutes a great danger to the free world in general and to the Jewish people in particular ... we must not forget what the Germans have done to us when they were united'. From this one understands that Israel and East Germany had a common, very important interest, namely, to oppose the unification of East Germany with West Germany.

In response to a question posed by a *Haaretz* reporter on the possibility of establishing ties between his country and Israel, Fischer declared that this issue would certainly be raised soon and that it was 'obvious' that his country was 'interested in improving' relations with Israel, but added that 'goodwill and a sense of what is realistic are required of both sides' – meaning that Israel must also exhibit interest. Regarding the question of his country's willingness to pay compensation to Holocaust victims, Fischer responded, 'This is certainly one of the topics we should discuss; however, this is not a matter for statements in the press'.

2. In another interview with *Haaretz* (19 November 1989), Modrow said that his country 'was interested in normal relations with Middle Eastern countries, including Israel'. Regarding the Arab-Israeli conflict he added, 'East Germany supports the right to self-determination for the Palestinians while at the same time supporting the right of Israel to exist within secure borders.' The *Haaretz* correspondent added that the prime minister 'had shown interest in what was going on in Israel, and said that he hopes to promote relations between the two countries'.

3. Statements by the deputy foreign minister of East Germany, Dr Heinz-Dieter Winter, on 13 December 1989:

> An interview with acting East German Foreign Minister Dr Heinz-Dieter Winter by East German News Agency (ADN) reporter Corinna Seide was sent with a missive (15 December 1989) from Plaschke to Israel's ambassador in Bucharest, Zvi Mazel, requesting that it be conveyed to Israel's Ministry of Foreign Affairs in Jerusalem.[25] Since these were official statements made for the first time by a senior government personage in East Germany concerning the issue of ties with Israel, and since they contained a kind of summary of the 'current situation' in East Germany, in the present and expectations for the future, on the advancement of East Germany's relations with Israel, we felt it fitting to cite

here the main points of the questions (that had certainly been pre-arranged) posed to the interviewee and his complete responses to them:

Question: Why does the GDR not have diplomatic relations with Israel?

Answer: The State of Israel was established on 14 May 1948 and more than a year later, on 7 October 1949, the GDR was established as an anti-fascist state. For a long time, it existed in diplomatic isolation. Israel, as a state already in existence, did not take any action at that time to recognize the GDR and to establish normal relations with it. In 1967, when the war broke out in the Near East, the Warsaw Pact countries, excluding Romania, decided to sever diplomatic ties with Israel as a sign of solidarity with the Arab countries under attack. This decision did not apply to the GDR since it had no relations with Israel. However, following the war, the GDR adopted the Warsaw Pact countries' policy.

Question: Considering the ties of Poland and the Soviet Union with Israel, whether at the level of Interest Offices or consular delegations, at what levels has the GDR established contact with Israel? What is the nature of those contacts?

Answer: For two years, the GDR has been maintaining contact with Israel – more intensively than in the past – at various levels and in various fields. For example, Israeli representatives visited the GDR for the commemoration of the fiftieth anniversary of the fascist pogrom in Berlin. We are also intensively fostering contact in the areas of religion and culture. The Leipzig Radio Choir, conducted by Kurt Masur, and the Berlin Ensemble have already made a round of appearances in Israel. Last July, the GDR participated for the first time in the Jerusalem Film Festival. The East German Ministry of Foreign Affairs consciously encourages this contact, since we are interested in conducting dialogue with Israel. We would like to inform Israel about our policy, about the foundations of our foreign policy, and we ourselves are interested in becoming better acquainted with Israel's policy. The most important connection that we had until now was by means of the visit of the state secretary for religious affairs in Israel, Mr Löffler, at the beginning of the year, at the invitation of the Holocaust Martyrs' and Heroes' Remembrance Authority, Yad Vashem, and of the WJC. He was accompanied by two of our senior workers who also held talks in the Foreign Ministry. Thus, we are interested in continuing to foster connections with Israel; it would certainly be a welcome development for the Israeli minister of religious affairs to respond positively to the invitation to visit the German Democratic Republic.

Question: Deputy Prime Minister and chairman of the socio-democratic Labour party of Israel, Shimon Peres, called the GDR a 'German country that due to the Holocaust, and, later, due to the Middle Eastern anti-Israeli policy, has sunk deeper into guilt regarding Israel and the Jewish people'. In a *Haaretz* interview, Foreign Minister Oskar Fischer said the question of compensation must be discussed. Where do we stand on this issue?

Answer: First – the question of guilt. It would be quite difficult to blame the founders of our anti-fascist country, who fought against fascism and the Holocaust, for the dark chapter in German history. Of course, our country does bear a large historical responsibility. From our beginnings, we set for ourselves the mission of vigorously fighting racist hatred and anti-Semitism in order to permanently root them out of our country. Any rejuvenation of those phenomena must be thwarted. Therefore, we stand committed to anti-fascism. As to the question of compensation, the GDR bears an obligation that stems from the rights of the nations in accordance with the Potsdam Agreement. The territory which at that time was under Soviet occupation and later became the GDR, met its obligation regarding claims that were included in the Potsdam Agreement; therefore, we do not have any more obligations regarding the rights of nations. It seems there was a misunderstanding, but in the past we made it clear in our contacts with Jewish organizations that the GDR is willing to discuss the issue of humanitarian aid to Jewish victims of fascism. This is the position of the Foreign Ministry. We will submit a fitting proposal to our government, when the need will arise, through the talks with Israel.

Question: Should we anticipate the establishment of diplomatic relations (with Israel) in the near future? Or, on what does this depend?

Answer: The GDR, in any event, is ready for that at any time, to begin talks in this direction. By my saying, that ultimately, when the relations of the GDR with Israel will become normal, I would like to stress, at one and the same time, that during the conducting of talks on this subject, neither side should demand preconditions from the other side. (Two days earlier, through the AND [Allgemeiner Deutscher Nachrichtendienst], it had been published that Foreign Minister Fischer had announced the readiness of the GDR to establish relations with Israel, without any preconditions.[26]) We do not feel that our relations with Arab countries are of an anti-Israel nature. And just as those relations were not directed against Israel, the possible relations with Israel will not be aimed against Arab or against third world countries. Clarifications from Israeli politicians that we should have amended our relations with other countries do not constitute a helpful factor, in our opinion. Our political positions concerning the Middle East question are based on UN resolutions, which were accepted by most countries of the world. Obviously, the GDR will not deviate from them. It supports the right of the Palestinian people to self-determination, just as it supports Israel's right to exist within secure borders. On the basis of this position the GDR is ready to have normal relations with all states in the Middle East, and this, obviously, includes Israel.

Question: Does this mean that the GDR is now taking intensive measures in this direction?

Answer: There are contacts with Israel and Israel must recognize our perception. We are still not familiar enough with Israel's perceptions. If a signal in this direction came from Israel, then we would submit a fitting proposal to the government.

Subsequently, there were consultations with Foreign Minister Arens, with the participation of the director general of the Ministry of Foreign Affairs, Reuven Merhav, the deputy director general, Eytan Bentzur, and myself, the deputy director general for Eastern Europe. The foreign minister and the director general accepted my proposal to instruct the Israeli ambassador in Bucharest to respond to his East German counterpart, that as a result of their appeal to us through me (during my mission as Israel ambassador to Bucharest) and in light of statements made by the new GDR leaders, including an interview of the deputy foreign minister to ADN, that made us aware of their readiness to discuss the establishment of diplomatic relations between his country and Israel and to talk about the complex of problems that had been obstacles in the past, we were willing to reply to their petition and begin political dialogue with them, and we were waiting to hear their proposals.[27] The message was not conveyed to Israel's ambassador in Bucharest, firstly, owing to the fact that the GDR ambassador was absent from Bucharest at that time and, secondly, because of events occurring in Romania – the revolution that resulted in the collapse of Romania's communist regime and the execution of Ceauşescu. Therefore, it was decided to convey the message to an East German ambassador in another European capital.

Meanwhile, on 29 December 1989, an additional interview was published in the *Jerusalem Post* by the journalist

Yehuda Litani, in which Fischer retracted much of what he had said in the ADN interview, but twice underscored the great importance that his country attributed to establishing diplomatic relations with Israel. Without his referring again to the need to establish them 'with no preconditions', he explained the 'great importance' in their establishment, first, to the joint struggle against the revival of nationalism, fascism, and anti-Semitism, and second, in the joint struggle against the reunification of Germany, so as to set the legitimacy of the independent existence of East Germany on a firm basis in the international arena.

In both interviews, Fischer, like East German leaders, used the word 'fascism' instead of 'Nazism', both when referring to his country's Nazi past and also with respect to neo-Nazism, which he called the revival of 'fascism'. In response to that and to his ignoring the need to admit to the Nazi responsibility towards the Jewish people, Hanan Bar-On, vice-president of the Weizmann Institute of Science and former deputy general director of the Foreign Ministry, wrote to him on 4 April 1990, following his interview in the *Jerusalem Post*.[28]

4. From the statements by the East German minister of culture, Dr Dietmar Keller, on 12 December 1989:

> We know that the issue of reparations to the Jewish victims of the Holocaust looms before the two countries. We know this very well and we shall find a solution for it … We recognize the right of the Jewish people to its own state and to its sovereignty, the same way we feel that the Palestinian people should have the possibility of their own home.[29]

5. From the statements by the East German minister of culture, Hans Modrow, to the *Haaretz* correspondent, Daniel Dagan (17 December 1989): 'We turned to Israel in an official manner with a request to discuss the establishment of diplomatic relations. My government is interested in such relations, and I hope that Jerusalem's response to

this will be positive.' (Modrow apparently was referring to the appeal by his country's ambassador in Bucharest to his Israeli counterpart, which was indeed transmitted, immediately, to the Foreign Ministry in Jerusalem, but in turn it decided to postpone the reply.)

As to the question whether East Germany would be willing to pay reparations to Jewish survivors of the Holocaust, he said, 'We are definitely willing to discuss the issue with authorized representatives of the Jewish organizations involved in this and with Israel. My government is open to talks on this subject and this is an inseparable part of the complex of topics that we must discuss.'

6. From the statements by Dr Gregor Gysi, chairman of the Socialist Unity Party (the Communist Party) of the GDR, to the *Haaretz* correspondent, Daniel Dagan, 17 December 1989. In response to his question as to whether a change had occurred in the hostile stance of the GDR towards Israel, he replied,

> Certainly there has been a change. All of us here agree that we must reconsider the attitude that was accepted towards Israel and towards the past. We must look at the history of Israel in a new light. The German past places a special obligation on us, and I think awareness of this is constantly growing.
>
> We are interested in relations with Israel in all areas, including, of course, diplomatic relations. This does not mean that we agree with Israel on every topic. Yet, we have relations with many other countries with which we differ on various issues ... I have great sympathy for Israel, and I seriously appreciate its achievements. I see a clear German responsibility towards Israel, and I will give this expression in my public appearances.

And in his interview to a *Yediot Aharonot* correspondent, Shlomo Shamgar, on 22 December 1989, Gysi said, among other things:

For me the establishment of the State of Israel was a

historic, justified, fitting decision. I am in favour of diplomatic relations between the two countries. And we shall recommend them. Israel has the right to accept the proposal or reject it. At the same time, I am also in favour of self-determination for the Palestinians. I support secure borders and co-existence between the two nations. Aside from the PLO I do not see any other representative Palestinian organization. It is nearsight-edness not to speak with them. It is impossible to see the PLO as merely a terror organization. It contains differ-ent streams, as does Israel. Even the PLO is changing, just like my party … I have the impression that over the years the GDR saw Israel and the Jewish people as connected to the United States. The time has come to develop towards each of them an independent attitude, including full relations. I know that Prime Minister Hans Modrow proposes relations with Israel and I am supportive of this – there is no need to impose obstacles – and of finishing this quickly.

To Shlomo Shamgar's response, 'But Israel demands, as a precondition, that the GDR take upon itself part of the responsibility for what happened in Hitler's time', Gysi replied:

They have to formulate precisely for us what they are asking for. The GDR must recognize its part in the responsibility for the Holocaust, fascism and anti-Semitism. This also goes for the issue of individual reparations for the injured parties. The question, of course, is what we are able to pay, in our situation, in this regard we are not like West Germany.

At the conclusion of the interview, Gysi noted,

I am party to the anxiety voiced in Israel, in face of the calls for the unification of Germany, in which there are practically no Jews. Here you have an example of joint interests that will lead to identical voting of Israel and the

123

GDR in the UN. The danger of anti-Semitism is the source for this worry. Even in the GDR, in which there are almost no Jews, there is anti-Semitism. This is an import: the danger will become more severe, the more open movement between the two Germanys develops.

In the calls of East German leaders to establish relations with Israel, a certain difference was discernable between their content and tone ('no preconditions'; 'The GDR intends to discuss the payment of compensation to the victims of fascism'; 'The GDR will not be able to pay compensation – certainly not while experiencing financial difficulties – but would be willing to offer humanitarian aid to Holocaust victims', and so on). However, their interest in discussing the establishment of diplomatic relations and their awareness of the question of compensation to Holocaust victims was obvious. Aside from East Germany's interest in improving its image in the West and obtaining Israeli/Jewish investments to rehabilitate the economy, it seems that the reason for the 'offensive' – as expressed in interviews to the press – was also due to the assumption that East Germany viewed Israel and world Jewry as partners in opposing German unification, which West German leaders, and a large part of the East German population, supported. East German leaders were determined to preserve, as far as possible, the independent character of their country. The establishment of diplomatic relations with Israel was likely to give the new regime of East Germany the political seal of approval, while it was still ridding itself of the systems of the previous regime. Therefore, it seems that it was important to the East German leaders to enter as quickly as possible into a dialogue with Israel, so as to reinforce its standing among its countrymen and among the Western states.

7. Talk between the East German Ambassador in Brussels with the Israel Ambassador there. On 4 January 1990, Israel's ambassador in Brussels, Avi Primor,[30] received the GDR ambassador to Belgium, Ernst Wolkowski.

Ambassador Wolkowski said that he was asked by a GDR delegation to propose to the Israeli government that talks for the purpose of normalizing relations between the two states be held at whatever level Israel deemed appropriate. He mentioned Fischer's offer to meet with Arens during the most recent UN General Assembly in New York, and expressed his country's regret that this offer was not accepted. The venue of the proposed meeting could be Berlin or Jerusalem, or anywhere in the world, except Bonn.

Wolkowski mentioned the talks that had taken place in Bucharest between his counterpart, the East German ambassador, and the Israeli ambassador, and noted that everything proposed then was still valid. The GDR was interested in developing its relations with Israel in every area – economics, culture, air and sea transportation, ties between Israel and the Jewish community in the GDR and visits of large groups of Israelis to the GDR, and so on. Wolkowski said the reason the GDR wanted to normalize relations with Israel was due to the urgent need to jointly combat the rise in neo-Nazism and anti-Semitism in the world, in general, and in Germany, in particular, especially in the GDR. He noted that Israel would encounter great understanding on the part of GDR leaders on the issue of recognition of war crimes and even on the question of compensation, although he assumed that the fact that his country was experiencing financial difficulties was clear to Israel. In this context he mentioned the talks that representatives of his country had conducted with Edgar Bronfman, president of the WJC, and with his representative in Europe, Maram Stern.

Wolkowski added that East Germans were astonished at the ability of nationalists from West Germany to penetrate the GDR and that he was convinced that a partnership with Israel would greatly contribute to the effectiveness of the struggle against this phenomenon. And in conclusion, Wolkowski reiterated that the East Germans were determined to maintain a separate and independent state, which would evolve into a Western democratic society.

Ambassador Primor promised Ambassador Wolkowski to transmit the message immediately to the Foreign Ministry in Jerusalem and to return to him with a reply.

Based on the decision that had already been made in Jerusalem to begin talks, Primor was authorized to convey a positive response to his East German counterpart. Both sides agreed to meet in Copenhagen under the aegis of the Danish Foreign Ministry.

Stage Four: Clarification Talks towards the Possibility of Establishing Diplomatic Relations between Representatives of the GDR and Israel

For the first time in history, representatives of the GDR and Israel convened to clarify for themselves the parameters for the possibility of establishing diplomatic relations. The East German representatives were willing to come to an immediate agreement, while the Israelis first requested clarification on a series of issues. Three rounds of talks, which were defined by the Israelis as 'clarification talks', meaning 'non-binding', took place. The first was held on 29–31 January 1990; the second on 7–9 March 1990, and the third on 2–3 July 1990. The three were conducted on a military base near Copenhagen. Although significant progress was apparent during the three rounds of talks, they did not lead to the attainment of the ultimate goal. Nevertheless, the talks were very important because they reflected the positions of both sides. East Germany entered the negotiations having changed its political view of Israel, either owing to the revolution that it had recently undergone, or because of the East German desire to gain the support of Israel for maintaining its independence and sovereignty, which it sought as a response to the threat of German reunification. Israel's new attitude was to recognize the positions held by East Germany in respect of Israel, and to consider its own expectations of East Germany, before deciding to establish diplomatic relations. Below we will survey the main discussions in each of the three rounds, in which the first aimed at defining opening positions, on the basis of which, so it seems, the talks of the other two rounds were conducted.[31]

FIRST ROUND

The participants on the Israeli side were Michael Shilo, counsellor to the foreign minister for Diaspora affairs, Shmuel Meirom, deputy director of the East European Department in the Foreign Ministry in Jerusalem, and Michael Arbel, counsellor in the Israel Embassy in Copenhagen. On the East German side were Reiner Neumann, head of the Middle and Near East Section in the GDR Ministry of Foreign Affairs, Reiner Babbe, first secretary, director of the Middle and Near East Department in the Middle and Near East Section in the East German Ministry of Foreign Affairs, and Dr Angelica Timm (translator) of Humboldt University, Berlin, as well as Thomas Bergmann, second secretary in the GDR Embassy in Copenhagen.

THE EAST GERMAN POSITION

Reiner Neumann welcomed the Israeli delegation and expressed his pleasure at their visit and to their becoming mutually acquainted on a professional level. He referred to the talks between the two sides that had been held in Bucharest and in Brussels and to the visit of the East German minister of religious affairs to Israel. He reviewed at length the great changes that had occurred in East Germany, since the change of regime on 7 October 1989, stressing that 'currently our first task is to ensure the existence of the GDR as a sovereign and independent country in Europe ... In both the GDR and FRG other forces are demanding immediate unification. We feel that such a unification is an erroneous concept.' And as to Israel, Neumann mentioned the statements by Prime Minister

Modrow who had declared his country's readiness to have normal relations with all states of the Middle East, and that 'concretely this means that we are ready for proper relations with Israel', adding that he had been authorized on behalf of the foreign minister of his country to propose to the Israeli delegation,

> the establishment of diplomatic relations between Israel and the GDR, to exchange special, authorized ambassadors between the two countries and to establish embassies in Tel Aviv and Berlin ... I clearly understand that it is not possible to sign immediately an agreement between the two countries and to establish relations. Until now there had been no contacts between the two ministries, except for my colleague Babba, who had had a meeting in the Foreign Ministry in Jerusalem. But you can rest assured that we want to implement these things in a constructive manner.

Neumann concluded his opening remarks by proposing to make use of this meeting to speak about issues relating to the establishment of relations and that he felt it possible to find mutual understanding for clarification of all issues openly. 'We will reach complete understanding of our positions and we will ask each other detailed questions. This is, in effect, the official charge that I received from my foreign minister and I would be happy to hear your opinion.'

ISRAEL'S POSITION

Michael Shilo expressed his appreciation for the presentation of the issues and asked to read from a written text the paragraphs of a 'position paper' at the opening of the talk (on the basis of a document that had been prepared by the Foreign Ministry in Jerusalem),[32] which were as follows:

> Israel agrees to the universal principle of diplomatic relations between states and is striving to maintain proper relations with each nation, with no difference as

128

to their regimes or ideologies. However, ties with Germany (both countries) present special difficulties to Israel, as one may understand by anyone who knows the history of the twentieth century. Recently we received information from a number of sources and we have read interviews published in the press, according to which the GDR wishes to clarify the possibilities for establishing relations with Israel. In response to that, the foreign minister, Moshe Arens, has decided to send a delegation to gain direct impressions and clarifications regarding the GDR's positions. The most important question is the issue of moral responsibility. As far as I remember, to date no acceptance of responsibility has been voiced for the crimes carried out in the Nazi period against the Jews. These crimes were perpetrated by Germans, without any link to their place of residence. The Wehrmacht officers of the SS and SA, the guards and the operators of the concentration camps and [perpetrators] of mass exterminations, the overlords of forced labour, came from both East and West Germany alike. So it is that the GDR came into being in 1949 as an equal successor to the Reich, neither less nor more than the FRG. What is demanded is open, public recognition of these facts in a specific, direct manner that will be aimed at the Jewish people and the State of Israel.

Yet, declared recognition of moral and historical responsibility is not enough. The question will be how the GDR intends to reinforce this recognition and to continue it through educational means, curricula, efforts at distributing fitting information, legal steps and others, on the one hand, and to fight the resurgence of neo-Nazism and anti-Semitism, on the other; to enable youth, students, teachers, journalists and researchers to understand Israel and Judaism, and to confront their past fairly. One way to carry on with the recognition and responsibility is a declaration of readiness to enter into a serious dialogue on Jewish material claims. As early as the beginning of 1951, Israel addressed the GDR about this issue, through the USSR, and it never received a reply. We ask, therefore, whether the Claims Conference (a committee representing world Jewish organizations) will be invited to discuss Jewish communal property and heirless individual property that remains in the GDR. And if yes, how and when does the GDR plan to open a dialogue with Israel on material claims as a result of the rehabilitation in Israel of Holocaust survivors? What will be the mechanism of such negotiations?

Another problem in need of immediate resolution, on the part of the GDR, is the hostile attitude and slanderous voices prevalent there against Zionism. Zionism is the national liberation movement of the Jewish people. This movement is what established Israel. Through it the desolate soil of Israel has been turned into a flourishing garden of living, modern culture and a fortress of democracy. It was Zionism that made possible the rehabilitation of tens of thousands of (Jewish) refugees. But, on the other hand, Zionism has become the victim of curses from the cynical coalition of the automatic majority at the UN that compared Zionism to racism. The question is how does the GDR intend to cut itself off from the slandering of Zionism, how does it plan to inform its people of this divestment, and whether it will join the enlightened democracies in an attempt to annul the infamous UN resolution.

During its forty-one years of existence, Israel has grappled with unceasing aggressiveness on the part of the Arab countries neighbouring it and with Arab terror organizations. Throughout that entire period the GDR supported by word and deed Israel's worst enemies. Various terrorist organizations were trained by the GDR and on its soil. Weapons and ammunition were given to Arab countries, the GDR was among the first to allow the PLO to open an official legation in its capital, without even asking the organization to amend its covenant, which calls for the destruction of Israel.

We ask how the GDR intends to rebuild its Middle East policy so that it will be more balanced and whether we are able to begin cooperation between Israel and the GDR in the struggle against international terror. Clarifications by East Germany on these issues will help further and promote this dialogue.

Neumann asked to present a fundamental question, 'Are these questions conditions for establishing diplomatic relations? And is it possible to find first a way to establish diplomatic relations and afterwards to deal with these problems?' Since in their estimation, 'the time is ripe for reaching an agreement about establishing relations and its rapid implemention'.

Shilo responded to that by saying:

Neither we nor you have come to conclude and sign on establishing relations. All we have come to do here is to examine and hear directly what we have heard in another manner through the embassies of Israel in Bucharest and Brussels and through your declarations that we have read in the press. We wanted to present things according to our understanding and to clarify them, and that is what we have done.

And here are the main points of Neumann's reply, in response to the presentation of Israel's position, as written down by Shmuel Meirom:

- They agree that there is a need to precede the establishment of relations with a clear declaration on the GDR's accepting moral and historical responsibility for German crimes against the Jews during the period of the Second World War.
- They are ready to translate the acceptance of responsibility referred to above into practical steps. In this context, they will agree to consider a letter of intent which will discuss steps such as educational reforms, changes in study material, the sending of a youth

delegation to Yad Vashem in Israel and to concentration camps, determining memorial days, a television programme, legislation against anti-Semitism, establishment of friendship leagues, and so on (in this context both sides asserted that it was clear that the implementation of such steps need not necessarily be carried out before the establishment of relations).

- They will examine the possibility for conducting negotiations at the level of experts, both with the Claims Conference and with the government of Israel, concerning material claims. Yet, it was important to add that owing to the serious economic situation of the GDR, he sees no chance, at this stage, for payments in foreign currency. They could at the most deal with a limited number of personal cases on the basis of humanitarian aid.

- On the whole the topic of reparations, owing to it importance, will be transferred for discussion in the government and Parliament of the GDR. They noted to themselves that the Israeli side felt that before or simultaneously with the establishment of relations there would be a declaration of intent by the GDR according to which it will conduct talks with Israel on this topic.

- Support of the GDR for the Zionism equals racism equation was a mistake. The picture they received of Zionism was fashioned by the former GDR leadership. They obligate themselves to re-examine the topic and promise that within framework of the new positions on foreign policy that the GDR will adopt, this issue too will be examined, but a specific declaration on this topic will be made within the general framework of the new relations between the two countries.

- The opinion of the GDR differs from that of Israel on the issue of the Middle East. It considers the PLO the legitimate representative of the Palestinian people

and supports the convening of an international
conference for the solution of the Israel-Arab conflict,
with its participation. Yet, it is striving to attain a
balanced policy on the Middle East, among others,
through the following steps:

a) The GDR will refrain from shipments of
armaments to areas of tension and will define the
Middle East as an area of tension. It will also refrain
from training people from these areas.
b) The GDR will refrain from automatic votes in
international bodies and will oppose any attempt to
expel Israel from any international organization.
c) The GDR will be ready to declare its readiness to
struggle against terror, but it is not convinced that the
PLO is included in that category.

The two delegations agreed on the summation of the talks –
each of which was formulated separately – for the purpose
of handing them on so as to inform their governments.
Similarly, they agreed to continue with the talks and
determined that the technical arrangements on this issue
would be made through the embassies in Copenhagen.
That was how the first round of talks ended.

About two weeks after concluding the first round of
talks in Copenhagen, Foreign Minister Moshe Arens,
accompanied by Michael Shilo, was received by the
chancellor of the FRG (West Germany), Helmut Kohl, and
by its foreign minister, Hans-Dietrich Genscher, in Bonn.
Arens asked his interlocutors how they regarded the possibility of the establishment of diplomatic relations between
Israel and the GDR.

Genscher responded, 'Should you progress in your talks
with the GDR government in this direction, I am telling
you without hesitation, that we are not against it and that
we regard this development positively' (yet, he asked that
it should not be publicized). Whereas Kohl answered that
although he shared Genscher's position, he still expressed

some reservations, suggesting that the matter should not be dealt with in the next four weeks (that is, until the general elections in the GDR).[33]

SECOND ROUND

At the opening of the second round of talks (7 March 1990), with the same composition of participants as the first round, the East German delegation brought with it a letter from the prime minister of the GDR, Hans Modrow, written on 2 March 1990, addressed to the prime minister of Israel, Yitzhak Shamir, in Jerusalem, in the name of the GDR government. Here is the text:

> The GDR recognizes the responsibility of the entire German people for the past. This responsibility results from the deep guilt of Hitlerite fascism, which in the name of the German people, perpetrated most obnox-ious crimes against the Jewish people. The GDR remains staunchly committed to its pledge to do everything against racism, Nazism, anti-Semitism and hatred against nations so that never again will war and fascism, but only peace and international understanding emanate from German soil.
>
> The GDR has fully met its obligations under interna-tional law ensuing from the Potsdam Agreement. It recognizes its humanitarian commitment vis-à-vis the Jewish people who survived Nazi oppression, and reaffirms its preparedness to render material solidarity and support to Jewish persecutees of the Nazi regime.

To this announcement, he added two sentences of his own: 'At this opportunity I wish to announce that the GDR is ready to discuss a solution for the property claims that will be submitted by Israeli citizens. I assume that this has created the preconditions for achieving an agreement on the establishment of diplomatic relations in the near future.'

To the reading of the letter at the Foreign Ministry in

Jerusalem, I responded immediately in my memorandum of 9 March 1990 to the foreign minister and to the directorate of the ministry.[34] I pointed out that this was the first letter of its kind sent from the prime minister of the GDR to the prime minister of Israel and its main importance derived from its components:

1. *Declaration on the responsibility of the German people for the Nazi crimes against the Jews.*

It is identical in formulation to the letter that the GDR prime minister had sent a day earlier (1 March 1990) to the president of the WJC, Edgar Bronfman. It is rather general and does not contain the other elements whose clarification we requested (even though it had been submitted during the talks of the two delegations in Copenhagen), and they were:

   a) An obligation to make a radical revision in the education system and in research related to the Holocaust.
   b) Annulment of the condemnation of Zionism.
   c) An obligation by the GDR to not help PLO terrorist materially or militarily.

2. *Readiness to discuss aid for those persecuted by the Nazis*

3. *Readiness to discuss property claims by Israeli citizens*

(The Claims Conference is not mentioned and it does not refer to the willingness to hold negotiations with the government of Israel but with Israeli citizens.)

4. *Readiness to establish diplomatic relations with Israel*

In summary, the letter does not meet our expectations, although one must take into consideration that it was intended for publication and as such it might be that the prime minister of East Germany refrained intentionally from specifying the obligations that the GDR had taken upon itself and therefore was phrased in general formulations, the specifying of which he had left for the clarification talk between the two delegations.

CLARIFICATION TALK

The letter from the prime minister of the GDR served as a main topic in the discussion at the second round of talks. Neumann tried to clarify its essence and to underscore its innovations, while referring to the paragraphs of the Israel position paper that had been read to the East German delegation, at the first round of talks. Here are his main points:[35]

1. *The GDR accepting responsibility for German history*

Here, he said, a most important step had been taken as a result of the comments by the Israeli delegation during the first round of talks. In this paragraph the following two points were stressed: first, not only condemnation of fascism but reference to Nazism; second, no longer spoken of was obligation towards Jewish organizations but humanitarian obligation to the remnants of the Jewish people who had suffered under Nazi rule. 'We are convinced thereby that we have solved the most difficult issue barring the path to establishing diplomatic relations between us.'

2. *Material claims*

As to the proposal of the Israeli delegation 'to take on an official obligation concerning this', Neumann asked to divide the problem into three secondary points:

> a) The government of the GDR is ready to enter negotiations about property claims that will be submitted by Israeli citizens. This is a matter of principle. 'We in the GDR felt that this is a great burden ... it includes everything noted by Shilo in the first round of talks, that is, private property, community property, and the like.'

b) Continuation of the talks on humanitarian aid to persons of Jewish origin persecuted by fascism (which had been started by representatives of the Claims Conference).

c) A fund will be established in the GDR to provide aid in the psycho-social field, a kind of branch of Amcha [an organization, supported by the Claims Conference, that offers psychological and social assistance to Holocaust survivors], with capital of a few million marks. The GDR government will grant this year, 1990, 100,000 marks for this purpose.

d) The GDR government will also decide about payment for recuperation vacations for the persecuted and for children from Israel. 'We will enable persons of German origin and children to spend time and relax among us.'

e) It has been proposed to the GDR government that it should grant fifty million marks to the synagogue and Jewish research centre (in Berlin). The money will be given from the sums that were held by the Communist Party. 'According to our proposal the government will decide to grant to the board of the Jewish community a sum of 1.3 million marks.'

f) A 'personal comment' that Neumann wished to make: 'I am convinced that this is the limit of our (financial) possibilities. There is an ever-increasing criticism from our public. This, of course, is our problem not yours. We must answer the public's complaints, and we have to explain why the GDR has to award such huge sums as these to Israel. Our youth does not understand these issues, but as I have said, this is our problem.'

3. *The GDR's position regarding Zionism*

Prime Minister Modrow instructed the foreign minister 'to prepare a new stance towards Zionism and to re-analyze our position. We have already begun this in our Foreign Ministry, which is responsible for this issue and we are including in this researchers from important universities, for example, Humboldt University. We will make the results public through the communications media. In essence, we understand that if we accept responsibility for the Holocaust, we are working out a new approach to Zionism ... the GDR has no right to criticize Zionism since it is the movement that the Jews have chosen to solve their national problem ... things will move along in the coming weeks more than they have in the past twenty years.'

4. *The education system*

The GDR government will decide tomorrow (8 March 1990) that 23 April will be the Memorial Day for the Holocaust in the GDR. Every year the government will organize on that date a memorial ceremony. Likewise, we are working on a new curriculum in the framework of which 'we will try to overcome "the dark stains" in our history about which we have not spoken until now.'

5. *The GDR policy towards the Middle East*

In talks conducted with Faruk Qaddumi, head of the Foreign Affairs Department of the PLO, during his visit to Berlin, a few days ago, the GDR position was presented to him in four points, as follows:

a) The GDR supports a solution of a just and stable peace in the Middle East. This includes Israel's right to exist within secure, recognized borders together with the right of self-determination of the Palestinian people.
b) The GDR is interested in normal relations with all countries of the region, and it is conducting talks with Israel on the establishment of diplomatic relations with it.
c) The GDR supports a dialogue between Israel and the Palestinians.
d) The GDR stressed that its dialogue with the parties must take into consideration the interests of all sides.

Neumann's personal comment was as follows:

> I say these things as head of the Middle East Section in the
> Foreign Ministry. Since, of late, we have been the object of
> increasingly severe criticism on the part of Arab countries,
> including states from which I had not thought to be
> sources of criticism. In our talks with these partners, we
> explain that establishing normal relations between the
> GDR and Israel is no less normal [a thing] than relations
> with Arab countries, and they should understand this. In
> that way the GDR can attain a more balanced position in
> the Middle East, whereas until now our policy had not
> been so. Such a balanced policy would also include
> relations between the GDR and Arab countries and
> between the GDR and Israel. It is very important to clarify
> to them that it is necessary and worthwhile establishing
> diplomatic relations with Israel. It is not easy for the Arab
> countries to get used to these positions, and I, as one who
> is working in this field, clearly see how things are taking
> place. I was never as important in the GDR as I have been
> since my return from the talks in Copenhagen, and I see
> this as a good sign that many among our public under-
> stand the need for relations with Israel.

He added,

> I want to sum up by saying that on the part of the GDR
> a situation has been created that will enable the estab-
> lishment of diplomatic relations. I am ready for any step
> that may be required because of that and I also am autho-
> rized to decide on every step. This is the first official letter
> from the government of the GDR to the government of
> Israel, and that gives it special importance.

Michael Shilo, in his remarks in response to his interlocutor Neumann, thanked him for his clarifications and for the
letter from Prime Minister Modrow, the very transmission of
which he defined as 'an important development and positive
step in the discussions between us'. As for its content, Prime

Minister Shamir will have to refer to it since he is the addressee. Then, Michael Shilo turned to all the other points in Neumann's remarks concerning, among other things:

The Material Claims

Shilo mentioned that during the first round of talks he had noted that there were two types of material issues: the first issue, that of Jewish community property and heirless Jewish private property that had to be discussed with the Claims Conference of the Jewish organizations; and the second issue, that related to Israel 'as a country absorbing and rehabilitating Holocaust survivors', a topic that must be discussed with the government of Israel. 'Therefore, what must be made is an announcement by the GDR on its agreement to open parallel negotiations, simultaneously and soon, with two teams – a team with Rabbi Miller (president of the Claims Conference) and a team with the government of Israel.'

As for the financial and economic situation of the GDR, Shilo made it clear that

> we are not speaking about payment on condition of political advancement but on the recognition in principle of a debt and the need to carry out negotiations. Obviously, in any agreement that will be achieved the element of the economic capabilities of the GDR will be taken into consideration (just as in the Luxembourg Agreements of 1952). But it must be clear that it is not only symbolic gestures that are to be discussed.

In this context, Shilo turned over to Neumann a document, covering two points that he had prepared for him, in German, to clarify his statements, which were:

1.   We are awaiting a solution that is not based per se on the situation of the GDR regarding foreign currency but on its economic potential. The modalities of payment are an issue for negotiation.
2.   Arranging for question of reparations for those

persecuted by the Nazis, on the one hand, and global recompense to the State of Israel, on the other, cannot be solved within a framework of symbolic gestures. The distress of the persecuted and the burden with which Israel is laden that derives from care of the persecuted are not, unfortunately, of symbolic dimensions.

In the continuation of the clarification of his statements, Shilo cited, for example, the issues of the similar claims that had been discussed with the GDR on the topic of payments and reparations that had been incorporated, afterwards, in the signing of the Luxembourg Agreement in 1952, and which were spread over twelve years. The Israeli side and the German side then said that since Israel had absorbed Holocaust refugees and rehabilitated them, it required 4.5 billion marks from Germany. The German side then said that it took upon itself only two thirds of the debt, since one third was located over the border (which is how the Israeli side understood it at the time). This principle of two thirds also applied to the agreement signed between the GDR and the Claims Conference regarding community and heirless individual property, with the remaining third supposed to apply across the border (which is how the Claims Conference understood this).

Comparison of Zionism to Racism

Shilo reminded Neumann that when referring to this topic he had said, among other things, that 'there is no right or permission to denigrate Zionism, if this is the way chosen by the Jewish people to solve its national question'. Shilo asked him to include this sentence 'in an agreed upon and official manner', in a document that would be worked out by the negotiators.

Middle East Policy of the GDR

When explaining Israel's policy on the issue of the Arab-Israeli conflict and its attitude towards the PLO that supported the eradication of the State of Israel, in stages,

141

Shilo noted that 'we anticipate that the GDR will give some expression that will set a limit to its support for the PLO ... at the time when you determine your policy anew'.

At this stage Neumann asked to speak privately with Shilo. Issues were stated frankly and they verified our supposition that the political offensive for establishing diplomatic relations with Israel was intended to slow down the rate of the unification of the two Germanys. Neumann's remarks are cited here in full:

> Prime Minister Modrow is providing us and you the best opportunity for establishing relations under conditions that are almost the same as those required by you. In another ten days Modrow will go to the opposition. Whatever will be agreed upon until then – will be valid, but whatever remains open will not obligate the next government. The question is whether, on the basis of Modrow's letter to Shamir, you are prepared to announce Israel's readiness to establish relations. Obviously, time is short and we will understand if you tell us that you want to leave everything for after the elections [which were scheduled to be held on 18 March 1990], but that might put us back to square one. Now, you have at least clear recognition of the responsibility and readiness to speak about Israel's material claims and a number of positive announcements in the spirit of your demands concerning Zionism and Middle East policy. If you can arrange the authorization for yourself, we will both be able to sit and compose a memorandum of understanding on what we achieved in our talks and to summarize the document in a sentence saying: Hence, the two governments agree to establish relations between them.
>
> In such a case, I would be happy to extend my stay in Copenhagen, but if not, then it would be better for us to separate now and continue after the elections, in line with the will of my new supervisors who will assume their roles at the end of the month. The reason I am interested that this business move along just now is that

there is a struggle within each of the two Germanys between those who wish to speed up the unification at any price and those who want a slow, controlled unification. This has no personal link to Modrow, since in any event he will be in the opposition. I ask that you inform me by Friday afternoon [the following day] which way the wind is blowing on your side ...

The next day (9 March 1990) – the last day of round two – Michael Shilo told Reiner Neumann the content of the statements transmitted to him one hour earlier, by telephone, from the deputy general director of the Foreign Ministry, Yosef Govrin:

We express our appreciation to Ambassador Neumann for the clarifications that he had brought with him to this round of talks. Unfortunately, we cannot meet the timetable that he proposes. The statements made in the letter (by the prime minister of the GDR) and the oral clarifications must be discussed and brought to a government decision. Perhaps this issue will even be discussed in the Knesset. What is lacking, at first glance, from the letter, is the explicit readiness (of the GDR government) to discuss with the government of Israel the material topic, since moreover under discussion is the readiness to compensate Israeli citizens.

Neumann replied that he completely understood Israel's decision and that he clearly understood that it was difficult to make decisions when pressed for time. He would report to Prime Minister Modrow and to the prime minister who would succeed him 'about the progress in the talks and the willingness of the Israeli government to proceed with the process that we have begun'. Shilo reiterated the main commitments required to move the process along, among them 'an unequivocal determination by the GDR on the readiness to enter negotiations on material claims'.

Thereby concluded the second round of talks, which was characterized by the drawing closer of the positions of the two delegations on the topic of accepting moral and material responsibility of East Germany for the Holocaust, on the institution of a revision in its education and information system regarding its role in the Holocaust, its attitude towards Israel and Zionism, and readiness to delineate a more balanced policy, than had been associated with it in the past, on the topic of the Palestinian-Israeli conflict. Yet, remaining open was the issue of its willingness to conduct negotiations with the government of Israel on the payment of reparations to Israel.

THE REUNIFICATION OF GERMANY

On 18 March 1990, for the first time in its history, free elections were held in the GDR. The Christian Democratic Union (CDU), sister party of the one to which the prime minister of West Germany, Helmut Kohl, belonged, won a majority of votes (40 per cent). The CDU was charged with establishing a new government, headed by Lothar de Maziere, which combined the Sozialdemokratische Partei Deutschlands (SPD) and the Freie Demokratische Partei (FDP). Together they accounted for 70 per cent of the electorate. This was the first time that the GDR was headed by a non-communist government. One of the main tasks of the coalition was to establish contact 'quickly and responsibly' with the West German government in advance of unification, which was scheduled to take place on 31 August 1990.

On 12 April 1990, the Volkskammer (People's Chamber of the GDR) unanimously adopted a statement requesting forgiveness from the Jewish people, the State of Israel, and the Jewish community in East Germany for the pain and suffering inflicted on them. The statement recognized East German responsibility for the Nazi crimes against the Jewish, Polish and Czech peoples. The parliament declared that it would make every effort to establish diplomatic relations with Israel, to rehabilitate the Jewish community in the country, to aid Holocaust survivors and to compensate them for material loss.

Since under discussion is a historical document, we will quote here the first paragraph relevant to the Jewish people and Israel. The second paragraph asks forgiveness from the USSR and the countries of Eastern Europe.[36]

> We, the first freely elected parliamentarians of the GDR, acknowledge the responsibility of the Germans in the GDR for their history and their future and unanimously declare before the international public:
>
> It was Germans who during the time of National Socialism inflicted immeasurable suffering on the peoples of the world. Nationalism and racist madness led to genocide, particularly among Jews from all European countries, among the peoples of the Soviet Union, the Polish people, and the Sinti and Roma. The guilt must never be forgotten and we want to perceive it as the source of our responsibility for the future.
>
> The first freely elected parliament of the GDR accepts, on behalf of the citizens of this country the responsibility for the humiliation, expulsion and murder of Jewish women, men and children. We feel sadness and shame as we acknowledge this burden of German history.
>
> We ask the Jews all over the world for their forgiveness. We ask the people in Israel to forgive the hypocrisy and hostility shown in official GDR policy towards the State of Israel and to forgive the persecution and degradation of Jewish compatriots also after 1945.
>
> We declare that we will do everything we can to help heal the mental and physical wounds of the survivors and to bring about just compensation for material losses.
>
> We are aware of our obligation to give particular care to fostering Jewish religion, culture and tradition in Germany and to constantly care for and preserve Jewish cemeteries, synagogues and memorial places.
>
> We regard it as a particular task of ours to educate the youth of our country to respect the Jewish people, and

> to disseminate knowledge on Jewish religion, tradition and culture.
>
> We advocate that persecuted Jews be granted asylum in the GDR. We declare that we will strive for the establishment of diplomatic relations and for wide-ranging contacts with the State of Israel.

Israel's Ministry of Foreign Affairs welcomed this statement. It seemed to have met Jerusalem's requirements, as presented during the first and second round of talks between East German and Israeli representatives in Copenhagen, except for the Israeli government's claim to reparations for the absorption and rehabilitation of tens of thousands of Holocaust survivors in Israel.

In mid-May 1990, Prime Minister de Maziere dispatched a missive to Edgar Bronfman, then president of the World Jewish Congress, in which he disavowed the decision of the communist regime in his country to vote for the UN resolution equating Zionism with racism. Parallel to that, Sabine Bergmann-Pohl, president of the Volkskammer, de Maziere, and the new foreign minister, Markus Meckel, sent congratulatory telegrams to Israel's president, Chaim Herzog, Prime Minister Yitzhak Shamir, and Foreign Minister Arens on the occasion of Israel's forty-first independence anniversary. In his telegram to Arens, Meckel proposed the renewal of talks. Arens thanked him for the good wishes and expressed willingness to renew the talks in Copenhagen, with the aim of establishing mutual diplomatic relations.[37]

For the first time, on 25–27 June 1990, Bundestag President Rita Süssmuth visited Israel with her East German counterpart, Bergmann-Pohl. During their appearances at various forums, including the Knesset, Bergmann-Pohl called for the establishment of diplomatic relations between the GDR and Israel as soon as possible. She said she regretted her country's attitude, during the time of the communist regime, toward the Holocaust, Jews and Israel. She invited Knesset members to form a delegation to visit East

Germany. The MKs, for their part, suggested they establish an inter-parliamentary friendship association, similar to the one already in existence between West Germany and Israel.

The statement in April, the congratulatory messages sent from the GDR heads of state to their Israeli counterparts in May, and the visit of Süssmuth and Bergmann-Pohl in June were the main catalysts toward the resumption of talks between East Germany and Israel in Copenhagen on 2–3 July 1990. In a meeting with the director general of the Foreign Ministry, in preparation for the coming round of talks, it was decided that the document on the establishment of diplomatic relations between the two countries would include a commitment by the two sides to establish a joint commission of experts to conduct negotiations over reparations. It suggested that the East Germans convene this commission within one month of the initialling of the agreement in Copenhagen, and that actual negotiations on reparations not be conducted at the talks.[38]

THIRD ROUND

The participants of the third round of talks operated on the assumption that this would be the final set of talks and that they would be signing an agreement on the establishment of diplomatic relations between the two countries. Both sides brought with them, from their capitals, drafts for the summary of the agreement to be initialled. This presumption was also expressed in the composition of the participants.

On the East German side were Reiner Neumann, head of the Middle and Near East Section in the East Germany Ministry of Foreign Affairs; Dr Angelica Timm (translator), lecturer at Humboldt University; Schoffen, a Protestant minister and long-time activist in the Middle East faculty of Humboldt University; Reiner Babbe, director of the Middle East Department Ministry of Foreign Affairs; and Stephan Meltzer, a representative of the Legal Department in the GDR's Ministry of Foreign Affairs.

On the Israeli side were myself, in my role as deputy director general in the Foreign Ministry for East European Affairs; Michael Shilo, counsellor to the foreign minister for Diaspora affairs; Dr Robert Sabel, legal adviser to the Foreign Ministry; and Mordechai Benaya from the Israeli Embassy in Copenhagen.[39]

Neumann began by saying that the purpose of the current round was to reach an agreement on the establishment of diplomatic relations between the two countries and that 'our function is to overcome all the obstacles and together to find solutions to the existing problems'. He assessed the current session as having two goals: first, to speak about conciliation between the two nations; second, to announce that the Germans, GDR citizens as well, take upon themselves responsibility regarding the past, 'with all that this entailed'. To this he added:

> The process of the unification of the two Germanys is now a very swift one. We are interested in attaining unification with a joint position of the two Germanys, our and theirs. And as for the Jewish-Israeli topic:
>
> We are aware of the pressure of time. It is already very difficult to maintain control over the process taking place in the GDR and it is hard to prophesy what will be tomorrow. Yesterday [1 July 1990] was a decisive day in German history. Yesterday, the unification of the currency of the two Germanys went into effect. That means that we have transferred part of our independent rights to the other side. Now two stages remain: dividing the GDR into various states and holding a referendum/elections. We think that the elections will take place as early as the end of the year. The precise time has not yet been set, but it seems this is how it will be. From the latest talks between us, in January and March, one may see that there are still two open issues: (a) a new declaration by the GDR regarding the UN resolution about Zionism; (b) overcoming the past regarding material claims. So let's begin with the issue of Zionism:

The starting point is that the GDR (today) has disso-
ciated itself from the former position supported by it. It
disagrees with the identification 'Zionism-racism'. This
identification is not possible and cannot be justified. The
second point is that the GDR begins from the premise
that it is a matter for the Jewish people to define and
determine its historical and spiritual roots by itself. The
GDR accepts with understanding the episodes important to the Jewish people, according to which Zionism is
the spiritual and ideological basis important for the
political movement for the maintenance of Jewish
identity and the right to self-determination. We begin
from the supposition that a large number of Jews chose
Zionism as their orientation for personal and national
life. Simultaneously, we see the variety and complexity
of the thoughts that the Jews create for themselves. The
main thing is that it cannot be that the Germans will
define the nature of Zionism. This is the exclusive right
of the Jewish people ... The government has no claim to
define ideological premises for other countries ... this
was a mistake of the previous regime in the GDR that
defined the nature of Zionism and that is how the issue
ended up as a UN resolution equating Zionism to
racism.

The third point is that we are working in the GDR in
such a way that a positive view of Zionism will be
distributed not only among the government but also
within the Parliament, the image of Zionism as you have
defined it in the past. We wish to speak about the unbal-
anced approach the GDR had towards Zionism and you
have already heard about that during the visit of Ms
Sabine Bergmann-Pohl in Israel. The government will
discuss that and even take unilateral steps concerning
this ... one may, of course, raise the issue at the UN, but
I am not certain that it is possible to attain a majority in
the UN. Perhaps most of the developing countries have
remained as they were. The GDR declared its new

position even before the topic will be discussed at the UN.

As for point two, the most important issue for us is the declaration of the GDR Parliament on 12 April. This is the most important starting point for us ... The declaration states that the German people accepts responsibility for its past in connection with the Holocaust – the time preceding 1945. In addition, there is a plea for forgiveness concerning the time or period after 1945 [his country's policy towards Israel]. The declaration further states that we wish to establish diplomatic relations. There still remains the open question of material claims. Your request on this issue is parallel to that of the Conference on Material Claims against Germany. The official talks with the Claims Conference regarding Germany began a week ago. I wish to tell you now of the readiness of the GDR government to begin negotiations with the State of Israel about 'contributions' to victims of the Holocaust. Mr Shilo was in the United States when our prime minister spoke about reparations. We do not wish to use the German expression *Wiedergutmachung* ('to make well again') for two reasons: (a) It is not possible to repair what was; (b) the German term means that there is no longer any need to thinks about it.

There is another problem: If in our discussions we speak about *Widergutmachung*, then another twenty or thirty countries that were members of the anti-German coalition will knock on our door and also want reparations. Among us everyone argues that this is impossible. These countries will ask why only Israel should get reparations and not them. This is a very difficult point. We must now come to an agreement with the FRG, and we have no other option on this point. The FRG argues that it is not possible to begin negotiations with forty or more countries. So, therefore, we must search together for another word. Not to speak about

150

Wiedergutmachung but to find a compromise we can live with. We think that these are the two remaining points for clarification on the way to establishing relations. Perhaps Mr Govrin will want to refer to what has been stated thus far.

I replied as follows:

I would like to express my appreciation for the course of these talks until now. As a result of the two latest rounds it was possible to hold a third round, with the aim thus far to clarify our position, as Mr Shilo did with great skill. Since then, the central event that has occurred was expressed in the declaration by the Parliament of the GDR on 12 April 1990. And in effect, the most important events, since then, were the free elections held in East Germany and the decision by the Parliament about the declaration to which we have just referred. Additional events are the visit by the speaker of the GDR Parliament in Israel and our very gathering here. As you know, Mr Neumann, we welcomed the Parliament declaration. We saw it as an expression of all the factions of Parliament that represent the people of the GDR and this may be termed a historic turning point towards us – in the attitude of the GDR to the Jewish people and the State of Israel. We hope and believe that the principles embodied in this declaration will be implemented. I will stress a number of its aspects:

First comes revision of the education system for everything concerning the presentation of the history of the Jewish people in its different periods and especially what happened during the Holocaust. We feel that the distortions of the previous regime were quite significant and now demand basic work to correct them. One may assume that the anti-Semitic–fascist movement in our days is nurtured from the negative image that was intruded into the falsified education. On this topic we, the government of Israel and its institutions (educational, research, cultural), will be ready to extend aid in carrying out the proposed revision.

The second, we believe and wish to hope that the Parliament will enact a law against anti-Semitism, also as part of the education system as well as a deterrent. I am happy to note with satisfaction the declaration about Zionism and think that it corrects to a great extent the prejudice and hostility of the previous regime towards Israel. The president of the United States, George Bush, has addressed a call to the countries of the world to amend the UN decision accepted for political and ideological reasons by a bloc of countries whose aim was the annihilation of the State of Israel.

The third, expressing faith and hope that there will be no repetition of acts of support of terrorists, including training terrorists on German soil, in light of our tragic past, acts which were aimed at eradicating the State of Israel and that were operated both directly and indirectly from East Germany. This has especially tragic meaning.

The fourth, the issue of reparations. My colleague Michael Shilo was right when he said that we have not accepted the concept of 'to make well again'. At every opportunity since then, we have noted that what was discussed with the government of West Germany in Luxembourg, in 1952, was an agreement whose aim was to help Israel absorb thousands of refugees who had been under Nazi occupation. For that reason we used the term *Global Recompensation* also for the part of East Germany. We welcomed the beginning of the talks between representatives of the GDR and those of the Claims Conference for advancing this subject.

We propose that a joint committee of both countries be established that will guide the negotiations between them on this topic. Similarly, it would be good to determine a time, within thirty days, for a meeting of a team of experts to discuss the issue of reparations. We even suggest that a time be set for the end of these talks on the basis of the declaration by the GDR government made on 5 April 1952 and Luxembourg Agreements from 10 September 1952. If we could include all these elements, together with what was voiced and will be heard, in a summary document, we would be able to recommend to our government that it act towards the establishment of diplomatic relations. We have gathered here as a result of the historic declaration of Parliament and also as a response to the proposals of the prime minister of the GDR to the prime minister of Israel. Finally, I wished to note that we are sensitive to the attempt to draw comparisons between our case and what happened in twenty or thirty other countries. Our instance, to our sorrow, is completely different from any other instance. There is no need to state that the policy and actions of Nazi Germany to annihilate us was unique.

Neumann referred to my statements about the help that East Germany provided for terrorists against Israel by saying that regarding the training of terrorists, 'the GDR has a clear position according to which there is no way such a thing should recur in light of the new policy of the GDR', since moreover he could state 'with complete certainty that there will not be military cooperation between the GDR and the PLO'.

From here on, the talks focused on the topic of reparations. Ultimately, it was this issue that eventually blocked the signing of an agreement. The crux of the disagreement was the Israeli delegation's demand that the basis for discussions be the reparations agreement of 1952; however, the head of the East German delegation announced that they were not ready to agree with every reference in the 1952 Luxembourg Agreement and that if the Israelis insisted upon this, they would insert their own concerns into the agreement. He said that neither they nor the West Germans had any intention of paying one third of the amount agreed upon in 1952. In his estimation, 'all monetary matters should be discussed with West Germany'. He added that the GDR intended to pay sums for personal compensation, which meant giving material donations (*Materielle Leistungen*) to Holocaust victims, such as scholarships, payment for summer camps in East Germany, support for old-age homes, and so on.[40]

In light of the differences of opinion about the formulation of the summary document, the Israeli delegation was dissatisfied with the text of the proposed agreement, did not initial it, and returned to Israel for consultations.

The Israeli delegation's recommendation to its Ministry of Foreign Affairs was that 'the issue should be passed on to the West German government to clarify its position regarding payment of one third of the reparations according to the 1952 agreement. If the West Germans are willing to view the 1952 agreement as a basis for negotiations, we do not see any reason not to sign the draft proposed by the East German delegation'.[41]

Below is the text of the document proposed to the Israeli delegation by the East German negotiators which was never signed:

The German Democratic Republic and the State of Israel by declaring as their starting point the partnership of the GDR in responsibility for the crimes perpetrated by the Nazi regime during the Holocaust against the Jewish people, as expressed in the declaration by all factions in the legislature on 12 April 1990,

- Through special consideration of the need to teach the youth the history, culture and travails of suffering of the Jews and the need to promote cooperation between the two countries so as to achieve this goal,
- By their censuring terror and by their deciding to take hold of the proper means according to the norms of international law so as to prevent any form of participation or support in acts of terror,

- By their disagreeing with UN Resolution 3379 from 1975

They have agreed:

1) The German Democratic Republic and the State of Israel will establish diplomatic relations between the two countries with the inception as of ... and special, authorized ambassadors will be exchanged. This process will be carried out according to the Vienna Convention on Diplomatic Relations of 18 April 1961. Details of the implementation of the establishment of relations will be authorized separately between the two governments.
2) The German Democratic Republic and Israel have agreed to begin talks on material claims of the State of Israel that are related to its absorption of Holocaust survivors, with the aim of attaining as soon as possible an agreed-upon arrangement.[42]

Ultimately the document went unsigned and the question of the establishment of diplomatic relations between the two countries remained open. Upon the return of the Israeli delegation to Jerusalem, a discussion took place, headed by (newly appointed) Deputy Prime Minister and Foreign Minister David Levy, in which I raised the following questions and answers:[43]

Question: Firstly, is West Germany for the establishment of diplomatic relations between Israel and East Germany?
Answer: The assumption is that it is, since this would be a sort of stamp of approval for the unification of the two Germanies. Moshe Arens (former foreign minister) received West German approval for the establishment of relations between Israel and East Germany in his consultations with West German leaders in Bonn (before the East German elections), and the Israeli ambassador in Bonn was told by a minister in Chancellor Kohl's office 'that he would prefer that the West German embassy in Israel also represent the GDR'.

Question: Secondly, is it politically wise to establish diplomatic relations with the GDR when in a few months it will be incorporated into West Germany and it refuses to bear its part in providing reparations to Israel (which was defined as fulfilling its part in absorbing Holocaust survivors from Germany and countries that had been under Nazi occupation)?

Answer: The East German government proposed the inclusion of a clause in the joint agreement that would state that Israel and the GDR have decided to convene their experts 'to discuss material donations', and if we insist, it will say 'to discuss Israel's material claims against East Germany that are related to Holocaust victims', no more than thirty days from the signing of the agreement on the establishment of relations.

Question: What are the advantages in establishing diplomatic relations with East Germany?

Answer: It would be an achievement in Israel's foreign policy with respect to the PLO and Arab countries, which enjoyed the political and military support of the GDR for close to forty years. The GDR is now turning its back on them by establishing diplomatic relations with Israel, by its public disavowal of the UN resolution equating Zionism with racism, and also by condemning terror. In addition, the establishment of a framework within which to negotiate reparations creates a dynamic that will continue to exist even with a unified Germany. (West Germany's chancellor declared that after reunification, he would honour all of East Germany's financial obligations.)

Question: What are the disadvantages in establishing diplomatic relations with East Germany?

Answer: One disadvantage would be the granting of a 'stamp of approval' to the GDR in advance of its political unification with West Germany, without it bearing its share of the reparations, as we would have expected, according to the Luxembourg Agreements. Moreover, receiving the version proposed by the East German delegation after it had announced to us that it had no intention of basing discussions on the Luxembourg Agreements could be interpreted as acquiescence on our side to the GDR's refusal to oblige the West Germans to negotiate with us on the basis of these agreements. Lastly, the lack of feasibility of establishing relations with a country that will not exist in a few months would be another disadvantage.

Once the pros and cons had been weighed, Israel's Ministry of Foreign Affairs, as authorized by the foreign minister, David Levy, decided not to establish diplomatic relations with East Germany, thus ending the last stage of negotiations. Israel's demands of the GDR on all issues except for reparations were satisfactorily fulfilled with the GDR parliament's unanimous decision on 22 July 1990 – a decision which in the history of the GDR can be termed historic – to declare its total disavowal of the anti-Israel policies maintained by the GDR for decades. The parliament also declared its nullification of the GDR's vote for the UN General Assembly Resolution 3379, of 10 November 1975, equating Zionism with racism.[44]

CONCLUSION

Although Israel did not establish diplomatic relations with the GDR, which disappeared from the map of Europe, one should not view the diplomatic process that preceded it as a passing episode in the annals of the two countries' foreign relations. The GDR, which was among the strongest supporters of the PLO and the Arab states hostile to Israel, publicly reversed its policy. Moreover, due to Israeli pressure, it publicly condemned terror and changed its anti-Israel and anti-Zionist policies. East Germany responded to Israel's demands in taking moral responsibility for Nazi crimes against Jews and implemented a change in its education systems. It seems unlikely that had relations with Israel been established, it would have done anything to delay the GDR's unification with West Germany. Nevertheless, it is certain that had the GDR managed to establish relations with Israel, its image in the US and the West would have been greatly improved and its demise more seriously mourned, than had been reflected in reality. The GDR could have reaped greater benefit, in the economic and political areas, than it had earned in all the years of its existence.

NOTES

1. An abridged version of this chapter appeared in *The Israel Journal of Foreign Affairs*, 2, 3 (Jerusalem, 2008), translated from Hebrew by Yvette Shumacher.
2. On the Potsdam Conference that was held on 27 July–3 August 1945 an on the agreement signed during it, see Alexander Werth, *Russia at War 1941–1945*, vol. 2 (Tel Aviv: Maarchot, 1968), pp.669–72. According to the agreement, East Germany paid compensation to the USSR, and it in turn allotted an amount to Poland from the sum it received in compensation from East Germany, while West Germany pledged to pay compensation to the United States, Britain and other countries, except the USSR. That being the situation, East Germany was under no obligation to pay compensation to other countries.
3. Documents concerning the agreement between the government of Israel and the FRG (signed on 10 September 1952 in Luxembourg), Foreign Ministry, Jerusalem 1953.
4. Cited by Angelika Timm, *Hammer, Zirkel, Davidstern. Das gestorte Verhaltnis der DDR zu Zionismus und Staat Israel* (Bonn: Bouvier, 1997), p.84.
5. Letter by Eliezer Doron, director of the East European Department in the Foreign Ministry in Jerusalem to the Israeli legations abroad, on 16 May 1965. File 103.1 grz, Israel State Archives (ISA).
6. File grz 103.1, 30.4.1981, ISA.
7. Documents about the agreement between the government of Israel and the FRG, Foreign Ministry, Jerusalem 1953.
8. Timm, *Hammer, Zirkel, Davidstern*, p.145.
9. Yosef Govrin, notes from his talk with Gysi, 22 March 1991, File 103.1 grz, ISA.
10. *Yediot Achronot*, 22 December 1989 [Hebrew]; *Haaretz*, 17 December 1989 [Hebrew].
11. *Deyukan*, 18 November 2005 [Hebrew].
12. Report by Dr Gerhard Riegner of the WJC, Geneva, 15 March 1985, following his visit to the GDR on 28 February–8 March 1985, File 103.1 grz, ISA.

13. Timm, *Hammer, Zirkel, Davidstern*, p.307; SWB (Summary of World Broadcasts), 8 June 1988, 0172/EE Europe 1/1A; telegrams from the Israel Embassy in Bonn for 7 and 15 June 1988, as heard in reports by Galinski, File 103.1 grz, ISA.
14. Timm, *Hammer, Zirkel, Davidstern*, pp.563–6 (complete minutes of the Honecker-Rotstein meeting).
15. SWB, 017/EE, 8 June 1988.
16. Report by Herzl Inbar, consul general of Israel in New York, about his talk with Rabbi Israel Miller, president of the Claims Conference, 9 October 1985, File 103.1 grz, ISA.
17. Timm, *Hammer, Zirkel, Davidstern*, pp.300–3.
18. Ibid., p.311.
19. V. Struminsky, Yad Vashem: a précis of the statements by the state secretary for religious affairs at a press conference at Yad Vashem, 2 February 1989, File 103.01 grz, ISA.
20. Agreement between Yad Vashem, the Holocaust Martyrs' and Heroes' Remembrance Authority, Israel, and the Directorate of the State Archives of the German Democratic Republic, 4 December 1989, Yad Vashem Archives.
21. See n.18 above.
22. File grz 103.01, 2.2.1989, ISA.
23. Report by Yeshayahu Anug, 2 February 1989, File 103.01 grz, ISA.
24. Report by Yosef Govrin, 10 March 1989, File 103.01 grz, ISA.
25. Letter from Zvi Mazel, 18 December 1989, File 103.01 grz, ISA.
26. *Jerusalem Post*, 11 December 1989.
27. Memorandum by Yosef Govrin, 26 December 1989, File 103.01 grz, ISA.
28. H. Bar-On, Office of the Vice-President, Weizmann Institute of Science, Rehovoth, 4 January 1989 (should be 1990).
29. *Jerusalem Post*, 13 December 1989.
30. Report by A. Primor, Brussels, 4 January 1990, File 103.01 grz, ISA.
31. Notes of the talks between the East German and Israel delegations, Copenhagen, 4 February 1990, File 103.01 grz, ISA.
32. Yosef Govrin, Points for the Talk, 15 January 1990, File 103.01 grz, ISA.
33. Michael Shilo, memorandum on Arens' talk with Genscher, 18 February 1990; Israel's ambassador in Bonn, telegram, 20 February 1990.
34. Yosef Govrin, 9 March 1990, File 103.01 grz, ISA.
35. Notes of the talks between representatives of East Germany and Israel, Copenhagen, 12 March 1990, File 103.01 grz, ISA.
36. The parliament's decision was transmitted to the Foreign Ministry in Jerusalem, in a French version, by the Israeli ambassador in Abidjan on 24 April 1990 and in an English version through the Israel appointee in charge of the Israeli legation in Ankara on 2 May 1990. In both instances the GDR Embassies forwarded the document to the diplomatic legations of Israel in those locations. The German version is cited in Timm, *Hammer, Zirkel, Davidstern*, pp.588–9.
37. Timm, *Hammer, Zirkel, Davidstern*, p.354.
38. Memorandum of the East European Section from 17 June 1990, File 103.01 grz, ISA.
39. Third meeting between representatives of Israel and the GDR, Copenhagen, Notes, 20 August 1990, File 103.01 grz, ISA.
40. Telegram from the Israeli delegation in Copenhagen, 3 July 1990, File 103.01 grz, ISA.

41. Ibid.
42. Ibid.
43. Yosef Govrin, 10 July 1990, File 103.01 grz, ISA.
44. Timm, *Hammer, Zirkel, Davidstern*, p.397.

6. *Milestones in the Diplomatic Relations between Israel and Hungary: From Severance (1967) to their Renewal (1989)*[1]

HISTORICAL BACKGROUND

Bowing to pressure from the Soviet Union, Hungary joined the Eastern Bloc satellites in their decision, on 12 June 1967, to sever diplomatic relations with Israel following the Six Day War. Of those countries, only Romania continued to maintain relations with Israel. Hungary, unlike the Soviet Union, Czechoslovakia and Poland, however, continued to maintain trade relations with Israel, even in the absence of diplomatic relations. Moreover, Hungary's anti-Israel propaganda was less vitriolic than that of its allies. However, in the UN, Hungary tended to vote with the Communist Bloc in favour of all anti-Israel resolutions that were proposed by the Soviet Union and Arab states. Years later, Hungary was to become the first country in that group to renew diplomatic relations with Israel on 18 September 1989.

From 1948 to 1967, relations between Hungary and Israel were quite chilly, a fact attested to by David Giladi, the last official representative of Israel's legation in Budapest.[2] This was true except for two brief periods: the first, during Israel's early years of independence, when all Soviet-led Communist Bloc countries accorded the Jewish state de jure recognition and supported it politically and

161

militarily. The second period occurred in 1956, during Hungary's brief liberal revolution.

For Israel, the most important issue on the agenda, immediately after the establishment of diplomatic relations with Hungary in 1948, was obtaining the right to emigrate to Israel for the thousands of Jews who wished to do so.[3] However, the Hungarians refused to acquiesce, claiming that there was no anti-Semitism in Hungary and that Jewish citizens had assimilated into the Hungarian nation.[4] Nevertheless, permission was granted for several thousand Jews to leave for Israel on condition that Jerusalem would allow Israelis of Hungarian origin to return to Hungary. Yet by comparison with the other Soviet satellites (except for Romania during the Ceauşescu era), Hungary's Jewish community was given a relatively free hand in running its communal Jewish life. A rabbinical seminary was even allowed to function in Budapest, the only one in the Soviet Bloc, as well as a Jewish high school.[5]

In 1949, Hungary was the first communist country to sign a trade agreement with Israel. However, due to difficulties, primarily on Israel's side, the potential for that agreement, which provided for a substantial flow of trade, was not fully realized.[6] In the years to follow, new trade agreements were signed, but they were less ambitious. The diplomatic representation in both countries was at the legation level, and until the severance of diplomatic relations, for the most part, an accredited representative headed the Israeli legation in Budapest.

Frequent changes in leadership occurred in the Soviet Union during the 1980s after the deaths of Leonid Brezhnev (1982), Yuri Andropov (1984), and Konstantin Chernenko (1985). Following these events, Mikhail Gorbachev rose to power (1985), soon becoming the architect of the political and economic reforms (glasnost and perestroika) that were very much in tune with the liberal, economic and political policies of Hungary's leader, Janos Kadar. Consequently, Hungary's dependence on the

Soviet Union lessened, and it broadened its ties with Western countries.[7] This included furthering relations with Israel in the areas of economics, trade, sport, tourism and culture at an unprecedented level.

Hungary accepted Israel's initiative to establish diplomatic contact – with Gorbachev's consent[8] – which led, initially, to the signing of an agreement (14 September 1987) to open Interest Offices in Budapest and Tel Aviv. These offices operated under the patronage of the two foreign embassies that respectively represented them. Israel's office in Budapest was located in the Swiss Embassy, and Hungary's office in the Swedish Embassy in Tel Aviv. Two years later, both countries renewed full diplomatic relations (18 September 1989).

Against the backdrop of the economic, social and diplomatic changes occurring in the Soviet Union, and in light of Hungary's efforts to broaden ties with the West and Israel, bilateral relations between the two countries were initiated in the early 1980s, with the blessing of their respective governments. This was an exceptional phenomenon among Communist Bloc countries, and which laid the groundwork for the next two stages; these were the opening of the interest offices and the full renewal of diplomatic relations. The three stages lasted from 1983 to 1989.

MAIN STAGES IN THE RENEWAL OF DIPLOMATIC RELATIONS

Stage One: Major Milestones in the Bilateral Relations of Hungary and Israel, 1983–1985

- On 1 July 1983 an agreement was signed between the Bank of Israel and the Hungarian National Bank to broaden mutual trade by opening reciprocal credit lines and making arrangements to establish mutual economic relations.[9]
- A comprehensive book called *Jerusalem* was published in Hungary with a print run of 70,000 copies. The book was written by the Hungarian

163

Daniel Rapcsany and illustrated by Jerusalemite painter Yossi Stern. The author visited Israel as a guest of Israel's Ministry of Foreign Affairs prior to publication. That volume provided an excellent and balanced portrait of daily life in the city among the three major religions, against the backdrop of Jerusalem's historical and religious importance.

- In 1983, an association to promote Israeli-Hungarian ties was established at the initiative of Moshe Sanbar (former governor of the Bank of Israel) and with the encouragement of Israel's Ministry of Foreign Affairs. A short while later, Sanbar visited Hungary at the invitation of J. Gostony, former director general of Hungary's Foreign Ministry and secretary general of the Budapest-based Association of Hungarians in the Diaspora. Sanbar conveyed a message from the Bank of Israel to the economic ministries in Budapest which stated that it wished to broaden mutual trade relations. The Israeli Ministry of Foreign Affairs suggested that he raise a series of issues to promote scientific and cultural ties between the two countries.[10]

- Three Israeli writers travelled to Hungary to conduct talks with the head of the Europa publishing house there. These were Ben-Zion Tomer, chairman of the General Union of Writers in Israel, Asher Reich, editor of the Hebrew-language journal *Moznayim*, and Itamar Yaoz-Kest, poet. This visit came about as a result of an agreement which the three writers had signed with Hungary's publishing house Europa to publish an anthology of modern Israeli poetry in Hungarian, as well as an anthology of Hungarian poetry in Hebrew. Israel's Ministry of Foreign Affairs and the World Zionist Organization funded their trip.[11]

- A groundbreaking agreement was signed between Hungary's State Documentation Authority and Yad

Vashem on the exchange of archival material dealing with the period of the Holocaust and the history of Hungarian Jews. The agreement enabled Yad Vashem researchers to photocopy archival material that had previously been inaccessible to them. Historians from both countries exchanged visits to discuss the historiography of the Holocaust.[12]

- For the first time, a delegation of Hungarian Jewish community leaders visited Israel to participate in an international conference of Jews of Hungarian origin, held in Jerusalem.[13]
- At the end of 1984, an official delegation from Hungary came to Tel Aviv for the opening of an exhibit at Beth Hatefutsoth (the Museum of the Jewish Diaspora) on Hungarian Jewry. Most of the items on display at the exhibition were obtained from Hungary's national museums and from the Jewish Museum in Budapest.[14]
- Significant changes were made by the Hungarian authorities that eased the way for Israelis who wished to visit Hungary, whether for personal reasons or for business. Israeli citizens could now obtain visas on the spot at Hungarian legations in Europe, or upon entering Hungary.[15] Consequently there was a considerable rise in tourism from Israel to Hungary as well as an increase in the scope of business between the two countries.
- A World Jewish Congress delegation visited Hungary in February 1985 and met with official representatives. Accompanying the delegation was the director of the Diaspora Department of Israel's Ministry of Foreign Affairs, Moshe Gilboa, who played an active role in all talks focusing on the issue of cooperation between Israel and Hungary, and between Hungary and world Jewry.[16] This was the first time since the severance of diplomatic relations between the two countries that a foreign ministry departmental head

165

from Israel had visited Hungary in an official capacity.
- Hungary, for the first time, participated in the International Book Fair, held in Jerusalem in May 1985. As part of the event, the Hannah Szenes Prize was awarded to Daniel Rapcsany, the Hungarian author of *Jerusalem*.[17]

These and other milestones laid the groundwork for the renewal of bilateral relations that branched out over time into the areas of economics, trade, culture, tourism, science and relations with the Jewish community in Hungary, all during the period when diplomatic relations remained severed, and particularly after their resumption.

Stage Two: Diplomatic Contact Involved in Opening Interest Offices
- Within the framework of UN General Assembly discussions, in September 1985, Deputy Prime Minister and Foreign Minster Yitzhak Shamir met for talks (initiated by Israel's Ministry of Foreign Affairs) with Hungarian Foreign Minister Dr Peter Varkonyi. This was the first meeting between the two foreign ministers since the severance of ties. Both praised the development of bilateral ties and expressed the hope that these would be strengthened. Even though the talks were held in an atmosphere of goodwill, the Hungarian foreign minister was cautious in discussing the possibility of re-establishing diplomatic relations between the two countries in the near future. The reasons for this, he claimed, were, first and foremost, Hungary's 'sensitivities' regarding its obligation to uphold the decision of the Soviet Bloc countries to sever ties with Israel. Another factor was Hungary's linkage to the issue of the progress achieved in the peace process between Israel and its neighbours, via an international conference in which the Soviet Union, the US, Israel and the PLO would participate. However, he left room for hope when he promised that 'if we see there is an opportunity for a

general improvement, I will recommend this step'.[18]

- Within the framework of discussions at the UN General Assembly in September 1986, the two foreign ministers, Shamir and Varkonyi, held another meeting, which they characterized as 'outstanding in its warmth and friendliness'. The Hungarian foreign minister asked Shamir for his opinion about the idea of convening an international conference to discuss possible solutions to the Arab-Israeli conflict. The answer he received was, 'We believe in direct negotation.' The topic quickly changed to the issue of promoting mutual relations. Shamir suggested that Hungry look to Poland as an example of how to proceed (that is, establish mutual interest offices), which he said was 'not an ideal example, but one route to take'. The deputy director general of Israel's foreign ministry, Hanan Bar-On, who was present for the talks, suggested the possibility of opening consulates, headed by consuls general, as was the case with Hungary and Spain at that time. Varkonyi responded that they were 'willing to discuss the suggestions that were raised', but did not note how, and at which diplomatic rank, contact would continue.[19]

- During my mission as Israel's ambassador in Bucharest, I had many conversations with my Hungarian counterpart, Ambassador Pal Szüts, on the topic of relations between Israel and Hungary. In that context, I was asked to convey to Szüts a letter from newly appointed Deputy Prime Minister and Foreign Minister Shimon Peres to the Hungarian foreign minister. The letter, dated 14 November 1986, stated:

> The meeting held in New York between the foreign ministers of our countries was, of course, brought to my attention. Now, as I embark upon my role as foreign minister of Israel, I am of the

opinion that perhaps the time has come to discuss the issues raised during the conversation, regarding establishing relations between our two countries. As you will remember, the two ministers discussed the possibility of opening general consulates or interest offices. As for myself, I am of the opinion that it is certainly possible to implement the idea of opening a consulate general, in light of the increasing flow of Israeli tourists to Hungary. If this suggestion seems interesting to you, we will, of course, be willing to discuss the necessary steps to be taken to implement it, at a venue of your choice.[20]

From a conversation with Szüts on the topic of Israeli-Hungarian relations (a few days before I received the letter from Peres), I understood that after discussing the issue, the Hungarian leaders had decided to take things 'step by step'. In his estimation, the timing was not right for the establishment of diplomatic relations. This was so for two reasons: first of all, the fear of losing the Arab market, which was so important to his country's economy; secondly, the fact that this issue would lead to tensions 'within the family'. To be sure, such tensions already existed, and the conservative communists were critical of the 'Hungarian road to Socialism'. Therefore, they would take the decisive step only when 'Big Brother' consented. In light of this reaction, I recommended to Peres that he delay sending the letter. My recommendation was accepted.[21]

The decision to proceed 'one step at a time' undoubtedly indicated the dilemma facing the Hungarian leadership. On the one hand, it feared an angry reaction from Arab countries, which could be manifested in serious harm to their economic relations if Hungary strayed from the consensus of the Communist Bloc to establish ties with Israel. It also feared confrontation on this issue with the Soviet Union. On the other hand, how could Hungary broaden economic and cultural ties, and enhance tourism with Israel without formally establishing diplomatic relations? Such a move, in itself, would improve Hungary's status in the West and among Jewish organizations in the US, a long-sought objective. This dilemma was apparent in the response of Hungarian Communist Party Secretary for Foreign Affairs, Matyas Szuros, to the following question, posed to him in a radio interview: 'Can we expect the establishment of diplomatic relations between Hungary and Israel?'

> In weighing the decision of whether to establish diplomatic relations, we must take into account the fact that the reasons that led to the severance of relations still exist. However, to this question, which deserves a thorough response, there are both historical and humanitarian components. One of these is that our intensive relations with Arab countries are long-term. The other is that in our country, there is increasing interest in Israel's ancient culture, and its many recent cultural, historical and artistic achievements ... More than 200,000 Israeli citizens are Hungarian speakers, many of whom have even kept their Hungarian citizenship. Therefore, their attachment to the homeland and their relatives living here has stayed constant over the years. We are aware of the fact that the majority of consular problems arising as a result of cultural, humanitarian and economic ties are increasingly difficult to solve under the present circumstances. We are certainly interested in finding a satisfactory solution to these problems, and, as I mentioned, developing economic ties, fair representation, and maintenance of our interests. But, I would like to emphasize that we are only discussing these considerations, and not a renewal of diplomatic relations.[22]

The attempt to solve this dilemma led the Hungarian leadership to consult with Gorbachev himself on the matter. To that end, Prime Minister Karoly Grosz travelled to Moscow and reported upon his return that he had a positive answer from Gorbachev.[23] Before he left, Grosz disclosed to World Jewish Congress President Edgar Bronfman, who, in July 1987, had been visiting Hungary at the invitation of the Hungarian government, that he supported the establishment of official relations with Israel. However, Hungary, he said, would not be able to proceed alone; according to Grosz, it required a decision taken by the Soviet bloc as a whole. He noted that he was going to consult with Gorbachev on the matter, in order to understand what was being discussed by Soviet and Israeli representatives regarding the idea of exchanging consular delegations as a means of establishing relations between them. He added that soon (that is, after returning from his consultations in Moscow) they would know if and how these measures (of the Soviets towards Israel) would influence Hungarian-Israeli relations.[24]

After receiving Soviet consent, Hungary suggested (via the Swedish Embassy in Tel Aviv) that they secretly meet the Israeli officials in Vienna, on 9–12 August 1987, to discuss the establishment of diplomatic relations between the two countries. Israel immediately agreed. The deputy director general of the Ministry of Foreign Affairs, Yeshayahu Anug, represented Israel at these talks; the Hungarians sent Janos Görög, head of the Department for International Law of Hungary's Foreign Ministry, who would eventually become Hungary's first ambassador to Israel after the resumption of diplomatic relations between the two countries. The two sides decided to open Interest Offices in the near future – no later than six months from the meeting. The official document describing the opening of the offices and defining the parameters of their activity in the consular, economic, trade, cultural, scientific and tourism realms was signed in the Swiss Foreign Ministry in Bern, in the presence of the president of Switzerland and the Hungarian and Israeli ambassadors in Bern, on 14 September 1987. The staffs of the offices were granted diplomatic immunity and all the rights associated with it. The heads of these offices would eventually present their credentials to the host country. In actual fact, free access to the foreign ministries of their host countries was given to them on all topics which they felt should be raised in order to advance bilateral relations.[25]

On the very day Yeshayahu Anug and Janos Görög signed the document, Deputy Foreign Minister Laszlo Kovacs informed the ambassadors of Arab countries and the PLO, who were accredited in Hungary (as well as the ambassadors of Warsaw Pact countries), and, separately, the ambassador of Iran, that a document had been signed stating that Interest Offices would be opened in each country, under the patronage of the foreign embassies representing their respective interests. According to Kovacs, the Arab representatives' reactions were 'unfriendly'; the exception was the Egyptian representative, who displayed satisfaction upon hearing the news. The reactions of the ambassadors of Syria, Libya, Algeria and the PLO were hostile in tone. Iraq's ambassador was of the opinion that this step would have a negative impact on relations between his country and Hungary, whereas Iran's ambassador reacted by saying that 'Israel is a cancerous tumour on the world which was to be excised.'[26]

The fact that the Arab and PLO ambassadors were invited to meet with Hungary's foreign minister to discuss the matter is a testament to the sensitivity of the Hungarians to the Arab countries and Iran, and of their concern that mutual relations might be harmed. Parallel to this, the Hungarians displayed a similar, if not identical, sensitivity towards the Soviet Bloc, when it decided to sever ties with Israel following the Six Day War.

Shmuel Meirom (who was accredited as Israel's first ambassador to Hungary after the resumption of diplomatic relations between the two countries) was appointed head of the Israeli Interest Office in Budapest. Jeno Geynis was appointed to head Hungary's Interest Office in Israel.

The decision to open mutual Interest Offices rather than renew diplomatic relations represented somewhat of a compromise on both sides. Hungary could claim to the Arab countries that the arrangement was not a resumption of diplomatic ties. The same applied to the Soviet Bloc consensus 'not to renew diplomatic relations with Israel as long as there is no change in the peace process between Israel and the Palestinians'. Israel did not insist that the establishment of ties be conditional upon a renewal of diplomatic relations. It definitely regarded the opening of its Interest Office in Budapest as a positive step (similar to its office in Warsaw) in accelerating the development of ties. To be sure, it was an important step in the preparation for the gradual renewal of diplomatic relations. Clearly, this compromise was acceptable to both sides and could serve Hungary's interests in Israel and the West, and Israel's interests in Eastern Europe and the international arena.

Stage Three: Renewal of Diplomatic Relations

A period of two years passed between the signing of the document, in Bern, by the representatives of Israel and Hungary, and the signing, in Budapest, by the two countries' foreign ministers of the protocol for the renewal of diplomatic relations. During this period, relations branched out into all areas, including diplomacy. Israeli ministers visited Hungary and Hungarian ministers visited Israel. Deputy Foreign Minister Laszlo Kovacs, who paid an official visit to Israel in April 1989 and who met for talks in Israel's Ministry of Foreign Affairs, spoke of the revolution that had occurred in the political views of the Hungarian leadership and government. Hungary, he said, was changing from a communist regime to a democratic and independent state, and Kovacs emphasized his country's aspiration to integrate as quickly as possible into European organizations, including the Common Market, without weakening relations with Warsaw Pact members. He noted with satisfaction the progress that had occurred in bilateral relations but did not hide his disappointment over the unfulfilled promises made by Israel's Ministries of Finance and Industry and Trade. In this context, he suggested signing agreements with Israel for ensuring investments, preventing double taxation, and reducing import taxes. It was made clear to him – by Deputy Director General Yeshayahu Anug and Deputy Foreign Minister Benjamin Netanyahu – that these documents could be prepared by teams from both sides, which would discuss them in their entirety, and could be signed upon the resumption of diplomatic relations.[27] From this, the Hungarian Foreign Ministry concluded that it would be possible to obtain these agreements after the resumption of diplomatic relations. And so they were.

Foreign Minister Moshe Arens was invited to Budapest by his Hungarian counterpart, Gyula Horn, to sign the protocol for the resumption of diplomatic relations. The signing ceremony was held at the Hungarian Ministry of Foreign Affairs in Budapest on 18 September 1989 in the presence of the media. Their speeches reviewed the history of negotiations to date, and expectations for the future in terms of advancement of mutual relations and the willingness to contribute to the achievement of peace in the Middle East. Gyula Horn's main points were:

After twenty-two years of severance of diplomatic relations between Hungary and Israel, this resumption of relations expresses the desire of the Hungarian people and also a new political reality in international relations, as well as the correction of a past error. Good relations exist between the two countries and the two peoples. This step expresses the fondness we feel for one another. I am convinced that the developments that have occurred in our relations since the opening of the interest offices demonstrate this very well. With the resumption of diplomatic relations, we will further strengthen these ties. It is possible that there are, and will be in the future, differences in political attitudes, but we must not deal with differences by confrontation, but rather by creating opportunities for dialogue. I am convinced that the resumption of our relations can be beneficial to [resolving] the problems of the Middle East.

The protocol that we signed for resumption of diplomatic relations between Hungary and Israel is not directed against the interests of any country in the world. Hungarians wish to continue their good relations with all countries and are interested in strengthening their relations with them. We hope Israel will have the opportunity to make peace and will do everything to contribute to that.

Moshe Arens' main points were:

The agreement signed today is a historic document, and I feel that we must regard this moment from the historical perspective of relations between Israel and the Jewish nation and Hungary. Our relationship also encompasses sad chapters: the large Jewish community in Hungary was almost totally destroyed during the last months of the Second World War. Most of the survivors of this community now live in Israel. Today we are strengthening the basis for friendly relations between our peoples and countries. I have no doubt that the decision of the Hungarian government to renew diplomatic relations with Israel required courage, and we in Israel view this as part of the courage that typifies Hungarian leadership when dealing with difficulties. Some countries believe that diplomatic relations should be conditional upon ideological agreement. Neither of us believes this, and we are of the opinion that diplomatic relations are beneficial to both countries.

We very much appreciate your interest in the Middle East peace process. In this realm as well, we believe that signing the protocol for renewal of Israeli-Hungarian relations can contribute to it ... we hope that the agreement we are signing today will allow us to exchange information that will benefit us all. One thing that has become clear in recent years: cooperation – particularly economic cooperation between countries – can bring about vast benefits that were hard to imagine in the past. This is apparent in the progress made in each of the countries of the European Community. Countries that live in solitude are punishing themselves. There are many things that can be done together for the benefit of both nations. This can be regarded as a starting point.[28]

In answer to one of the journalists who asked if there was an element of national soul-searching that perhaps typified all the Eastern European Communist Bloc states which had decided to sever diplomatic relations with Israel following the Six Day War, Horn declared, 'A few years ago, when we started to discuss the idea of normalizing relations with Israel, we carefully studied the documents of 1967 and the causes of the severance of relations with Israel. I must say that my personal impression is that not only did ideological prejudices play a role in this decision, but also the fact that we were not properly versed in the details of the war and everything that happened in it.'

EPILOGUE

Thus, this chapter in history, in which diplomatic relations between Hungary and Israel were disrupted, finally came to a close. A short while after resumption of relations, the agreements for cooperation between the two countries were signed, as suggested by Hungary's deputy foreign minister, Kovacs. Later, in the early 1990s, other agreements were signed as well. These agreements broadened and deepened the bilateral relations in all possible areas. Similarly, official ties were also strengthened between the two countries. Presidential visits were exchanged, as well as visits by prime ministers, foreign ministers, and others. In the UN, Hungary adopted more balanced perspectives on the issue of the Israeli-Palestinian conflict and to support the idea of a solution in a way that would be acceptable to both sides.

The Jewish community in Hungary – the largest in Eastern Europe after the Soviet Union – numbered 80,000 at the beginning of 1990. Its institutions conducted religious, social and national activities with renewed vigour after the establishment of democracy in the country. However, the democratization and liberalization of Hungary allowed extremist nationalistic groups to take advantage of freedom of speech to engage in anti-Semitic incitement, particularly during the April 1990 elections. Both the president and prime minister of Hungary denounced these manifestations of anti-Semitism and took action against the inciters. Among those condemning these manifestations of anti-Semitism were both the Catholic and Protestant churches. A survey published in May 1991 found that anti-Semitism in Hungary was less virulent than in other Eastern European countries. However, this situation has considerably changed. In the last Hungarian parliamentary elections (second round, 25 April 2010) the extreme right party, Jobbik – known for its anti-Semitic and anti-Romani policies – gained, for the first time, a relatively high percentage of the total votes in the general elections: forty-seven seats out of 386 in the parliament. It will therefore now be eligible to join the parliament as the third party (after the Socialists with fifty-nine seats). According to statements made by the leader of the central-conservative party Fidesz, which gained the majority of the votes (263 seats) and will form the new government, and by the head of the Jewish community, there is no intention of entering into any coalition with the Jobbik party. Time will show to what degree Jobbik will gain or lose power in Hungary.[29]

Hungary was the first Communist Bloc state to renew diplomatic relations with Israel. In addition to its democratization (following its decreased dependence on the Soviet Union) and its aspiration to increase its cooperation with the West and Israel in order to promote its political and economic interests, the mutual affinity between the large Hungarian Jewish community and Israelis of Hungarian origin played an important role in achieving this goal. Hungary regarded this affinity as a means to build a bridge to the free world.

NOTES

1. An abridged version of this chapter appeared in *The Israel Journal of Foreign Affairs,* 1, 2 (2007), 107–18, translated from Hebrew by Yvette Shumachers.
2. David Giladi, 'The Russians Pressured and the Hungarians Severed Ties', *Ma'ariv,* 22 September 1989 [Hebrew].
3. Yehuda Marton, 'The Jews of Hungary', in Ya'akov Tsur (ed.), *The Diaspora: East Europe* (Jerusalem: Keter, 1976), pp.239–68 [Hebrew]; A.A. Ben-Asher (pseudonym of Katriel Katz), *Foreign Relations 1948–1953* (Tel Aviv: Ayanot, 1957), pp.210–11.
4. Ben Asher, *Foreign Relations 1948–1953.*
5. *Encyclopaedia Hebraica,* Supplement 2 (Tel Aviv: Sifriat Poalim, 1983), entries 428–9.
6. Ben Asher, *Foreign Relations 1948–1953,* pp.210–11.
7. From testimony of Laszlo Kovacs, former deputy foreign minister of Hungary, in a collection of interviews made into a documentary film. The text of the interviews was published in the booklet entitled *A Historical Sketch: Five Decades of Diplomatic Relations between Hungary and the State of Israel,* written and directed by Peter Bokor, producer Pal Schiffer (Budapest, 1995–1997), part 1, p.4.
8. Ibid., part 2, p.2.
9. Memorandum of Y. Govrin, director of the Eastern Europe Department of Israel's Ministry of Foreign Affairs, 5 May 1985, Hungarian File 103.1, Israel State Archives (ISA).
10. Memorandum of Y. Govrin, 12 April 1984, Hungarian File 103.1, ISA.
11. Ibid.
12. Memorandum of Y. Govrin, 15 May 1985, Hungarian File 103.1, ISA.
13. Ibid.
14. Ibid.
15. Ibid.
16. Report of Moshe Gilboa, director of the Diaspora Department of Israel's Ministry of Foreign Affairs, 13 May 1985, and memorandum of Y. Govrin, 28 May 1985, Hungarian File 103.1, ISA.
17. Memorandum of Y. Govrin, 28 August 1985, Hungarian File 103.1, ISA.
18. Report of Aharon Ofry, Israel's Diplomatic Mission to the UN, 26 September 1985, Hungarian File 103.1, ISA.
19. Report of Raphael Gvir, Israel's Diplomatic Mission to the UN, 29 September 1986, Hungarian File 103.1, ISA.
20. 24 November 1986, Hungarian File 103.1, ISA.
21. Report of Y. Govrin, Israel's ambassador to Bucharest, 26 November 1986, Hungarian File 103.1, ISA.
22. Taken from an interview on Radio Budapest later published in the Hungarian Communist daily *Nepszabadsag,* 11 February 1987.
23. Testimony of Karoly Grosz, former prime minister of Hungary, in Bokor, *A Historical Sketch,* part 2, p.9.
24. Report of Johanan Bein, Israel's Diplomatic Mission to the UN, 22 July 1987, Hungarian File 103.1, ISA.
25. Letter of Janos Görög to Yeshayahu Anug, 7 September 1987, detailing the agreements reached in their talks in Vienna, Hungarian File 103.1, ISA.

26. Testimony of Laszlo Kovacs in Bokor, *A Historical Sketch*, part 2, p.12.
27. Report of S. Meirom, deputy director of European Department 3, Israel's Ministry of Foreign Affairs, 14 April 1989 and 17 April 1989, Hungarian file 103.1, ISA.
28. Record of Tova Herzl, Foreign Minister's Office, 20 September 1989, Hungarian File 103.1, ISA.
29. *Haaretz*, 11, 12, 13, 26 April 2010 [Hebrew].

7. Milestones in the Diplomatic Relations between Israel and Poland: From Severance (1967) to their Renewal (1990)

The Polish government, under the leadership of Wladyslaw Gomulka, secretary of the Polish United Workers Party, followed the line of the Soviet Bloc (except for Romania) when, in a letter handed to the Israeli ambassador in Warsaw, Dov Sattath, on 12 June 1967, by the Polish deputy foreign minister, Marian Naszkowski, it announced the decision to sever its diplomatic relations with Israel in the wake of the Six Day War. At the same time, it indicated 'that it would be ready to reinstate them, when Israel would withdraw from the territories of Arab countries that it had occupied during the war, and would cease its aggressive policy towards those countries'. No mention was made of the events that caused the outbreak of the war. The letter was accompanied by a humiliating, hostile attitude towards the staff of the Israeli Embassy, which was ordered to leave Poland within a few days and by an anti-Israel demonstration at the Warsaw airport on 19 June 1967, when the ambassador, his wife and the embassy staff were leaving Poland on their way to Paris. All this took place in front of foreign ambassadors who had come to the airport to take leave of the Israeli Embassy staff, led by the ambassador of the Netherlands, Albrecht Frederik Calkoen, who had been appointed – from that time until the resumption of diplomatic relations between Poland and Israel – to represent Israeli interests in Poland.[1]

HISTORICAL BACKGROUND

In the history of the Jewish people in Eastern Europe, Poland held a special place for a number of reasons: 1) The Jewish community that had lived within its territory, for a thousand years before the Holocaust, was one of the largest in Eastern Europe. It numbered some 3.5 million people on the eve of the invasion of Poland by Nazi Germany, on the one side, and by the Soviet Union on the other.[2] Over the course of its thousand-year existence, the community wielded a decisive influence on the shape of Judaism and subsequently on the development of Jewish history – in Poland itself and beyond, in the domains of society, culture, and religion; 2) On its soil most of the Jews, victims of the Holocaust, were murdered by the Nazi occupiers. To this day, Poland is considered the largest cemetery of the Jewish people; 3) The rebellion of the Jews against the German army of occupation that took place in the ghettos and concentration camps in Poland became the symbol of Jewish heroism in the annals of the Holocaust; 4) Anti-Semitism: although the mass murder and extermination of the Jews were carried out in Poland by the German occupying forces, there were also a number of notorious pogroms that were perpetrated by local Polish communities out of their own fierce anti-Semitism. Such attacks occurred both during the time of the Nazi occupation, and even afterwards, which was the case with the horrific slaughter of dozens of Holocaust survivors by Poles in the city of Kielce in July 1946, over a year after the end of the Second World War. Despite the strong condemnation of this outrage by Cardinal Hlond, head of the Polish Catholic Church,[3] the pogrom at Kielce was definitely an expression of the deep-seated anti-Semitism that had seeped into a sizable portion of the Polish people, throughout the long period of the growth of the local Jewish community. In contrast, there were also many Poles who risked their lives in rescuing thousands of Jews during the Nazi occupation. Thousands of such rescuers have been recognized by Yad Vashem, The Holocaust Martyrs' and Heroes' Remembrance Authority, as Righteous among the Nations; 5) The Polish authorities demonstrated a sympathetic attitude to the eighty to one hundred thousand Holocaust survivors and to the additional tens of thousands of refugees who returned to Poland from the USSR in two waves at the end of the war (in accordance with the repatriation agreements between the USSR and Poland). This is seen in the support they gave to enable the Jews to re-establish religious, cultural, research, social, and educational institutions, including Jewish schools and a Jewish press. Similarly, the Jews were allowed to migrate to Israel.[4]

Poland, along with the other countries of the Soviet Bloc, was among the first countries to recognize the State of Israel de jure on 18 May 1948. During the period of the political struggle in the UN forum that preceded the Declaration of Israel's Independence (according to the UN Resolution of 29 November 1947) and during the months of the War of Independence (that followed the seven Arab states' invasion of Israel's territory), the Polish government demonstrated its support for Israel. It was the Polish foreign minister who initiated a decision at a conference of foreign ministers of the Soviet Bloc that welcomed the State of Israel, upon the declaration of its independence, and censured the aggressiveness of the Arab countries towards Israel. And even before the War of Independence broke out, the government of Poland allowed the emissaries of *Haganah* ('The Defence' was a Jewish paramilitary organization in what was then the British Mandate of Palestine from 1920 to 1948, which later became the core of Israel's Defence Forces) in 1948 to organize on its territory a training camp for 1,500 young people, who underwent intensive preparatory exercises towards their migration to Israel where they were to join the ranks of the fighters in the War of Independence. In August 1948, an Israeli legation was established in Warsaw – one of the first in the world – and the Israel emissary, Israel Barzilai, presented his credentials to the president of Poland as the first Israeli minister plenipotentiary in September 1948.[5] Diplomatic representation was raised to ambassador level in 1963, the same as in relations between the USSR and Israel. The level of diplomatic representation in the other countries of the Communist Bloc (including Yugoslavia) remained at the level of legation, until their severance of relations with Israel, following the Six Day War.

With the cooling of the attitude of the USSR towards Israel, from 1950 to 1955, Poland's relations with Israel worsened, as it did with all the other countries in the Soviet Bloc. In 1953, after the Prague Trials, Israel's minister plenipotentiary, Arye Kubovi, was declared *persona non grata* both in Prague and in Warsaw.

Mutual relations improved with Gomulka's ascent to power, in autumn 1956, and with the implementation of the limited liberal reforms in Poland regarding internal and foreign matters. As a result an Israeli minister plenipotentiary, Katriel Katz, was appointed to Warsaw after an absence of three years of an Israeli diplomatic representative there. The improvement in mutual relations was expressed, inter alia, by giving permission on a large scale for Jews to immigrate to Israel, something denied to them previously, despite unceasing pressure from Israel on their behalf.[6] From then on, until the breaking of diplomatic relations, economic, scientific, and cultural relations between Israel and Poland expanded – including exchange visits of ministers, performing artists, and writers – on a scale unknown for the other countries of the Soviet Bloc. A particularly prominent event took place in May 1966, when a conference of Israeli ambassadors to Eastern Europe led by Foreign Minister Abba Eban convened in Warsaw for the first time with the approval of the Polish authorities. During the course of the gathering Abba Eban met with his Polish counterpart, Adam Rapacki, for a talk that was defined as friendly, on the topics of the development of the mutual relations between the two countries and international issues. This was the first visit of an Israeli foreign minister in Poland.[7]

Signs of a turn for the worse began to appear in mid-May 1967 and were expressed in the conducting of a malicious anti-Zionist and anti-Israel campaign in Poland's state media, with the aim of voicing Polish support for Egypt in the international as well as internal arenas. Dov Sattath, in a summary report on Poland after the severance of relations, cited the telegram from the president of Poland, Gomulka, to the Egyptian president, Nasser, on 28 May 1967 (that is, nine days before the outbreak of the Six Day War), which was published in the Polish state (controlled) media, that stated, inter alia:

> We are following closely your efforts to maintain national sovereignty and the integrity of your lands. By Egypt's fighting shoulder to shoulder with the Arab countries, it is combating imperialist countries that stand behind this enemy. The Polish people does not hide in any ways its full and unconditional sympathy and support of nations fighting for their freedom, sovereignty, and honour. We, therefore, boundlessly support [our] friend the Egyptian people in the struggle it is waging with courage and resoluteness against the imperialist aggressor. The Polish people believes that the ultimate victory shall be yours.

In addition, the anti-Semitic policy followed by the government of Poland under the leadership of Gomulka, after the Six Day War, was manifested in the removal of Jews, including those known to be members of the Communist Party, from any key position in government offices. As a result, some 12,000 of the 20,000 Jews then in Poland migrated to Sweden and Denmark – which were willing to accept them – and some to Israel. Commentators saw in this wave of anti-Semitism an act of distrust towards these elements, many of whom had expressed orally and in writing their sympathy for Israel during the Six Day War, and had even congratulated the Israeli ambassador on Israel's victory in the war, a phenomenon that absolutely contradicted the Polish government's strict anti-Israeli policy.

This was the anti-Semitic image of Poland in the world, which apparently influenced Poland's new leadership, as headed by the party secretary, Edward Gierek (after the ousting of Gomulka from power, at the end of 1970, and from his membership of the Party's Central Committee in 1971), to initiate contact with Israel in 1977. Gierek's intention was to create a congenial atmosphere for political exchanges, whether for the purpose of improving Poland's negative image in the West, or with the goal of making preparations for the renewal of diplomatic relations in the future, when Poland might receive the USSR's authorization to do so. In the decade between 1967 and 1977, there was a total freeze on mutual relations in the political sphere as well as in the areas of commerce, tourism, and culture. In the ensuing we shall survey the stages of rapprochement of Poland with Israel, beginning in 1977, with the establishment of interest offices in 1986, to the renewal of diplomatic relations in 1990.

MILESTONES TOWARDS RENEWAL OF DIPLOMATIC RELATIONS

1. April 1977. The Visit to Israel of the Editor of 'Kultura'

Dominik Horodenski, the editor of the Polish weekly magazine *Kultura*, was the first Polish journalists to visit Israel during the period of severed diplomatic relations. He arrived in Israel as the official guest of Rakah (the New Communist Party). The visa to Israel in his diplomatic passport was given at the Israeli Embassy in Vienna, with the authorization of the Foreign Ministry in Jerusalem, after a direct application by the Polish Embassy in Vienna to the Israeli Embassy there. During the course of his visit he asked, through the Government Press Office in Tel Aviv, to speak with someone from the Israeli Foreign Ministry. I received him for a talk in the Foreign Ministry in Jerusalem by virtue of my position as director of the East European Department, on 28 April 1977. Below are the main points of his statement, which he read from a prepared text:

> The time has come 'to turn a new page' in Poland-Israel relations with an eye to the future. Poland supported the establishment of Israel, and it always stresses Israel's right to exist. Poland helped Israel to transfer Jewish repatriates from the USSR to Poland and afterwards to Israel, even though a sizable percentage of them had not held Polish citizenship in the past and they had never set foot on Polish soil. The current Polish government, under the leadership of Gierek, has demonstrated a different attitude towards the Jewish communists who had to leave Poland in 1968. It has uprooted any previous tendency that might be understood as anti-Semitism. In contrast to what has been published in Israel, Poland is not an anti-Semitic country.

Of course, he did not have statistics on the number of Jews resident in his country, but he did know that in Poland a Jewish daily, *Volksstimme*, appeared and a Jewish theatre operated regularly in Warsaw. 'One may note', he said, and this he came to realize also in his meetings in Israel, 'that we have a common history that was expressed in the common anti-Fascist struggle in occupied Poland'. His authorities – he did not specify which – had asked him to go to Israel, to gain an impression of the attitude towards Poland, to enter discussions with anyone willing to talk, to think about what could be done to achieve normalization of the relations between the two countries, and upon his return, to offer recommendations towards attaining this goal. Since a rapid switch from one extreme to another would be unrealistic, he suggested preparing a fitting atmosphere towards this aim, perhaps through cultural exchanges, invitations of to journalists, and commercial ties. He asked what Israel's attitude was towards the reconvening of the Geneva conference for the settlement of the Arab-Israeli conflict, and from this one could discern, as it were, that the opening of the conference could serve as a convenient catalyst for the renewal of diplomatic relations with Israel.

In my reply I tried to clarify for him Israel's position concerning the convening of the Geneva conference and the obstacles standing in our way: the inability to conduct negotiations with the PLO on the basis of its covenant and its aspirations to destroy us. I stressed our longing for peace, our support for maintaining diplomatic relations with all countries of the world, without taking into account their regimes, and that 'even now there are already direct commercial ties with a number of states in Eastern Europe'. At that point he asked, 'Really direct?' And when I made it clear that they were 'indeed direct', I added that the creation of a congenial atmosphere between our two countries was important in itself but could not stand in place of official relations. I pointed out that in Israel there was great disappointment over the behaviour of his country towards us, that is, in the breaking of relations with us – precisely his country, on whose soil the horrific Holocaust had taken place. This act not only distanced Poland from Israel, but also did not contribute to the advancement of peace in our region. I asked him what his concrete suggestions were 'for the creation of normalization in our mutual relations', and to that he replied that he had nothing concrete to propose and he requested that we, too, think about what might be done. I responded that the ball was now in the hands of the Polish government and that our stance had always been that the party that had broken relations had to initiate their renewal, if they so desired. At the conclusion, he asked if he would be able to make his suggestions known to the Israeli ambassador in

Vienna and to that I replied positively. I drew his attention to the fact that the ambassador in Vienna, Avigdor Dagan, had served in the past as ambassador in Warsaw and had previously held the position of director of the East European Department.[8]

As a result of this talk, I presumed that Horodenski had come to Israel as the emissary of the Polish government to inquire whether we were willing to renew our relations with Poland in light of our considering it an anti-Semitic country. Apparently, their conscience was troubled by their attitude towards us following the Six Day War and the feelings towards the Jewish communists who were hounded in 1968, for which the Polish government was accused of anti-Semitism.

I did not discern in his statements that the Polish authorities really did intend to renew diplomatic relations with Israel at the current stage, but rather that the aim was to create a fitting atmosphere and an array of relations that would lead to their reinstitution at the proper time.

Three facts became clear shortly after this talk: (a) Horodenski made no contact with the Israeli ambassador in Vienna. Instead, in October 1977, he initiated the invitation of the Israeli correspondents in Paris, Edwin Eytan and Micha Limor, to visit Poland to survey its 'Jewish life' with the aim of improving the 'Jewish image' of Poland in the West; (b) Poland under Gierek had encountered many economic problems: throughout the country many demonstrations had taken place protesting against food shortages and price rises, while Poland's foreign debt was continuously increasing. It may be that the country's leadership was seeking a way to improve its image in the West so that Poland could be helped to emerge from the crisis in which it was enmeshed; (c) The visit, in any event, did have positive results in laying a foundation for further contacts between the two sides and for spotting issues for the promotion of relations between them.

2. December 1977. The Visit to Poland of Eli Zborowski, Deputy Chairman of the World Federation of Polish Jews and Chairman of the Association of Friends of Yad Vashem in the United States

For the first time, a delegation of the World Federation of Polish Jews, which was located in the US, left for Poland to conduct negotiations with the authorities on obtaining historical documents and Jewish ritual and cultural objects, on the creation of memorials at Holocaust sites, and on the fate of Jewish (public) property that remained in Poland. Eli Zborowski, who was part of the delegation, visited Israel on his way back to the US to give his impressions of the visit to the Foreign Ministry in Jerusalem. His main points were the following: The members of the delegation met with the minister of religions and minorities, with the secretary of the Polish government and with Polish Foreign Ministry staff members. The talks took place in a congenial atmosphere, and there was an exchange of letters dedicated to the topics mentioned above that mainly expressed the Polish government's readiness to begin serious negotiations with the organization – something the Polish authorities had refused to do for many years. Similarly, there was explicit discussion of transferring a number of historical documents to Israel.

On the final evening of the delegation's stay in Poland, Eli Zborowski was invited for a discussion with the minister of religions and minorities, Jerzy Kuberski, who knew that his guest was going to visit Israel on his way back to the US. The minister asked that he transmit 'to whomever he considered appropriate among the proper authorities in Israel' the main points of his message that the time had come to renew relations with Israel. Poland would not wait until the USSR would do so, and it was preferable to have resumed relations before 19 April 1978 (Holocaust Remembrance Day). Moreover, the minister said that the groundwork for this could be arranged by the invitation of Polish journalists to visit Israel, or through the Israeli representatives conducting the negotiations towards the setting up of the Jewish Commemorative Museum at the site of the Auschwitz extermination camp, or by Israel agreeing to allow the Polish Press Agency (PAP) to post a representative in Jerusalem. The minister went on to say that he himself would look positively at an invitation to go to Israel as part of a delegation from Poland of the Righteous Among the Nations that would visit on the occasion of 19 April (Yad Vashem had such a programme).

Zborowski added that, in light of my proposal on the eve of the delegation's departure for Poland, he had drawn Minister Kuberski's attention to the injustice the Poles had done to Israel and its Holocaust survivors by severing relations with Israel, a break that was accompanied by open anti-Semitic agitation, as well as to the damage that the severance had caused to the system of proper relations. To Zborowski's inquiry as to what to reply to Minister Kuberski, I replied that he should write to him that he had reported the essence of his statements to the Foreign Ministry in Jerusalem. I made it clear to him that, as far as I understood, the Polish government's willingness to renew diplomatic relations with Israel was not under discussion, but rather an attempt to renew ties towards resumptions of diplomatic relations at some undefined point in the future. Likewise I added that the way in which the message had been delivered attested to the great interest of the Poles in repairing 'its Jewish image' among world Jewry in the US in order to obtain increased economic credit and to attract Jewish tourism from the US to Poland. I assumed that it was against this backdrop that one should understand their readiness to begin negotiations with the World Federation of Polish Jews.[9]

3. *May 1978. Interview of First Secretary of the Polish Communist Party Edward Gierek with a Reporter from the Polish Newspaper 'Trybuna Ludu', 3 May 1978*

In reply to the reporter's question, 'Is there any possibility of the renewal of diplomatic relations between Poland and Israel?', Gieriek responded:

I think that final decisions have not yet been made, the type that one cannot go back on. Similar to the way in which we once had diplomatic relations with Israel and were among the initiators of the establishment of the State of Israel, so it may be in the future that we will generate diplomatic ties. We never had hostile intensions towards the Jewish people. We thought, and we are still convinced and will continue to think, that the Jewish people, Jews like other nations, have the right to have an independent state, and this right must be ensured through international agreements. I feel that our attitude towards history, to all that we endured in common, constitutes the best proof of, and attests to our attitude to the Jewish people and the Jews. In our country, one must never forget this history. Quite the opposite, it is vital to erect such relations that will make easier in the future rapprochement and normalization of the relations between our countries and our nations. When will this happen? The answer does not depend only on us. The issue is that Israel must also draw the correct conclusions from what is now happening in the Middle East. The thing is that sustainable relations in the Middle East must be based on friendly relations between the peoples living in this region of the world. We are convinced that it is impossible to reach such an agreement without solving the Palestinian question and our opinion over this is still valid.[10]

This was the first public expression by a Polish leader on this issue since the severance of Israeli-Polish relations. This formulation – which was intended to be balanced – meant to say that Poland did not have a hostile attitude towards Israel and did not have any objection in principle to the renewal of diplomatic relations, but for that to happen it was expected that Israel would do its part to bring peace to the Middle East. This text represented Poland even after Gieriek was forced to leave office in September 1980 and was replaced by Stanislav Kania, who was also replaced in October 1981 because of Poland's economic crisis and the increased power of the social protest movement, Solidarnoscż (Solidarity), founded by Poland's Association of Professional Trade Unions.

4. *January 1981. Visit to Israel by Poland's Minister of Religions and Minorities, Jerzy Kuberski*

The International Janos Korczak Association is devoted to disseminating the image and heritage of Janos Korczak, the Jewish physician and educator, who went to his death at the hand of the Nazis, together with his pupils. It conducts activities linked to the moral and social aspects of Korczak among Jewish youth in Israel and Diaspora. During 1980 the Association in Israel developed the idea to convene its directorate in Jerusalem. The permanent location of the group's secretariat was in Warsaw, while the membership included most of the countries of Eastern Europe, as well as the United States, France, Holland, and West Germany. Poland's minister of religions and minorities, Jerzy Kuberski, who chaired the International Janos Korczak Association, agreed to hold the meeting of the directorate in Israel and even expressed willingness to participate at the conference as the head of a twelve-member delegation. The general director of the Israeli association, Benjamin Anolik, a member of kibbutz Beit Lohamei Haghetaot and a member of the board of the Beit Lohamei Haghetaot Museum, had travelled a few times to Poland – with the support of the Foreign, Education, and Culture Ministries – to coordinate the planning of the visit and the conference with Kuberski. The Polish minister told Anolik directly that he was willing to meet with 'whomever would be ready to have a talk' with him, and even to be interviewed by the Israeli media.

In an internal Foreign Ministry memorandum on the political aspect of the visit, I noted, inter alia, that there was particular political importance to the visit by the minister and his entourage, since this was the first time a Polish minister would visit Israel in the period of severed diplomatic relations and an obvious signal to Israel about Poland's readiness to resume contacts and to conduct a political dialogue.

The conference was held in Jerusalem in January 1981, after a festive opening at the president's residence, attended by the Polish minister and the members of his delegation as well as delegations from Israel and other countries. During his visit – which was the object of extensive press and media coverage – the minister toured Yad Vashem and was received for a meeting with Foreign Minister Yitzhak Shamir, from which he emerged fully satisfied. In that discussion, Kuberski told Minister Shamir that he wanted to hear our thoughts about expanding mutual relations, and at his request, I met him for a discussion in his hotel on 17 January 1981. I referred to the following issues at that time:[11]

1. *Consular relations.* I mentioned to the minister the existing arrangement between Israel and Poland after his government's decision to cut off diplomatic relations, as a result of which only one member of staff of the Israeli Embassy remained in Warsaw. Yet, because of the difficult conditions and the hostile atmosphere, we had been forced to return him to Israel. If possible, that arrangement should be reinstituted – whereby he would be accepted as an Interest Officer acting under the aegis of the embassy representing the interests of his country there. This would ease the movement of tourists in both directions and perhaps even promote mutual commercial ties. I pointed out that Poland had a permanent representative at the Polska Kasa Opieki – PKO Bank – in Tel Aviv who could serve, if authorized, as a parallel link.[12]

2. *Commercial ties.* I pointed out that with the exception of Poland and the USSR, we were trading with all the countries of Eastern Europe that had broken their diplomatic relations with us at the time, and that commercial ties were being conducted in a proper manner and even more extensively than prior to the

severance, in June 1967, including with East Germany, with which we had never had diplomatic relations. In my estimation, there was significant potential for advancing mutual trade with Poland to the benefit of both sides. I presumed that our merchandise would reach Poland through a third country, something which would substantially increase the cost of their import to Poland, while in Israel there was no importing from Poland at all. That being the case, it would be advisable for representatives of commercial companies from both countries to meet in Jerusalem or Warsaw or anywhere else, to conclude between them the details for the renewal of mutual trade.

3. *Payment of allotments to Israeli victims of work accidents who had come from Poland to Israel.* I told him about the arrangement that had operated in the past, according to which those eligible received their payments in Israel through the Israeli Embassy in Warsaw, and of their cessation with the break in Polish-Israeli relations. I stressed the suffering of the designated recipients, beginning with their loss of physical ability in Poland and then their not receiving the allotments they deserved according to the decisions of the Polish courts for reasons unrelated to them. I asked for his help – first, in locating the funds that certainly had been deposited on their behalf in Polish banks, and second, the regular receipt and transfer of the stipends to them, whether through the Polish bank operating in Tel Aviv or through the Dutch Embassy in Warsaw that represented Israeli interests in Poland, or in any other manner that the Polish government would see fit. I indicated that under discussion was the solution of a humanitarian issue between the Polish government and its former citizens – who happened to live in Israel – and not between the government of Poland and the government of Israel.

The minister took notes and said that he would bring these

points to the attention of the authorities in his country and promised to send us a reply through a representative of the Polish PKO Bank 'within two months' or through Stefan Grayek, chairman of the World Organization of Jewish Fighters, Partisans, and Camp Inmates, who was scheduled to visit Poland in the near future – and who was a trusted liaison for the transfer of our messages to the Polish authorities and for receiving their comments. Indeed, Grayek heard from him in Warsaw, in April 1981, that he had submitted a positive report to the Central Committee of the Party about his visit to Israel and his handling of the issues I had raised in our talk. But during the course of the year, no progress was made in solving them. The three topics were supposed to be discussed anew with the foreign minister of Poland at his meeting with the foreign minister of Israel at the end of September 1981. Yet, Minister Kuberski told Grayek that he would deal with the exchange of delegations of writers and the visit to Israel of the Ida Kaminska State Jewish Theatre in Warsaw, and he did so.[13]

To these one must add that over the course of 1981, three visits to Poland took place and laid an important foundation for the process of advancing our relations and of cooperation between Israel and Poland:

1. A visit of Israeli historians to Poland to locate historical documentation in state archives related to the history of the Jews of Poland. During their stay they made significant progress towards obtaining the material.
2. A youth delegation that went from Israel to Poland which was organized by the Korczak Association in Israel, led by Gershon Bergson, director of the Jerusalem district of the Ministry of Education and Culture, for a visit to an international Korczak youth camp in Poland. The members of the delegation were received with demonstrative warmth and met with various individuals in the fields of education, communications, and government, as well as with remnants of local Jewish communities. The delegation's

194

hosts expressed their desire for cooperation in the fields of education and culture.

3. A visit of writers from Israel to Poland that consisted of Ben-Zion Tomer, Haim Gouri, Gabriel Moked, and Dvora Omer. According to reports they submitted to the Foreign Ministry in Jerusalem, they were welcomed enthusiastically everywhere. Meetings with the general public were arranged for them as well as many lectures and appearances on television and radio, addressing literary and cultural topics with political overtones. They also met with prominent figures, ministers and writers. On the practical side, it was concluded that there would be a reciprocal visit to Israel by a delegation of writers from Poland, and that an anthology of Hebrew poetry and prose translated into Polish and a similar volume of Polish literature translated into Hebrew would be published.[14]

5. September 1981. (First) Political Dialogue between Israel's Foreign Minister Yitzhak Shamir and the Polish Foreign Minister Jozef Czyrek

Foreign Minister Yitzhak Shamir met for a talk, at our initiative, with his counterpart, the foreign minister of Poland, Jozef Czyrek, on 28 September 1981 within the framework of the opening of the discussions of the UN General Assembly in New York. This was the first discussion held between the foreign ministers of the two countries after a political hiatus of over fourteen years. The two ministers initially exchanged greetings, and each of them mentioned the shared elements that united the two countries and nations in light of the background of the common historical past of Jewish life in Poland for hundreds of years before the Holocaust. As to the expectations and limitations for the development of mutual relations in the present, each set out his approach at length, while referring to the problem of the Arab-Israeli conflict and the way to resolve it. The essence of their statements appears below.[15]

Foreign Minister Yitzhak Shamir:

> There have been times when the relations between our countries were friendly. But now an abnormal situation of lack of relations prevails. We regret this and find no justification for it. Our two countries have relations with many countries despite the lack of agreement about their policies. Recently we were gratified to see the beginning of contacts between us. I met with the Polish minister of religious affairs, Jerzy Kuberski, and there have also been contacts between the countries at the level of exchange of delegations in various fields. Positive work has been accomplished in the sphere of cultural links, cooperation between museums and commemoration of the Holocaust. Yet, this is insufficient and the cooperation should be expanded to economic and trade relations, exchange of political evaluations, and we on our part are ready for that.

Polish Foreign Minister Jozef Czyrek:

> As to official relations between the two countries, Poland is acting in coordination with its socialist allies. But to the extent possible, we are trying to expand concrete relations, such as in the field of culture. The Jewish theatre of Poland visited Israel, while Israeli artists have performed in Poland. Likewise, delegations of war veterans and partisans have visited Poland. There are contacts with Yad Vashem, which recognized Poles who saved Jews during the Holocaust as Righteous Among the Nations. There are phenomena, therefore, that have stirred a moral and political reverberation. Considering the circumstances, it seems to me that relations are developing in a positive way. As we have stated a number of times, diplomatic relations are related to the political background which is based on the declaration of the socialist states as well as on the declarations of the United Nations. There are differences of opinion between us on these issues and this has repercussions

on our mutual relations. Even so, we must seek ways to exhaust whatever may be done to promote bilateral relations … Whoever has visited Israel has told me about the positive attitude on the part of some of the citizens of Israel towards Poland and their forefathers' memories and so on. This creates special conditions for the beginning of cooperation of moral and historical value. Minister Kuberski cited an intention to establish in Warsaw a Judaica centre and a (Jewish?) museum of historical remnants. Regretfully, the restoration of the central synagogue in Warsaw has been delayed, but we would like to speed up the work on its refurbishment. The (Jewish?) centre that has been established in Auschwitz plays an important role as a cautionary factor against genocide and anti-Semitism. We would like to do more in the sphere of preserving the past and would like cooperation on your part and that of Jewish cultural and scientific centre the world over.

Foreign Minister Yitzhak Shamir:

I am aware that there is sympathy towards us and towards our struggle to build up our nation and our homeland. That explains why we are sometimes hurt when representatives of Poland in various forums, in the UN and the Security Council, support elements such as the PLO, whose philosophy calls for the physical annihilation of our people. I understand and appreciate your desire to work towards preservation of common memories and the development of cultural and historical relations. But that is not enough. As a practical Marxist you certainly understand that it is necessary to give expression to the history of the past for the present and the future. I do, of course, know that Poland belongs to the bloc that has adopted a policy of non-maintenance of any relations with us. This is totally unjustified, despite the differences in opinion between us. But the decision is in your hands. Yet, even within the framework of the current data, it is possible to do more for the opening of actual relations between us; if there were, for example, a decision on the economic issue, it would be beneficial to both sides. There is another topic, such as tourism, for which there is a need to allow residents of Israel to receive in Israel tourist visas for Poland. There is also the problem of pension payments. We must hold more meetings to discuss issues that are not currently covered ... We established our country despite the opposition of the Arab states since we believe that this is our homeland and we are now making an effort to attain peace. We have done much towards this aim. There is a peace treaty between us and Egypt. This, to be sure, is only a single country but it is an important one. We are looking for ways to achieve peace with other countries and hope to succeed. We only regret that you and the bloc you belong to are not encouraging in this regard.

Foreign Minister Jozef Czyrek:

Poland has been and remains a country that supports the existence and development of Israel. Some of my schoolmates emigrated from Poland to fight for Israel. That was the time of a very positive attitude towards Israel and its struggle. But we do not agree with your statements about supporting extremism in the Middle East. We support peaceful co-existence of all countries of the region, including Israel, and a peaceful solution, but we are divided on how to reach this. For example, we do not believe in separatist solutions with each one of the countries. We do believe that within the PLO there are tendencies and trends towards recognizing Israel, although they demand a solution for the Palestinians. After all, there is a Palestinian people that wants a homeland and country of its own. Thus, we do not think that the idea of a Palestinian state is against the interests of Israel, but that the two issues are congruent. We believe that it is possible to ensure peace and a sustainable

198

solution in the region. Extremists are to be found everywhere in the world, and we must find a solution that will remove the extremist elements. This will be an expression of a farsighted policy. We are greatly interested in a comprehensive peace in the region, and the solution to the Palestinian problem is a precondition and integral part of such a solution.

Foreign Minister Yitzhak Shamir:

In response to your comment about separatist solutions, I wish to note that we are living in the Middle East region, and we have past experience. We have been trying to explain all along that if a regional conference [for the solution of the Arab-Israeli conflict] of all the states in the region were convened, on such an occasion the extreme Arab line would win. This is the lesson [we have learned] from our experience with all international conferences to date. Even in the UN, this is the reality, and only the solution of step by step will lead to a treaty in an evolutionary way. … Despite the differences of opinion between us, I do not believe there is justification for the state of relations between us. This is not a normal situation and you and the bloc to which you belong claim that Israel has the right to exist, while at the same time you do not have relations with it. This is irrational.

The two ministers concluded their statements by stating that despite the disagreements between them, their talk had been important and beneficial. The Polish minister expressed satisfaction from the meeting and noted that the development of Israeli-Polish relations had a double function: both bilateral relations as well as the situation of relations in the wider world. 'We are bound and subordinate to the global situation and can only hope that this will develop towards world peace and security.' The minister likewise referred to the difficult internal problems plaguing his country and the efforts of its leadership to solve them 'through political means, while developing democratic socialism and introducing far-reaching economic reforms', and that his country needs 'time and material assistance' to solve its problems and, above all, requires 'internal and foreign peace' (that is, discussion between the leadership and the protest movement Solidarnoscz, without the intervention of the USSR). Foreign Minister Shamir was appreciative of the friendly statements by his colleague and expressed his hope that there would be additional opportunities for the exchange of opinions and ideas 'and perhaps relations will develop in a positive direction for your country and mine, with you and with me'. The Polish minister added, as his departing words, that 'our two peoples are innately optimistic, without this characteristic we would have been annihilated', and to that Shamir replied, 'I agree to be optimistic'.

From the statements and positions of the Polish foreign minister, one may reach the conclusion, heard more than once in the past, that Poland would be willing to renew diplomatic relations with Israel after 'the Union of Socialist States' (meaning the USSR)' had given its permission. Until this had taken place, the Polish minister suggested expanding the current circle of relations.

6. September 1984. A Second Political Dialogue between Deputy Prime Minister and Foreign Minister Yitzhak Shamir and the New Polish Foreign Minister, Stefan Olszowski

This discussion was held on 26 September 1984, again in New York, within the framework of the opening of the debates of the UN General Assembly. Three years had passed since Foreign Minister Shamir had conducted his meeting with Polish Foreign Minister Czyrek, which had indeed closed on an optimistic note, but in the area of mutual diplomatic relations no real turning point had been reached. It seems, therefore, that despite the change in the composition of the leadership and despite the political and social upheavals in Poland,[16] the Polish political leadership had not changed their stance that renewal of diplomatic relations would only become possible when progress could be discerned in the Middle East peace process according to the political line defined by their Soviet superiors. In practice this meant that without the agreement of the USSR, Poland would not be able to reinstitute diplomatic relations with Israel, even though it wished to do so. This tone was also evident in the statements by Foreign Minister Olszowski, and in that regard they held nothing new when compared with those of his predecessors. He did refer, however, to PKO, the Polish bank in Tel Aviv, by pointing out that it would be able 'to serve as the home base for the development of various activities, so as to become the basis for support in the material sense for relations between the two countries'. This was the first reference by a Polish minister to the possibility that I had raised with Minister of Religious Affairs Kuberski three years earlier, to permit us to appoint an Israeli interests officer in Warsaw under the patronage of the Dutch Embassy in Poland. Foreign Minister Shamir reiterated, more or less, the statements he had made to the previous foreign minister, Czyrek, about Israel's aspiration to expand cultural and economic cooperation with Poland. He even proposed that Polish and Israeli import/export specialists meet to work out a plan for joint efforts. He further recommended establishing 'some kind of framework for political discussion, since we already know Poland's positions, for there is no negative aspect to the two sides exchanging argument and opinion between themselves'. As to trading opinions on 'material issues', Foreign Minister Shamir proposed 'establishing an institution of Israel in Warsaw parallel to the PKO Bank'. Minister Olszowski responded to that positively – as if he had heard it for the first time – by saying that 'this is a practical idea and perhaps it would be possible to weigh proposals and to augment the staffing of the PKO Bank in Tel Aviv, in order to deal with economic cooperation'.[17]

Minister Shamir's proposal to establish in Warsaw an

institution parallel to the PKO Bank in Tel Aviv, without designating explicitly that under discussion was a suggestion to appoint an interests officer for Israel under the aegis of the Dutch Embassy in Warsaw, led, in my opinion, to two similar but unsuccessful ideas by the Polish side. These were communicated by the Polish ambassador in Bonn to his Israeli counterpart, Yitzchak Ben-Ari. One idea, voiced in June 1985, was that in tandem to staffing the PKO Bank with Polish diplomats, an Israeli representative would operate within the framework of a Jewish economic corporation. The other, aired in August 1985, was that an American-Jewish company would be set up in Warsaw (perhaps led by Eli Zborowski, a resident of New York, head of the Israel-United States Chamber of Commerce, and one of the leaders of the World Federation of Polish Jews) that could serve as cover for the activity of the Israeli representative there. The Israeli ambassador in Bonn was instructed, on my recommendation, to summarily reject the two ideas and to propose instead placing an Israel interests officer under the aegis of the Dutch Embassy.[18]

The political talks, whether at the ministerial level or at the senior level of state officials – between representatives of Israel and representatives of the Polish government – or whether at the level of representatives of Israeli public institutions and organizations, with representatives of the Polish government, became part of the system for the development of the proper arrangement of relations between the two sides. Undoubtedly, all of these exchanges contributed to the creation of a political and public atmosphere of an ever-expanding process in institutionalizing bilateral relations. One must assume, however, that the factor that catalyzed the Polish government at this stage to strive to find a compromise towards the establishing of relations, as part of the establishment of the interest offices in Tel Aviv and Warsaw and on the way to the renewal of diplomatic relations in the not too distant future, was the accession to rule of Mikhail Gorbachev, the leader of the

USSR, who was distinguished in his efforts for economic reforms (perestroika) and a new social openness (glasnost) within the USSR and among the countries of the Warsaw Pact. This came simultaneously with his working towards putting an end to the cold war between East and West and assuaging thereby the tension created as a result of the inter-bloc confrontation. As a result of his policy, the dependence of the Warsaw Pact countries on the USSR and its global policies weakened. Poland was the first among the countries of the Eastern bloc whose relations with Israel had been severed to understand the proper meaning of its official policy towards Israel.

7. September 1985. Acceptance of the Credentials of the Chargé d'Affaires of Israel under the Aegis of the Dutch Embassy in Warsaw and the Acceptance of the Credentials of the Polish Representative of Parallel Standing under the Aegis of the PKO Bank in Tel Aviv

At the initiative of the Polish government a work session was called for between representatives of the Polish and the Israeli Foreign Ministries in New York towards a meeting of the foreign ministers of Israel and Poland on 2 October 1985 within the framework of the opening of the UN General Assembly discussions. We held two meetings, on 23 and 26 September 1985, with the participation – on the Polish side – of Antoni Pierzchala, director of the Department for Asia and the Jewish World Diaspora in the Polish Foreign Ministry, Stefan Kwiatkowski, who was presented to us as an adviser to the Polish foreign minister, and Olszowski, who had served in the Polish consulate in Israel from 1953 to 1955. On the Israeli side, taking part were Hanan Bar-On, deputy director general of the Foreign Ministry, and myself, as director of the East European Department in the Foreign Ministry (I held this position until September 1985; from then until 1989, I served as Israel's ambassador to Romania); I had nurtured the issue of our relations with Poland from 1977 until the convening of the work sessions.[19]

MAIN POINTS OF THE FIRST SESSION (23 SEPTEMBER 1985)

1. *Presentation of the Polish Perspective*

The roots of the past constitute a highly valuable factor in the rapprochement between Israel and Poland. Poland plays an important role in Europe, particularly with regard to the German Question. The coming meeting between the foreign minister of Israel and the foreign minister of Poland (set to take place on 2 October 1985) will be very significant (that is, a kind of milestone in the history of mutual relations). Both sides have agreed to maintain contacts towards the expansion of relations, on the basis of their past connections, in the fields of science, culture, economics, and tourism, with the aim of advancing by stages towards renewal of diplomatic relations 'in accordance with political circumstances'. In the spirit of this principle, they propose the following three stages:

Stage One. The Poles will send to their PKO Bank, a deputy director, with the rank of counsellor in the Polish Foreign Ministry, and simultaneously Israel will send its representative, at the same rank in the Israel Foreign Ministry, who will work under the patronage of a world Jewish organization or will be a representative of an Israeli company registered abroad as a foreign company (in this context they mentioned Eli Zborowski), or will be a representative of the Korczak Association (this association, led by Benjamin Anolik, developed a range of activities in Poland and Israel and was an important bridge for Israeli-Polish rapprochement in the area of education and culture). These representatives would deal with the issues of the Foreign Ministry and Foreign Trade, would be authorized to grant visas 'and to carry out other actions', would hold national passports (not diplomatic passports or service passports), would be able to send mail, such as diplomatic communications, through one of the neighbouring countries (that is, not directly). They would be allowed to send telexes (secret telegrams were not noted).

Stage Two, which would be ready for implementation

between 1986 and 1987, would consist of the establishment of commercial consulates that would turn in time into general consulates.

Stage Three would see the establishment of embassies.

B. Presentation of the Israel Perspective

We summarily rejected implementation of the first stage for the following reasons: we would have no control over activity of the representative of the commercial company or Jewish organization. There should be no admixture of Israeli representation with that of Jewish organizations. We well remember the period of the early 1950s in which, unjustly, Jewish organizations were accused of Zionist activity. The camouflage of the representation would become known, which would have a negative impact. With all of our understanding of Poland, of its inability under present circumstances to renew its relations with Israel, we could not establish a type of relations of the sort proposed, since it would not be fair towards Romania that had decided at the time not to break diplomatic relations with Israel. As to Kwiatkowski's claim that making public knowledge of a Polish trade delegation visit to Israel would harm us, we argued that delegations from other East European countries came to Israel openly, with diplomatic passports and no concealment, since direct and regular commerce did exist with Hungary, Yugoslavia, Czechoslovakia and even with East Germany, with whom diplomatic relations had never been established. It was difficult to perceive how it was possible to trade between two states and to stimulate commercial elements to develop mutual trade without this becoming public knowledge.

With the aim of accommodating the Poles somewhat, by understanding their unique situation, and with the hope that any arrangement that would be reached would be a temporary one towards renewal of diplomatic relations, they were offered the choice of one of the following four options:

1. *Establishment of consulates general* (the break had been declared regarding diplomatic relations and not consular relations).
2. *Appointment of an Israel interest officer* who would function under the aegis of the Dutch Embassy (and simultaneously a Polish representative who would operate under the aegis of the PKO Bank in Tel Aviv).
3. *Commercial representation* of the Ministries for Foreign Trade of the two countries.
4. *Tourism representation* of the government company for tourism.

In each of the cases the representatives would carry diplomatic passports and work towards the expansion of existing relations. The Polish Foreign Ministry representatives admitted that the proposals we raised were pragmatic and contained some new elements. They said they would bring them to the attention of the Polish foreign minister (who was supposed to arrive the following day in New York, accompanying the prime minister of Poland, General Wojciech Jaruzelski, for an appearance at the UN General Assembly, and discuss the proposals towards preparation of the agenda of the talk between the two foreign ministers.

MAIN POINTS OF THE SECOND SESSION
(26 SEPTEMBER 1985)

A. *The Polish representatives* announced their agreement to accept the second proposal, accreditation of an Interest Officer who would act under the aegis of the Dutch Embassy in Warsaw. Towards their expression of agreement, premises were formulated that were read from a written text, stating that the Polish side expected the establishment of economic relations and economic cooperation with Israel and the Jewish Diaspora the world over, Israel's financial support of Poland, Israeli opposition to the anti-Poland campaign throughout the world, in which Poland was accused of anti-Semitism, assistance in creating a positive image in the world by presenting the common history in its true light so that it should serve the coming generations, and abstention from any contact with Solidarnoscz. (Shortly before these consultations, members of the Solidarnoscz office that represented the Polish trade union in Brussels had visited Israel as guests of the *Histadrut* [General Federation of Labourers in Israel].)

B. *On the Israeli side* – we heartily welcomed this decision as a first step towards renewal of diplomatic relations. We noted that within both Jewish and Israeli public opinion there was special sensitivity to Poland in light of events of the past, and obviously expressions of anti-Semitism and anti-Israeli acts (such as placing a wreath from the PLO at the memorial for the Warsaw ghetto victims) aroused a wave of reactions. Improving the relations between Israel and Poland would certainly create a calm atmosphere and pave the way for attaining the common goals.

The Polish representatives presented drafts of the summary of the talks. After acceptable emendations had been entered, a summary document was consolidated in nine points:

1. The two sides agree to exchange representatives.
2. The representative of each side will represent the Foreign Ministry and the Ministry of Foreign Trade of his country and will maintain contacts with the official institutions of both countries.
3. The Israeli side agrees that the Polish side will operate under the aegis of the Polish PKO Bank in Tel Aviv.
4. The Polish side agrees that the Israeli representative will be the chargé d'affaires of his country and will operate under the aegis of the Dutch Embassy in Warsaw.
5. The two representatives will be eligible for the privileges and immunity provided to embassy advisors in their fields.
6. The two representatives have the right to maintain a technical and administrative staff from their countries.

7. The two representatives will be ensured non-interfer-
ence in the right to diplomatic post and diplomatic
couriers.
8. The representatives will have the right to issue visas.
9. All of the above will be implemented after authorization
by the two countries' Foreign Ministries.

This document was an important milestone in relations
between the two countries since the severance of relations
in 1967. It was concluded that following the exchange of
this document, letters would be exchanged between the
two governments through their ambassadors in Bonn.
Both sides would bear the responsibility of working out
the details concerning the establishment of the Interest
Offices. We asked to be permitted to use the building of
our representation in Warsaw under a sign, 'Dutch
Embassy, Department for Israeli Affairs'. They replied that
they would consider this and inform us of their decision.
We also asked that our representative be allowed, even
though he was at the level of counsellor, to meet with –
when necessary – individuals at the senior level of the
Polish administration. We were assured that this would be
allowed. The two foreign ministers had to agree upon a
date for the publication of these conclusions and its form;
they determined that the working session set for 2
October would be accompanied, at the suggestion of the
representatives of the Polish Foreign Ministry, by a
luncheon in the Polish Consulate building in New York to
which they wished to invite, in addition to Hanan Bar-
On, deputy director general of the Foreign Ministry, and
myself, also the head of the Israeli UN delegation and the
general consul of Israel in New York. (I was unable to
participate at this event because I had to return to my
ambassadorial post in Bucharest.)

SUMMARY AND EVALUATION

To the summary of the two meetings that was sent to the Foreign Ministry in Jerusalem, I added my own evaluation:

At hand is an important breakthrough in Israel's relations with the East European countries that severed them with us in 1967. Actually, there is no precedent such as this in the East European foreign services. Our insistence over recent months not to agree to anything less than an interest officer has borne fruit. It is likely to serve as a precedent for the other countries of Eastern Europe and will not embarrass (so I believe) the Romanians. The path has been opened for secret, discreet contacts for a similar arrangement with the other countries of Eastern Europe. We must choose the proper staff to send to Warsaw … It is important for us in Israel to work through the list of technical needs for the discussion in Bonn … An advance team will have to set out for Warsaw to prepare the office, but no less significant,: the preparation of a basic work plan, in all possible areas, taking into consideration, of course, what can be realized under the current circumstances in Poland, which should lead gradually to a complete normalization of our relations. This achievement was obtained thanks to the painstaking work carried out for years in our ministry, with the help of Stefan Grayek, former chairman of the World Organization of Jewish Fighters, Partisans, and Camp Inmates and chairman of the World Federation of Polish Jews; Benjamin Anolik, director of the Beit Lohamei Haghetaot Museum and one of the leaders of the Janos Korczak Association in Israel and Poland; and Eli Zborowski, who negotiated with the Polish Consul General in New York, under our guidance. Also with the assistance of our dozens of Polish guests who had visited us in recent years and who, each in his own way, had endeavoured to prepare the groundwork. This achievement, perhaps, would not have been obtained at this juncture were it not for Poland finding itself in social and economic crises, with its eyes towards the Western world, including the Jewish world, that would rescue it from its troubles, and in this context, undoubtedly also taken into account was the value of American and Diaspora Jewry and the Jewish significance of Israel in the United States.

I further included my advice to act with restraint and modesty in our communications media. Even if this was a significant attainment, we should not present it as such, particularly as viewed by the East European countries, regarding whom there was still a chance for renewal of full diplomatic relations with Israel, as well as Romania, 'the only communist country that did not sever her diplomatic relations with Israel'– as the Romanians stated repeatedly.

As expected, the two foreign ministers affirmed the summary document at their meeting on 2 October 1985, and they decided, as anticipated, that the next step would be an exchange of letters confirming the agreement. Foreign Minister Olszowski stressed that this was 'only the first step' in a system of mutual relations, and Foreign Minister Shamir expressed the hope that there would soon be a possibility for establishing full (that is, diplomatic) relations between the two countries. He agreed to our suggestion that the Israel Interest Office be located in the building of the former Israeli Embassy in Warsaw. He proposed, and Foreign Minister Shamir agreed, that after the exchange of letters between the two countries, a detailed announcement would be published that would include an expression of hope for the development of cultural and economic relations between the two countries, and specific information about mutual representation.

They decided that in the interim, as suggested by the Polish side, a laconic announcement would be made that would not include direct reference to the agreement on the establishment of the interest offices but would note that 'the two ministers had discussed international issues relevant to the interests of their countries, the relations between them, and the importance they ascribe to their continued development'. The message also noted that the talks between the two ministers 'had been conducted in a productive, constructive atmosphere'. The text of the announcement was published on 2 October 1985. Only towards the end of October, however, did the government of Poland confirm, through Jerzy Urban, the government spokesman, the information disseminated by the Israeli media about the establishment of an Israel interest office under the aegis of the Dutch Embassy in Warsaw and a Polish interest office in the PKO Bank in Tel Aviv, following an understanding reached at the recent meeting of the two foreign ministers in New York. Yet, striking in his statement was the aim of playing down the importance of the agreement, which noted that the 'sections [and not Interest Offices] will deal with the issuance of tourist visas' – without mentioning other topics – and added that 'the agreement does not mean normalization of relations between the countries'. In a previous notice, Urban had asserted that 'at this time there is no intention of renewing diplomatic relations ... The aim of the exchange of representatives is to improve human relations, and Poland had not changed its stance regarding the Middle East'.[20] Thus an intentional gap was drawn between the conclusions of the political talks that the foreign ministers of Israel and Poland conducted between themselves and the official reporting on them. What was the reason behind this?

At a meeting of the WJC (World Jewish Congress) leaders with the Polish prime minister, General Jaruzelski, that took place in New York on 28 October 1985, the latter related, inter alia, that the USSR had given some range of action to the advancement of the relations of his country with Israel, and yet despite this, he was being pressured in the opposite direction by the Arabs. At that same discussion, Jaruzelski asked for the help of the WJC in its efforts to improve Poland's image in the United States and assistance in developing commercial and economic ties between Poland and the United States.[21] In a second talk that a WJC delegation held with him in Warsaw, at the beginning of December 1985, Jaruzelski noted that he had hoped that 'the relations with Israel would develop quickly and have real content but it had turned out that one must demonstrate patience', since 'the development will be slow'. This stemmed from 'the exaggerated and premature notification of it in the Arab countries and Africa'. The 'superfluous fuss' that Israel had made about its relations with Poland had prompted Arab pressure on Poland.[22]

Jaruzelski's statements attest to the difficult political dilemma facing the leaders of Poland concerning its relations with Israel on the one hand and its links with the Arab countries on the other. Israel was perceived in Poland's political orientation as a factor with sizable influence on public opinion in the West, and in the United States in particular, which could help it to improve its connections with the US. Moreover, owing to Jaruzelski's attitude towards the Solidarnoscz movement, which he had declared illegal – with the result that the United States authorities now looked sympathetically upon the struggle of this protest movement – the United States had, in 1982, frozen its trade agreement with Poland according to which Poland had been recognized as a 'Most Favoured Nation' in mutual trade. This annulment was accompanied by other economic sanctions and was severely detrimental to Polish exports to the United States. Under these circumstances, or so Poland thought, the more its connections with Israel expanded, the greater would be the benefit towards improving its standing in the United States, and following that, to a renewal of its status as a 'Most Favoured Nation'. This did indeed happen in February 1987 when the United States lifted the economic sanctions against Poland, after the latter had put an end to martial law and declared amnesty for hundreds of detainees who had fought against the rule of martial law, among them the leaders of the rebels, Lech Wałęsa.

Despite this, the Polish leadership then feared that its relations with Israel might cause great damage to its economic links with Arab countries, particularly those of North Africa. Thus a paradox was created: Poland ceased to be afraid of the USSR under Gorbachev's rule owing to the development of its connections with Israel, and it began to fear the wrath of the Arab countries, especially Libya, which supplied Poland with large amounts of fuel that the USSR was not able to provide, lest they invoke economic sanctions against it if it would renew relations with Israel. Poland worked in close cooperation with Arab states, mainly Iraq, Libya, Syria and Algeria. Polish companies operated in those country in paving roads and setting up industrial enterprises. Among others, the Polish Ravar company built the anti-aircraft warning system of Libya's leader, Muammar Kaddafi, and in 1988 the Polish arms industry exported weapons and ammunition to the value of 320 million dollars, in large part to the Arab states and countries of the Third World.[23] This explains the apologetic response of Polish government spokesman Urban concerning Poland's relations with Israel when he said that human relations were under discussion; he also noted that Poland's Middle East policy had not changed and that 'there was no room for fears, Poland would not renew its diplomatic relations with Israel as long as Israel had not withdrawn from the territories occupied in the Six Day War'.

8. September 1986. Opening of the Interest Offices in Warsaw and Tel Aviv

Jaruzelski had correctly estimated the slow pace of advancement in Polish-Israeli relations. For several months fatiguing negotiations were carried out between the Israeli ambassador in Bonn and his Polish counterpart over the formulation of the exchange of letters between the two foreign ministries. These were finally exchanged on 13 May 1986 and contained extensive detailing of the nine points agreed upon by the two sides half a year earlier. It was noted in Israel's letter, inter alia, that Mordechai Palzur, who had served until then as the Israeli ambassador to the Dominican Republic, would head Israel's Interest Office in Warsaw, under the auspices of the Dutch Embassy, in the building that had housed the Israeli Embassy until the break in Polish-Israeli relations, and that was considered the property of the State of Israel. It was agreed that a sign would be affixed to the structure stating, 'Dutch Embassy, Israel Interest Office'. Stefan Kwiatkowski was appointed as head of the Interest Office of Poland in the PKO Bank in Tel Aviv.[24] On 14 October 1986 Kwiatkowski arrived in Israel, while the head of the Israel Interest Office, Palzur, arrived in Warsaw on 7 November 1986. The staffs had arrived to prepare the offices about a month earlier.[25]

On 26 September 1986 the foreign ministers of Israel and Poland met for a talk, for the fourth time, as part of the opening of the UN General Assembly. This was the first meeting of Foreign Minister Shamir with the new Polish foreign minister, Marian Orzechowski, and as Raphael Gvir of Israel's Diplomatic Mission to the UN noted, who was present at the discussion and reported on it, it was not distinguished by 'excessive warmth', even though the two ministers – each in his own way – welcomed the opening of the Interest Offices. Minister Shamir expressed his confidence that with their firm establishment, 'we will begin to create new content in our relations. Until now we have been witness to fairly ramified scientific and cultural connections, but there is definitely room for the development of relations and their expansion'. For our part, he stated, we shall try to develop them: 'We are willing to do this without limit, but this depends on you'. Minister

Orzechowski responded by saying that the opening of the Interest Offices was, indeed, 'an important step reflecting the state of relations between us. But the chances for their development depend upon both sides, including the situation in the Middle East'. Improvement in that situation would have a positive influence on Polish-Israeli relations. He asked that no announcement appear in the press, explaining that such a step would cause difficulties in Poland's relations with the Arabs. He did request that we try to influence the Western media, especially in the United States, 'for the promotion of Polish interests in the West'. He concluded by saying that 'a year from now we will reassess the situation'. Hanan Bar-On, deputy director general of the Foreign Ministry, who was present at this discussion, commented that 'in our opinion a fitting announcement would not prevent, [but would] at least attenuate speculations. Ultimately, the opening of the offices is a public event, especially for us, so it is worthwhile reaching an understanding on an agreed press release, since the media, including the foreign media extensively represented in Israel, will in any event publicize this occurrence'. The Polish minister said that 'he would still look into the matter and get back to this issue', but he did not specify how. Raphael Gvir added his impression that 'the man lacks cordiality and it is noticeable that he is approaching renewal of the Israeli-Polish relations without particular enthusiasm'.[26]

On the surface, there was nothing new in the content of this dialogue: the Polish government tended to downplay as much as possible the importance of the establishment of the Interest Offices, for fear of what the Arab countries would say. In contrast, it asked for Israel's influence to make the American communications media 'work' to repair Poland's image in the USA and for the 'advancement of its interests in the West'. These approaches, however, attest to the anti-Semitic heritage that characterized the communist leadership in Poland, consciously or unconsciously. This is seen, first, in the aim not to deviate radically from the anti-Israeli, pro-Arab positions that had crystallized during Gomulka's rule and, second, in the assessment that the Jews controlled economics, policy, and communications in the Western world, a conclusion that coincides with the *Protocols of the Elders of Zion*: the Jews control everything. This instance – as with similar cases in other East European countries where government elements wished to make use of Israel to promote the status of their country in the West, especially in the US – more than once posed a dilemma for the Israeli representatives: whether we should deny the 'fact' that Israel did not have the influence on governments, statesmen, and communications that was attributed to it in the Western world, or if we were to agree to it, we would have to prove it incontrovertibly.

The request by the Polish foreign minister not to publicize the details of the agreement to set up Interest Offices was honoured by Israel. On 15 October 1986, the morning after the arrival in Israel of the head of the Polish office, *Maariv* published an article under a prominent headline, 'Today Poland and Israel Are Opening a New Era in Relations between Them after a 19-Year Break'. It stated, 'Sources in the Foreign Ministry in Jerusalem informed [us] that "Interest Offices" of Israel and Poland are to begin operation officially today. Through contacts between the two countries, it was agreed that there would be no ceremonies and no official announcement about this would be made.' This was a kind of an unsigned compromise between the two sides, more than a year after their official representatives had agreed between themselves about the establishment of the Interest Offices, and somewhat over three years before the foreign ministers of Israel and Poland each signed the protocol on the renewal of diplomatic relations between their two countries.

9. 1987–1990. The Final Stage towards Renewal of Diplomatic Relations

At the beginning of Ambassador Mordechai Palzur's period of activity in Warsaw as the head of the Israeli Interest Office, he was received in a friendly manner by the Polish Foreign Ministry, but he encountered difficulties and a great degree of alienation on the part of the leaders of the ruling party as well as from Polish citizens, who were apparently fearful of coming in contact, in the light of the harsh anti-Israel propaganda rife in Poland at that time. But thanks to his command of the Polish language and his diplomatic experience, he was able to make breakthroughs. A few months after establishing himself, he held a discussion with the Polish deputy foreign minister, Jan Majewski, and later with the foreign minister, Marian Orzechowski. Both were friendly and candid, by stating their aim of making mutual relations with Israel closer, without hiding the fact that within the Polish government there were differences of opinion on this subject, with those opposing the rapprochement process towards Israel sometimes taking the lead. The current situation of maintaining Interest Offices and developing reciprocal relations seemed quite good. In this way, Poland was not violating the decision of the Warsaw Pact concerning the severance of diplomatic relations with Israel, and it was not endangering its close economic ties with Arab countries. Palzur made proposals to Minister Orzechowski for the development of reciprocal relations, and he, on his part, promised to work towards implementing them. Palzur assessed this talk with the Polish foreign minister as a 'milestone marking the start of a long, convoluted process until reaching full normalization of relations, which went on for some three and a half years'.[27]

Indeed, in this period, the scope of bilateral relations grew sizably in the fields of economics, commerce, tourism and aviation (establishing direct flights by El Al and LOT between Poland and Israel), sport, education, culture and science. Likewise, visits were arranged for youth, ministers, and other personages from Israel to Poland, such as Minister of Religious Affairs Zevulun Hammer; the director general of the Foreign Ministry, Yossi Beilin; Minister of Tourism Avraham Sharir; Minister of Education Yitzhak Navon; Minister of Industry and Commerce Ariel Sharon; Knesset members from various factions, and others besides. The same was true for Polish ministers who made official visits to Israel. Another achievement, from Israel's point of view, was the initiative of Ambassador Palzur to remove Dutch patronage from the Interest Office in Warsaw and to make it independent. This was implemented at the beginning of October 1988, and from then on the Israel Interest Office in Warsaw operated as an embassy in every respect, even if it did not have official standing as such. The scope of political discourse between Israeli representatives and Polish representatives extended beyond its 'traditional' framework of an annual meeting as part of the UN General Assembly. Yet, the representatives of the Polish government did not have anything new to report in their talks with the Israeli representatives concerning the conditions that were still not ripe for renewal of full diplomatic relations with Israel. This remained so even after the Israeli representatives presented the argument that Spain had established diplomatic relations with Israel without damaging its connections to Arab countries. Moreover, they pointed out the absurd situation in which Israel conducted diplomatic relations with Egypt, and Egypt maintained an embassy in Israel, and Israel likewise in Egypt, while diplomatic relations with the East European countries, including Poland, remained severed.

Even though the range of bilateral links grew immeasurably, and this was public knowledge, the Polish authorities tended outwardly to denigrate their significance. A clear example is the statement by the Polish minister of information and Polish government spokesman, Jerzy Urban, at his weekly press conference on 23 February 1988. In response to a question by a journalist from the *Jewish Chronicle* on the possibility for the renewal of diplomatic relations between Poland and Israel in the near future, the minister replied,

> The chances for that are totally dependent upon progress in the Middle East peace process. The question of the advancement of Polish-Israeli relations towards the establishment of diplomatic relations is not connected to any Polish-Israeli problem, to any bilateral issue, but to the Middle East peace process and to the tendency to honour the just aspirations of the Palestinian people.

To another question by that same writer as to whether the present circumstances, under which the USSR and Poland maintained relations with only one side of the Israeli-Arab conflict, were normal, and was this not detrimental to the ability to influence the parties in conflict or to the participation in an international conference towards resolving the conflict, without acknowledging the position of the other side? Moreover, was not Poland marching along the Soviet path regarding relations with Israel? The minister answered:

> There is no difference in approach between Poland and the USSR on the Middle East question. Poland supports an international conference for the solution of the Arab-Israeli conflict, with the participation of the parties to the conflict, including the PLO, for the purpose of resolving the Palestinian problem and determining safe and just borders for all states in the Middle East, including Israel. Diplomatic relations between Poland and Israel can come about when the Middle East peace process will take on realistic dimensions, thus we will be able to assume that this is beneficial to toning down the Middle East conflict and that the causes that led to the break in relations will evaporate or can possibly disappear. We cannot give a more precise answer at this time, or more properly, a concrete answer.[28]

Undoubtedly this was the political line dictated to the spokesman by the Polish government, under the leadership of General Jaruzelski (albeit, not personally, as Ambassador Palzur attested to me, there was a positive attitude towards Israel). And as previously noted, the USSR as led by Gorbachev was no longer a disruptive factor in Poland's relations with Israel, while fear of a worsening of Poland's economic links with the Arab countries because of Poland's connections to Israel had been proven as unfounded.[29] What remained, then, was only the deep-rooted animosity towards Israel on the part of the communist ruling circles in Poland, which promoted a poisonous campaign against it, and against the Jews of Poland, in the wake of the Six Day War. It was Poland's severe economic and social crises that forced it to woo the American Jews and Israel so as to find a solution for the country's weighty problems. This brings us back to the paradox of hatred for Israel, on the one hand, and a tendency to exploit Israel and through it the Jews of the United States in finding solutions to its economic problems, on the other.

An assessment of the situation, written on 13 June 1988 by the East European Department of the Foreign Ministry in Jerusalem, on the internal political crisis in Poland, determined, inter alia, that

1. The extent of Poland's external debts had reached thirty billion dollars (which forced it to ask Western countries to reschedule their debt payments for a number of years).
2. The country's low production capacity did not provide for internal needs and did not allow export at appropriate levels of quality and quantity.
3. There was increasing inflation and low salaries (about $50 a month for a university professor).
4. A wave of strikes detrimental to the shaky economy had given rise to a tense atmosphere and feelings of instability.

5. Even though the Polish government had tried to obtain the nation's agreement, the October 1987 referendum for painful economic reforms (by raising prices and making factories more efficient) had failed. This came about because most of the voters negated the proposals, assuming that without political reform, one could not expect essential, positive changes in the economy.

6. Poland's main problem was the strong opposition in the ruling (communist) party to the implementation of liberal political reforms that would permit significant economic changes. The government leader, Jaruzelski – actually a follower of Gorbachev and his theories of perestroika and glasnost – estimated that in Poland it would not be possible to swiftly expedite a process of liberalization, since the process was liable to slip out of the grasp of the regime, thereby endangering the standing of the Communist Party and destabilize the entire Communist Bloc. This assumption proved true, over time.

The dramatic reversal in Polish policy, which was of decisive influence on the internal affairs of the country and on its foreign policy, including towards Israel, occurred in June 1989, when – for the first time since 1947 – free elections were held. As a result, the dominant Communist Party, lost control, and in its stead a coalition was created composed of Solidarnoscz with a few parties that had operated in Poland before the access to power of the Communist Party, and with representatives of the Communist Party who had renounced Marxist-Leninist principles.[30] The first government was assembled in July 1989. Tadeusz Mazowiecki was chosen as prime minister and Professor Krzysztof Skubiszewski was appointed foreign minister, both on behalf of Solidarnoscz, while Wojciech Jaruzelski was selected as president of the country.

The first inkling of a change in policy towards Israel

was already garnered from Prime Minister Mazowiecki's first speech in the Polish parliament, when he announced that 'Poland intends to renew its diplomatic relations with countries with which they had been severed'.[31] Even if Israel was not mentioned specifically in his statements, the message was understood as undoubtedly referring to it.

A second sign, this time explicit, was noted by Ambassador Palzur directly from Foreign Minister Skubiszewski, on the eve of his departure for New York to take part in the UN General Assembly in September 1989, when he revealed to the ambassador that he intended to 'normalize' his country's relations with Israel,[32] meaning, to renew the diplomatic relations of his country with Israel. In the talk between Foreign Minister Moshe Arens and his Polish counterpart, as part of the UN General Assembly, at the end of September 1989, Skubiszewski reiterated this intention. This decision, he said, was made by Poland and required no authorization from the USSR or the Arab states. Yet, 'even without directly linking things', he found it proper to reiterate to Minister Arens two arguments that we heard from previous foreign ministers: first, that Poland had a certain difficulty in implementing this goal because of its close economic ties with the Arab countries, and second, that Poland anticipated being helped by Israel and world Jewry to extricate itself from its economic difficulties. The entire talk was conducted in a congenial atmosphere, with both sides presenting general lines and ideas for cooperation in future activities.[33]

In an interview with *Haaretz* correspondent Roman Priester on 10 October 1989 Skubiszewski was asked about the issue of renewing diplomatic relations between his country and Israel:

> We have made a firm decision to institute full diplomatic relations with Israel, while maintaining proper relations with all the countries of the Near East ... severance of relations does not contribute anything, and even if there

are political or ideological differences of opinion
between the two states, the best way to work out and
clarify them is through unmediated relations ...
whatever will be, we have decided not to drag this issue
of diplomatic relations with Israel on forever. And I see a
solution of the problem in the very near future.

This was the tone in which the Polish foreign minister
spoke with the deputy prime minister and minister of the
treasury, Shimon Peres, when he paid an official visit to
Poland, at the end of November 1989. He was the first
top-level politician ever to visit Poland at the invitation of
its government, and he was received with all ceremonial
protocol. I accompanied him as part of my new position
in the Foreign Ministry as deputy director general for
East European affairs. Among the attendees at a large
reception that Ambassador Mordechai Palzur and his
wife hosted in his honour were Prime Minister
Mazowiecki and eighteen other government ministers.[34]
During the visit Peres met for talks with Foreign Minister
Skubiszewski, Polish President Jaruzelski, and Prime
Minister Mazowiecki. In each of these discussions,
carried on in a friendly, unofficial spirit, the need for the
renewal of diplomatic relations in the near future was
discussed. The reason that the diplomatic relations had
not as yet been renewed, noted Skubiszewski, was the
desire of his government to inform the Arab countries in
advance, so as 'to avoid problems'. He said further at this
talk, that Poland's breaking of relations with Israel 'was
an impulsive act that had gone on for a long time and
alleviating its results was not a simple issue', but he
immediately added that they would be renewed in the
first quarter of 1990.[35]

At the luncheon that Foreign Minister Skubiszewski
arranged in Peres' honour, Deputy Foreign Minister
Majevski told me – in reply to my question – that his office
was planning to hold a ceremony for the signing of the
renewal of diplomatic relations in the middle of February

1990. He asked for my view as to whether the ceremony should be held in Warsaw or Israel, and I replied, in Warsaw. I explained this by noting that from the communications aspect there would be greater impact than if it was held in Jerusalem. Moreover, it was in Warsaw that the Polish government had decreed the severance of relations with Israel on 12 June 1967. Albeit, I did say that I would forward the question for the opinion of Foreign Minister Arens. Similarly, he asked me whether it was worthwhile to have additional bilateral agreements signed on the occasion; I gave a positive reply. The deputy minister told me that he would send drafts of the agreements for our review through Ambassador Palzur.

On my return to Israel, I reported these exchanges to Foreign Minister Arens. The minister authorized Warsaw as the location for the ceremony for the renewal of diplomatic relations; his preference was that it should be held during the last week of February 1990. I notified Ambassador Palzur and requested that he pass on this information to Deputy Foreign Minister Majewski.[36] The two sides agreed to hold the ceremony on 27 February 1990, with the attendance of the two foreign ministers, their entourages, and the heads of the Interest Offices of Israel and Poland.[37]

At a press conference that Foreign Minister Skubiszewski convened in Warsaw on 9 February 1990, he announced, among other things:

> As to relations with Israel, for a long time now Poland has been involved with them, in a strange way called 'Interest Offices', which play the role of embassies in many respects. We want full normalization of diplomatic relations that will be accompanied by concrete steps, and we want closer participation between our two countries. During the coming visit by Israel Foreign Minister Arens in Warsaw, an agreement will be signed on the establishment of diplomatic relations and agreements for the encouragement of capital investments

and their protection, as well as cooperation in the cultural sphere.[38]

This was the first official announcement about the decision by the Polish government to renew its diplomatic relations with Israel in the presence of Israel Foreign Minister Moshe Arens in Warsaw.

VISIT BY FOREIGN MINISTER MOSHE ARENS TO WARSAW
AND THE SIGNING OF THE PROTOCOL ON THE RENEWAL
OF DIPLOMATIC RELATIONS BETWEEN POLAND AND ISRAEL

The ceremony for the signing of the renewal of diplomatic relations between Poland and Israel took place as planned on 27 February 1990, involving the two foreign ministers and in the presence of the Polish prime minister. The event was widely covered in the Polish press, including the communist media, in a report by the Soviet news agency, Tass, and in the Israeli press.

During the course of his visit to Poland, Foreign Minister Arens held working talks with his colleague, Polish Foreign Minister Skubiszewski, Polish President Jaruzelski, and Prime Minister Mazowiecki. Below are selections from their statements to illustrate the perception of the past and the present as they offered them, as well as their expectations for the future, with the 'closing of the circle' and the opening of the new chapter in mutual relations.[39]

Skubiszewski commented that Poland established diplomatic relations with Israel from the beginning of Israel's independence, which personified the realization of the Balfour Declaration. Poland regrets the break in its relations with Israel in 1967, and considered it a serious political mistake that was carried out under the command of the Communist Party of Poland and not in line with opinion of the Polish nation. Poland hopes to strengthen its relations with Israel, as they had been in their early days. Similarly, it looks forward to carrying out political contacts through the exchange of visits by the heads of state, and in this spirit Poland is interested in signing in the near future the following agreements with Israel: a) encouragement of capital investments and their protection; b) prevention of double taxation; c) cultural and scientific connections; d) establishment of cultural centres; and e) commercial exchanges.

Jaruzelski commented that in Polish history there have been warm episodes of Jews and Poles living together in the distant and recent past. He mentioned the Holocaust of the Polish Jews and the joint struggle against Hitler. Yet, 'there have been unpleasant moments' – the break in relations between Poland and Israel, as an expression of the policy of the (Communist) Bloc. Now, things have changed, and the Poland of today is capable of implementing the desired change in the renewal of relations with Israel. This resumption was preceded by other links. He praised the contribution of Ambassador Palzur for establishing and reinforcing them. 'Now, it is important to act towards a new quality of relations', in all fields: economic, political, moral (he did not specify), and historical. All of this was to be done with the aim of transmitting to the coming generations a heritage of a common past. They were interested in nurturing relations with Polish émigrés in Israel and in cooperation with Israel, in areas that hitherto had been inaccessible:

1. Building a centre for Jewish culture in Warsaw and a museum for Jewish heritage in Poland.
2. Building a hotel in Warsaw to accommodate tourists from Israel and the Diaspora dispersion.
3. Producing a joint film on the heritage of the past, for example, Anders Army.[40] This episode was totally unknown. There must certainly be a great deal of documentation on it in Israel and Poland that could be put to use.
4. On the whole, Poland could be a good partner for Israel in the establishment of joint industrial endeavours.
5. Poland was entering an era of reforms and a struggle

against galloping inflation. It would be interested in learning from Israel's experience in this area and in others, such as banking, infrastructure, administration, interpersonal relations, tourism, and in finding common solutions to shared problems.
6. Poland offers its good services towards the solution of the problems in the Middle East.

Mazowiecki commented that Poland's breaking relations with Israel was a fatal step. Renewing relations opens a new chapter of friendship and cooperation between the two countries. He expressed appreciation to the economic delegation from Israel, which accompanied Foreign Minister Arens, and he wanted to tell it not to be discouraged from the first impression gained from contacts with representatives of the economic ministries in Poland. There was a need for a great deal of patience.

Foreign Minister Moshe Arens welcomed their statements. He conveyed his hope that mutual relations would continue to grow stronger for the mutual benefit of the two countries, and he invited his interlocutors to visit Israel. At these talks, political topics were touched upon, in addition to interrelations, such as the implementation of the reforms in the USSR and the issue of the unification of Germany, the thought of which made the Polish leadership apprehensive. At the conclusion of the talks the minister met with the Jewish community leaders and paid a visit to the Auschwitz extermination camp. A correspondent from the Soviet news agency Tass reported on the event in an article published on 28 February 1990 with the headline 'Poland-Israel Diplomatic Relations':

> The foreign ministers of Israel and Poland signed on 27 February 1990 a protocol for the establishment of diplomatic relations between the two states. Attending the ceremony held in Warsaw was the prime minister of Poland.

Poland was the third East European country – after Hungary and Czechoslovakia – to renew officially its diplomatic relations with Israel, which had been severed in 1967. Poland and Israel also signed an inter-governmental agreement on air services between them. During the meeting between Foreign Minister Moshe Arens and the prime minister of Poland, which lasted two hours, the parties discussed possibilities for bilateral economic cooperation. The issue of the unification of Germany was also raised in the discussion. Foreign Minister Arens expressed complete understanding and support for the Polish position. He extended an invitation to the prime minister of Poland to pay an official visit to Israel. The invitation was accepted. The announcement by the Polish Foreign Ministry, which was published by the Polish news agency, stated that the establishment of diplomatic relations between Poland and Israel would not be detrimental to the interests of other states and nations. This is also not a factor towards a change in the Polish position regarding the establishment of a sustainable peace in the Middle East, which will be based on principles of international law and UN resolutions. Poland is ready to grant constructive aid towards this end. The president of Poland also met with the Israeli foreign minister.[41]

One must assume that the Polish Foreign Ministry was the source that provided these ideas to the Tass correspondent, with the aim of noting that Poland was not the first country in the Communist Bloc to renew diplomatic relations with Israel. No expression of regret over the break in relations was voiced in this announcement, apparently so as not to embarrass the USSR, which had dictated this move. In addition, it sent a calming message to the Arab countries.

The Israeli Interest Office in Warsaw, which operated independently from October 1988, now changed its name to the Embassy of Israel, and the head of the office, Mordechai Palzur, became the chargé d'affaires at the embassy until he presented his credentials to the president of Poland, Jaruzelski, at the Presidential Palace in Warsaw, on 18 April 1990, as the ambassador of Israel to Poland. This took place at a festive ceremony accompanied by the playing of 'Hatikvah' by the Polish army orchestra, after a break of twenty-three years in relations between the two countries. I am quite certain that for Ambassador Palzur, a native of Poland who had fled with his parents to the USSR to escape the Nazi invasion, this was surely a most moving event, 'closing the circle' in his life and in the history of his diplomatic service in Israel's Ministry of Foreign Affairs. This brought to a close the long process of the renewal of diplomatic relations between Israel and Poland, with the establishment of democratic rule there. Wide-ranging impetus was given to the continued development and reinforcement of relations, whose foundation had been laid by Ambassador Palzur during his four-year mission in Poland, in the areas of economics, trade, tourism, culture, education, science , and aviation (Warsaw served for a time, in the early 1990s, as a way station for immigrants from the USSR to Israel, thanks to direct flights between Poland and Israel).

A short time after the renewal of diplomatic relations, official visits were made at all levels, including exchange visits by the presidents of both countries. In the UN arena there was an appreciable change in Poland's position regarding issues affecting Israel, Zionism, and the Arab-Israeli conflict. Departments of Jewish Studies were established at Polish universities and friendship leagues were founded. Similarly, joint research expanded between Israel and Polish historians in studying the history of the Jews in Poland before, during and after the Second World War.

A side effect, however, of the democratization and liberalization processes in Poland was also a rise in anti-Semitism, which was expressed in the media, in nationalist publications, in the desecration of Jewish cemeteries, and even in the campaigns for the presidential elections in

November 1990. Under the influence of Cardinal Franciszek Macherski of Cracow (who in 1978 had signed the agreement with the Jewish organizations on the removal of the Carmelite monastery from the Auschwitz camp), the Polish Episcopate Conference distributed, in January 1991, a pastoral letter against anti-Semitism. The letter defined anti-Semitism as a sin against Christianity and rebuked those Poles who had assisted the Nazis in exterminating Jews. In March 1991, Poland's new president, Lech Wałęsa, established a presidential council for Jewish-Polish affairs to combat anti-Semitism.

THE JEWISH POPULATION

In 1990/91 the number of Jews in Poland registered within the framework of local Jewish communal institutions – religious, social, and cultural – operating with the assistance of the Joint Distribution Committee, the Lauder Foundation,[42] and the central government, was estimated at some 6,000. The number of Jews who were not listed with the community was considered to be a few thousand more. Despite their relatively small number among the general population of thirty-eight million people, their presence was striking in the communications media, literature, culture and academe. At the same time, the connections of the Jewish community with educational and cultural institutions in Israel grew ever closer. And even though the number of Jews is constantly declining, Jewish life in Poland continues as usual.

NOTES

1. Dov Sattath, Summary Report on Poland after the severance of relations, n.d. (written in January–February 1975), I File Pol 103.1, Israel State Archives (ISA). All documents and memoranda mentioned and cited in this chapter are found in this file.
2. Ezra Mendelson, 'Poland', in Ya'akov Tsur (ed.), *Tefutzah: Mizrah Eiuropa* (Jerusalem: Keter, 1976).
3. Ibid.
4. *Encyclopaedia Hebraica*, Supplement 2 (Tel Aviv: Sifriat Poalim, 1983), pp. 925–7;

Yosef Govrin, *Israel-Soviet Relations 1953–1967, From Confrontation to Disruption* (London:, Frank Cass, 1988), Chapter. 7, discusses emigration to Israel from the USSR and Eastern Europe. On the rate of migration from Poland between 1953 and 1967, see p. 139. On the repatriation agreements between the USSR and Poland, see pp.139–40.

5. A. A. Ben Asher, *Foreign Relations 1948–1953* (Tel Aviv:, Ayanot, 1957), pp. 196–200 [Hebrew].

6. Ibid.; *Hebrew Encyclopaedia*, Supplement 2, pp. 925–7; Katriel Katz, *Ambassador to Alienated Countries* (Tel Aviv: Sifriat Hapoalim, 1976) [Hebrew].

7. Abba Eban, *Pirkei Hayim* [Chapters of Life] (Tel Aviv: Sifriat Maariv, 1978), pp. 302–3.

8. Y. Govrin, Report on the visit of the editor of the Polish weekly magazine *Kultura*, 1 May 1977.

9. Y. Govrin, Report on the discussion with Zborowski, Poland-Israel, 27 December 1977.

10. The translation into Hebrew is found in a memorandum of the East European Department in the Foreign Ministry, Jerusalem, 8 January 1981.

11. Y. Govrin, Report on the discussion with the Polish minister of religious affairs, 9 February 1981.

12. The Polish bank PKO had operated on Allenby Street in Tel Aviv for over a decade before the foundation of Israel, including during the Second World War, when Poland was under Nazi occupation. Most of its clients were foreign citizens. The same situation applied during the period of severed Polish-Israeli relations. It was always headed by a representative of Poland.

13. Stefan Grayek, Report on his discussion with the Polish minister of religious affairs, 23 April 1981.

14. Y. Govrin, Report on the impressions of two Israeli delegations returned from a visit to Poland, 25 August 1981.

15. Yosef Ben-Aharon, Report on discussions, 28 September 1981.

16. *Hebrew Encyclopaedia*, Supplement 2, pp. 924–6, on the socio-economic foment in Poland from the mid-1970s to 1981; Supplement 3, pp. 775–6, covering 1981–89.

17. Arye Levin, Report on discussions, 26 September 1984.

18. Y. Govrin, Summary on Israel-Poland Relations and Proposals for Action, 4 June 1985.

19. Y. Govrin, Report on discussions, 13 October 1985.

20. Telegram from the East European Department, Foreign Ministry, to the Israel Embassy in Bonn, 27 October 1985.

21. Moshe Yegar, Israel General Consul in New York, in the Report on his discussions with Kalman Sultanik, 26 December 1985.

22. Stefan Grayek, Report to the East European Department of the Foreign Ministry, 3 January 1986.

23. Cited in the article by Roman Priester on Israel-Poland relations, *Haaretz*, 19 October 1989 [Hebrew].

24. *Maariv*, 15 October 1986.

25. Palzur, 'Poland – Renewal of Relations', in Moshe Yegar, Yosef Govrin, and Oded Aryeh (eds), *The Foreign Ministry, the First 50 Years* (Jerusalem: Keter, 2002), pp.505–519 [Hebrew].

26. Raphael Gvir, Report on discussions, 29 September 1986.

27. Palzur, 'Poland', p. 511.

28. Telegram from the Israeli representation in Warsaw (the Interest Office), 24 August 1988.

29. Mordechai Palzur, Report on his discussion with Polish Foreign Minister Orzechowski, 1 February 1989, p. 6. To Palzur's question, 'What were the Arab responses about our declaration of an independent representation?' the minister replied 'that there were questions but no protests and this step did not disrupt

231

our good relations with the Arabs'.
30. Review by the East European Department of the Foreign Ministry, 13 June 1988.
31. Telegram from Israel's representation in Warsaw, 22 September 1989.
32. Ibid.
33. Report to the Foreign Ministry by Israel's Diplomatic Mission to the UN, 28 September 1989.
34. Palzur, 'Poland', p. 518.
35. Y. Govrin, Report on the Peres talks with Polish leaders, 10 December 1989.
36. Ibid.
37. Palzur, 'Poland', p. 518.
38. Telegram from Israel's representation in Warsaw, 12 February 1990.
39. Y. Govrin, Discussions with Foreign Minister Arens in Warsaw, 13 March 1990.
40. Anders Army was formed by the Polish General Wladislaw Anders, in 1941, after the invasion of Nazi Germany into the USSR. Anders was at that time a Polish prisoner in Moscow, taken in the course of the Soviet invasion into Poland in 1939. Following the re-establishment of diplomatic relations between the Polish government in exile, in London, with the USSR, it was decided to form a Polish Army headed by General Anders, whose soldiers were Polish citizens (among them many Jews) who had fled to the USSR or had been imprisoned by the Soviet army during the Nazi and Soviet invasion to Poland. Anders Army was transferred (by Soviet-British agreement) via Iran to Iraq, the Middle East (Trans Jordan and Palestine) and from there to Italy where they fought with the British Army.
41. Tass report, 28 February 1990.
42. The Lauder Foundation is an American Jewish philanthropic organization dedicated to rebuilding Jewish communities in Central and Eastern Europe, mainly in the social, educational and cultural fields.

8. Milestones in the Diplomatic Relations between Israel and Yugoslavia: From Severance (1967) to their Renewal (1991)

HISTORICAL BACKGROUND

Yugoslavia, under the rule of Josip Broz Tito,[1] founder in 1946 of the People's Federal Republic of Yugoslavia (which comprised Serbia, Croatia, Slovenia, Bosnia-Herzegovina, Macedonia and Montenegro) was one of the initiators of the break in diplomatic relations with Israel among the countries of the East European Communist Bloc at the end of the Six Day War in June 1967. Yugoslavia was last among them to renew relations, in October 1991, except for the USSR, which reinstituted its relations with Israel at the consular level in 1990 and at the diplomatic level towards the end of October 1991. Yet, unlike the other communist countries of Eastern Europe – Bulgaria, Hungary, Poland and Czechoslovakia – which automatically supported the USSR position in their decision to break their diplomatic relations with Israel (except for Romania, which decided to continue them), Tito's Yugoslavia did so for independent considerations.

In fact, this was a decision taken by Tito, which he dictated to his government,[2] against the opinion of some of his ministers, including the foreign minister, Marko

Nikezic, who felt that such an extreme measure should not be taken against Israel because of the role of Arab countries in causing the outbreak of the war. Moreover, Nikezic felt that 'it was not good for Yugoslavia to position itself one hundred per cent behind one of the sides and to burn its bridges to the other, thereby limiting its power in the arena of political activity and in dealing with the crisis in the Middle East, even for the benefit of the Arabs'.[3] Tito's personal decision to sever relations was also in opposition to the opinion of most of the members of the Foreign Affairs Committee of the Yugoslav Parliament.[4] The question then arises, what were the motives behind Tito's initiative to break his country's diplomatic relations with Israel?

In light of the goals he had set for his policy, one may assume that Tito was operating from four main motives, namely: first, personal friendship with the ruler of Egypt, Gamal Abdel Nasser. Tito had not fought alongside him against Israel in the Six Day War, though he did use diplomatic weapons against Israel – punishing the state by severing relations with the aim of isolating Israel in the international arena. He threatened that sanctions would be applied if Israel did not withdraw from all Arab territory taken during the Six Day War, and on this issue he found allies in the East European Bloc led by the USSR.

Secondly, Tito belonged to the leadership of the Non-Aligned Movement – Tito was among its founding fathers, alongside Nehru and Nasser – and he was constantly striving to be its leader. He saw the strengthening of the movement as a kind of insurance to prevent a possible invasion by the USSR of Yugoslavia, under the aegis of the Warsaw Pact. This had indeed happened to Hungary in 1956, in line with the Brezhnev Doctrine, which supported military intervention in a communist state, if and when its regime was in danger of falling. Moreover, the non-aligned states were considered as the balancing element in a confrontation between the Eastern Bloc and the Western

Bloc during the period of the cold war, and many of them broke their diplomatic relations with Israel. Thus, Yugoslavia chose not only to be one of them but even the leader in this direction.

Third was Yugoslavia's close political but mainly economic ties with the majority of Arab countries, particularly its dependence on Libyan oil. Severing itself from Israel was intended to be a demonstrative act of solidarity with the Arab states that would also yield economic and political profit. And fourth, Yugoslavia's aggressive and consistent opposition to any occupation or holding of foreign territories captured in war, owing not a little to its fear of the Soviet threat hanging over it. The Yugoslav ambassador to the UN, Ernest Petric, expressed this quite clearly in the discussions of the UN Committee for Palestine to which Yugoslavia belonged, on 19 November 1976: 'There are no good or democratic occupations, nor can they be justified. Freedom and independence cannot be replaced by anything, and the best way of protecting one's own freedom is to respect the freedom of other peoples.'[5]

From this stemmed the condition that Yugoslavia demanded of Israel: as long as it did not withdraw from all the territories occupied in the Six Day War, Yugoslavia would not renew diplomatic relations. Yugoslavia held fast to this opinion during the entire period of severed relations, except for about half a year before their resumption.

Yugoslavia clung steadfastly to this policy toward Israel even after Israel had signed the peace treaty with Egypt (1979) and established diplomatic relations with Egypt (Nasser, Tito's friend, was no longer alive). Not only that, it vilified the peace treaty between Israel and Egypt in the UN arena, along with the other countries of the Communist Bloc (except Romania), and severely criticized the idea of establishing autonomy for the Arab inhabitants of Judea, Samaria and Gaza. Even after Tito's death (1980), Yugoslavia did not rush to renew diplomatic relations with Israel, and no essential change took place in its policy in the international arena. One may perhaps attribute this to the fact that the new Yugoslav chieftains tended not to deviate from Tito's heritage, being an interim leadership (whose president and vice-president changed after one year, according to the selection of the collective presidency, in line with a predetermined order of the six republics comprising Federal Yugoslavia). It was perhaps also significant that Yugoslavia, owing to internal difficulties, was deeply ensconced in problems concerning its stability and identity. This situation led to the power and national distinctiveness of the six republics and two autonomous areas, Kosovo and Vojvodina, overwhelming the central regime, a situation that eventually led to the dissolution of the Federal Republic of Yugoslavia.

Yet, during the entire period of the break in diplomatic relations, mutual exchange visits as well as commercial, tourism and sporting relations between the two countries continued as usual. And when the isolationist powers in the republics became predominant, from the mid-1980s onwards, the calls of the leaders of Serbia, Slovenia and Croatia also intensified for the renewal of Yugoslavia's diplomatic relations with Israel, to honour a common past and for the benefit of the national interest. These calls were also voiced in the Federal Parliament, in the press and in important journals.

Yugoslavia first became involved in the Palestine issue as a communist republic when it was appointed to the UN Special Commission on Palestine (UNSCOP), initiated by the UN, at Britain's request in 1947, to study the problem of Palestine and to present its recommendations for solving it. Most of the commission members – which included Yugoslavia and Czechoslovakia – proposed partitioning Palestine into two states: a Jewish one and an Arab one. Yugoslavia and Czechoslovakia were among the minority that demurred from this proposal and supported the establishment of a bi-national state in Palestine, at the end of the British Mandate. Yugoslavia's reason at the time was that a federative political framework such as its own would be suitable for other nations as well.[6]

When the proposal was raised at the UN General Assembly, on 29 November 1947, toward the resolution for the division of Palestine into two states, Yugoslavia was the only East European country to refrain from voting. In addition to the USSR, other East European countries that voted in favour of the resolution were Poland, Czechoslovakia and Hungary (at the time Romania, Bulgaria and Albania were not yet UN members). Despite this, Yugoslavia did give the State of Israel de jure recognition as early as the first month of its independence and, within a short time, diplomatic representations between them were exchanged.[7]

The period from 1948 until the severance of relations was characterized by close relations, particularly in the areas of economics, commerce and trade, sports, culture and tourism – except for the period of the Sinai Campaign (1956/58), during which relations in the political sphere degenerated but did not rupture, as did happen after the end of the Six Day War in June 1967. Moreover, when Yugoslavia was ousted from the Cominform (Communist Information Bureau) in 1948 and its relations with the USSR worsened as a result of the boycott that the USSR and its followers instituted, Israel – together with the European nations and the United States – was considered as an important political and economic support for Yugoslavia.

Regarding emigration to Israel, Yugoslavia placed no obstacles in the way of Jews who desired to migrate there, and it promised full rights to those who preferred to stay in its territory, whether in community self-organization and the fostering of the values of Jewish tradition and culture or through nurturing links to Israel, on the personal and institutional levels.[8] Etched into the common historical memory were a few significant facts: the fighting of many Jews among the ranks of the inhabitants of Yugoslavia, alongside the partisans led by Tito, during the Nazi occupation; Yugoslavia as a transit station for 'illegal' immigrants who reached it in 1946/47 with the aim of setting sail for the shores of Mandatory Palestine as part of the unauthorized immigration; and the passage of arms to Israel over Yugoslavian territory during the War of Independence in 1948.

In the years of severed diplomatic relations (1967–1991), Yugoslavia waged a fierce anti-Israel policy in the forum of the non-aligned nations as well as in internal propaganda. It provided military and political assistance to the PLO and to its delegation in Belgrade that had status equivalent to an embassy (although its head was not given the title ambassador) even before the Palestine National Council declared at its conference in Algiers, in November 1988, the establishment of the 'New State of Palestine'. Tito hosted the PLO chairman, Arafat, on his visits to Yugoslavia, with all the pomp awarded to heads of state. With the aim of demonstrating Yugoslavia's unlimited support for the Arab countries and with the goal of strengthening its standing as leader of the non-aligned nations, Tito arranged, in August 1967, about two months after the Six Day War, a series of state visits to Egypt (twice), Syria and Iraq. At the end of his round of visits, he declared, at a press conference in Alexandria, on 17 August 1967, that,

> It is well known, that Yugoslavia from the very outbreak of the aggression in the Middle East, made active efforts to find a solution to this problem most acceptable to the Arab countries ... It is understandable, that we wished first of all, to become acquainted with the views of the leaders of the states we had visited on what action was to be undertaken ... The talks in Cairo, Damascus, Baghdad and Alexandria showed that political activity is as necessary to the Arab countries as material assistance in aiding them to repair the damages of the war.[9]

At the end of August and beginning of September 1967, this political activity resulted in Tito's initiative to send emissaries throughout the world with proposals in hand. These proposals were summed up in five paragraphs and published the world over:

1. Withdrawal of Israel to the borders of 4 June 1967 under UN supervision.
2. Guarantees for the borders of all states of the region and for their security by the UN Security Council, or by the Four Powers, until a final solution to all the pending issues should be reached. For this purpose, perhaps, UN Forces should be stationed on both sides of the frontier.
3. Free passage [of Israeli ships] in the Straits of Tiran until a decision was taken by the International Court.
4. Passage through the Suez Canal [for Israeli ships] as by the convention prior to 5 June 1967 [meaning, no sailing].
5. After the implementation of the above paragraphs, the UN Security Council will deal with the remaining issues, and particularly with the refugee problem and that of Israeli [ships] passing through the Suez Canal.

Foreign Minister Abba Eban published the Israeli government's response to this initiative in an interview in the *New York Times* on 2 September 1967:

> The Yugoslav Government which had broken diplomatic relations with Israel was developing intense activity on matters affecting Israel's vital interests without any contact or consultation with Israel. This attitude reflects the absence of objectivity and impartiality in the Yugoslavian position. In the recent General Assembly session and thereafter Yugoslavia has been the constant advocate of the Arab position in favour of a return to the situation of June 4th which brought peril to Israel and to Middle Eastern peace.
> Israel will not allow her rights or interests to be affected in any way by proposals or initiatives from

Yugoslavia. It is to be hoped that all other governments approached by Yugoslavia will understand the one-sided and unauthorized nature of Yugoslavian proposals concerning Israel. According to reports, Yugoslav emissaries are proposing that Israel return to the borders that existed before the Arab-Israel war in early June in return of declarations or so-called guarantees by third parties. We totally reject this approach. The political and territorial situation of June 4th endangered Israel's security and existence. It can never be restored. The cease fire agreements can only be superseded by peace treaties directly engaging the responsibility of Israel and her neighbouring states. The former armistice demarcation lines, which are no longer in force, must give way to agreed and permanent national frontiers and security arrangements. The peace that we seek together with the regional cooperation that will flow from it can only arise from the direct contact and full mutual recognition of the sovereign states of the region. It cannot be from outside without mutual consent of the sovereign states concerned. Israel was not inviting any third-party participation in her dispute with her neighbours. So far as Israel is concerned there can be no substitute for a directly negotiated peace settlement with the Arabs.

The Foreign Ministry in Jerusalem directed its representatives abroad, on 4 September 1967, to hand over to the foreign ministries of the countries in which they were serving the text of the statement by Foreign Minister Eban that had appeared in the *New York Times* and to stress additional points in the spirit of Eban's response, mainly as follows: Tito was not qualified to act as a mediator since he had severed relations with Israel. He did not consult Israel before making his proposals public, and he positioned himself exclusively on the side of the enemies of Israel.[10] Indeed, if we were to judge by the reactions of the local press in a number of countries, Tito's initiative did not meet with the success he had anticipated. For example, a political weekly in Buenos Aires, *Primera Plana*, which reviewed the Middle East crisis in its issue of 12 September 1967, pointed out, among other things, that Tito's proposal would not gain many supporters since it did not mention the need for the Arab countries to recognize Israel and concluding peace treaties. It went on to say that greater success was anticipated for Romania since it maintained diplomatic relations with Israel, and even openly and persistently pleaded with the Arab states to come to terms with Israel's existence.[11]

In speeches by official representatives of Yugoslavia at UN institutions and other political forums, including those of the non-aligned nations, on the issue of the Arab-Israeli conflict, during the years of the break in Israeli-Yugoslav relations, the following approaches and appeals were given expression:[12]

- Israeli withdrawal from all Arab territory occupied in the Six Day War, including Jerusalem.
- Cessation of settlement activity by Israel in Judea, Samaria and Gaza and in Galilee and evacuation of the 'illegal' existing settlements.
- Recognition of the legal rights of the Palestinian people, including the right to self-determination, establishment of an independent state in the territory of Judea, Samaria and Gaza, and recognition of the PLO as the legitimate representative of the Palestinian people.
- Right of return of the Arab refugees who wished to return to their homeland and payment of reparations to those who did not wish to return.
- The immediate opening of talks on the settlement of the Arab-Israeli conflict, under UN auspices and with the participation of all sides to the conflict, including the PLO as the sole representative of the Palestinian people, with status equal to that of the other participants. This solution should include all elements noted above, while determining recognized borders between the State of Israel and its neighbours and the provision of security

guarantees on behalf of the UN as a means for ensuring peace and security for all states of the region including Israel.
*   Imposition of sanctions against Israel 'if it persists in its expansionist policy' (Tito at the Non-Aligned Movement Summit in Colombo, 18 August 1976). A year earlier this call had been voiced by the Yugoslav foreign minister at the UN General Assembly.

These calls, with their sharp tone, were reiterated until the mid-1980s. Afterwards and until the renewal of diplomatic relations in October 1991, they were attenuated and softened, especially when internal criticism of Yugoslavia's policy towards Israel increased and in light of the renewal of political contacts between Israel and the USSR and the other countries of the Communist Bloc towards renewal of diplomatic relations. But these demands had been qualified even before the changes of attitude in the Eastern Bloc, and had been accompanied by declarations on the legality of the existence of Israel. Tito, for example, declared for the first time, at a joint meal with the president of Romania, Nicolae Ceauşescu, while visiting Romania in December 1977, 'No one can dream about throwing Israel into the sea. Israel is a real fact, that country has been in existence for many years, it is recognized by the United Nations, and is a member of the United Nations ... any other view would be unrealistic.'[13] Tito repeated these remarks when speaking to senior officers of the Yugoslav Army: 'The Palestinians have the right to their own state, but the idea of throwing Israel into the sea is unrealistic since the Jewish state also has the right to exist',[14] and again during the visit of the Egyptian deputy foreign minister to Belgrade, at the end of January 1978, Tito declared 'the need for the Arab countries and the PLO to recognize Israel as an existing fact'.

Making such a statement to an Arab minister was a kind of innovation, but it may be understood in light of the negotiations between Israel and Egypt about a peace treaty. Or take, for example, the declaration by the Yugoslav foreign minister, in Stockholm, on 28 September 1978: 'All directly interested countries and all international bodies must respect the fact that both the existence of Israel as a United Nations member country, and its right to independence and security, and the need to establish an independent state for the Palestinian people and the right of this State to existence, independence and security, are historical realities which must be accepted.'[15]

Perhaps as a result of these declarations, Prime Minister Menachem Begin decided to send a letter to Tito, in early October 1978, through the Belgian Embassy in Belgrade, which represented Israel's interests in Yugoslavia, containing a clarification of the historical significance of the Camp David agreement and the possibilities it created for Israel and Egypt. Yet it appeared that Tito's basic stance towards Israel – regarding whatever concerned relations that might be interpreted as official – had not changed. A direct response to the prime minister's letter was not received. An indirect reply, however, was made through the spokesmen of the Yugoslav Foreign Ministry at a press conference on 2 November 1978, in which he noted that 'Tito has received two letters following the Camp David agreement, one from Yaser Arafat, the chairman of the PLO, and the other, from the prime minister of Israel, Menachem Begin.' As for the Israeli letter, the spokesman said, 'It is well known that Yugoslavia does not have diplomatic relations with and does not maintain political contacts with Israel. We shall not reply to the message.'[16] From his statements, one may conclude that Tito not only refused to have political relations with Israel, but he was even unwilling to respond to the Israeli 'signal'.

YUGOSLAVIA AND THE USSR – IDENTICAL AND CONTRASTING APPROACHES

Was Yugoslav policy towards Israel distinct from that of the USSR and its satellites in the period of severed relations with Israel? And if so, in what way?

By calling for Israeli withdrawal from all territories occupied in the Six Day War; by opposing the Camp David agreements (1978); by calling for the UN to provide security guarantees (after the withdrawal) to all countries of the region, including Israel; by supporting the right of the Palestinians to self-determination and an independent, sovereign state and recognition of the PLO as the exclusive representative of the Palestinian people – in all these, Yugoslavia did not differ from the USSR (although, at times, the Yugoslav declarations had a sharper tone than those of the USSR). Yet the Yugoslav calls for the halting of Israeli settlement in Judea, Samaria and Gaza and the evacuation of the existing ones as 'illegal', and for the honouring of the Palestinian right of return for the Arab refugees did differ from the Soviet position. However, when referring to 'the right of return', Tito sometimes specified 'to their homes', at another time 'to their homeland'; sometimes he spoke of the refugees of 1948, and then at other times of the 'refugees of 1967'. Here, the influence of PLO Chairman Arafat on Tito is more salient than the influence of Tito on Arafat concerning the legal right of Israel to exist. Finally, the Yugoslav position also differed from that of the USSR on calling for the imposition of sanctions on Israel if it did not withdraw from the occupied territories.

In the years 1989/90, the Yugoslav position towards Israel softened and this was expressed through two important issues. The first was by taking public exception to the UN General Assembly's resolution of 11 November 1975 which defined Zionism as a 'form of racism and discrimination' (Yugoslavia had voted in favour of this resolution along with seventy-one other countries, with thirty-five countries opposing, thirty-two abstaining, and three not in attendance. On 16 December 1991, the UN General Assembly revoked the resolution. One hundred and eleven countries voted for that step – Yugoslavia among them – twenty-five opposed, and thirteen abstained).[17] The second instance of Yugoslavia's more favourable attitude to Israel was demonstrated by their opposition to discussing a proposal from Arab countries to rescind Israel's credentials to the UN.

On the bilateral level, the difference between Yugoslavia's stance and that of the USSR, Poland, and Czechoslovakia is particularly evident. At times, this difference contradicted the declarations by Yugoslav representatives in the international arena and among the non-aligned nations. Not only were the commercial ties of Yugoslavia with Israel conducted on a regular basis, but their scope was greater than the trade with Romania (which had not severed its diplomatic relations with Israel) and certainly was greater than trade with Hungary and Bulgaria (which had not ceased as a result of the break in their diplomatic relations with Israel), as they had been halted with the USSR, Poland and Czechoslovakia. Economic missions from Yugoslavia visited Israel from time to time and Israeli delegations went to Yugoslavia. Connections in shipping, sports, culture and tourism also continued, although of a more limited scope than before the severance of relations. The Yugoslav authorities did not limit the activity of the Jewish communities in Yugoslavia nor their connections with Israel and other Jewish communities the world over. Jewish youth choirs were permitted to participate in the Zimriyah choir festival in Israel. Mapam (United Workers Party) delegations were invited for talks in Yugoslavia as guests of the League of Communists of Yugoslavia. Another exceptional phenomenon was that Yugoslav ambassadors held free conversations with their Israeli counterparts in Europe, Asia, Africa, the United States and Australia. For the most part they did not depart from the political line dictated to them from Belgrade regarding Israel, but they listened and always absorbed the versions of the official representatives of Israel, for example on the plain of Israel's policy towards the Arab-Israeli conflict or with regard to the wider question of Yugoslavia's position towards Israel.

Perhaps this phenomenon should be attributed to the relatively liberal regime in Yugoslavia versus the centralized rule in the USSR; perhaps it was Tito himself who instructed his ministers to carry on with bilateral connections, while at the same time ordering his government to break diplomatic relations with Israel. Testimony on this can be found in the protocol of the Federal Executive Council of 13 June 1967, which, while containing the 'decision' on the severing of relations, stated further, that the 'Federal Executive Council's Economic Committee, together with the State Secretariat for Foreign Affairs and the State Secretariat for Foreign Trade, should examine the overall relations between our country and Israel, and especially in terms of furtherance of economic relations, and to eventually suggest the adequate measures to be taken'.[18] We have at hand no testimony as to the results of the discussions of the three bodies mentioned in the protocol, but one may assume with certainty that their decision was to continue with bilateral relations between Yugoslavia and Israel as being in the Yugoslav interest.

MILESTONES TOWARDS RENEWAL OF DIPLOMATIC RELATIONS

1. *Letter from Foreign Minister Yitzhak Shamir to Yugoslav Foreign Minister Lazar Mojsov*

Israel apparently reconciled itself to the Yugoslav policy on the issue of the Arab-Israeli conflict and realized, with a great degree of justification, that as long as Tito ruled in Yugoslavia there was no chance to change its policy nor, in any event, to renew diplomatic relations.

The first attempt was made by Israel in May 1982, about two years after Tito's death, and a short time before the evacuation of the Sinai Peninsula by the Israel Defence Force (IDF) and its return to Egyptian sovereignty. Also in May 1982, Lazar Mojsov was appointed as the new foreign minister in the Yugoslav government, and statements by the Yugoslav ambassador from among the non-aligned states – at the final UN Emergency Session on the issue of the Arab-Israeli conflict – were characterized by a more moderate tone than in the past. Against the background of these developments the Foreign Ministry in Jerusalem initiated a direct appeal from Foreign Minister Shamir to the Yugoslav foreign minister, in a personal letter he sent to him on 20 May 1982, through Israel's ambassador to the UN, Professor Yehuda Blum, to be delivered to the Yugoslav ambassador at the UN, stating:

> Although, to our regret, there are no diplomatic relations between our two countries, I feel the need to share our thoughts with you – on the strength of the ties of friendship that existed between our countries until the Six Day War in 1967, and in view of the profound esteem in which our peoples hold each other, against the background of our common struggle against the Nazi scourge and the determination of both our peoples to maintain their independence and their sovereignty in the face of hostile forces from the outside.
>
> We are today entering a new historical era in our region. Our forces having been compelled, at one time, to rally in the defence of our homeland against the terrible threat to its very existence, have now withdrawn from the entire Sinai Peninsula, in accordance with the agreement signed between Israel and Egypt.
>
> Israel, for its part, has paid a heavy price, in strategic as well as economic terms, for the establishment of normal neighbourly relations and full diplomatic relations with Egypt, the largest of the Arab countries, after 30 years of hostility and warfare.
>
> From the nations of the world – and especially from those which in the past have maintained friendly relations with us – Israel expects understanding for the great effort it has made, and the high price it has paid, for the advancement of peace in our region.
>
> The normalization of relations between Israel and

Egypt should serve as a source of encouragement to all countries in conflict, as well as to those States that aspire to contribute their share to the settlement of international conflicts through peace negotiations.

Normal relations between countries and the carrying on of an active dialogue between them, can only lead to the consolidation of a well-functioning system of international relations and, thus, would contribute substantially to a deepening of the understanding between peoples and a strengthening of the cause of peace.

Israel is aware of the fact that not all the problems of our region have been resolved – problems which, much to our regret, have come about through the activity of hostile forces that aspire, to this day, to eradicate Israel from the map of the Middle East.

As always, Israel is prepared to contribute its share to finding a solution; and we are inspired by the hope and the confidence that this goal will eventually be achieved, in the only feasible way – the way of peace.

In these days, as we mark the evacuation of Sinai, together with the establishment of good-neighbourly relations between Israel and Egypt, I wish to share our gratification concerning these developments with the people of Yugoslavia, as we face the future – and the continuation of the effort to bring peace and security to all the States in our region …

At the same time that this letter was sent, on 20 May 1982, Foreign Minister Shamir dispatched a letter of congratulation to his counterpart on his appointment as his country's new foreign minister. The two letters received no reply. Moreover, about a week after Foreign Minister Shamir's letter was sent to his Yugoslav counterpart, Israel made initial inquiries among the Yugoslav authorities, through the Belgian ambassador in Belgrade, as to whether it would be possible to place an Israeli diplomat in the Belgian Embassy in Belgrade who would represent the interests of Israel in Yugoslavia; to this, Israel was given a negative response. Thus the conclusion may be reached that no change had occurred in the Yugoslav government's position on the issue of the renewal of diplomatic relations with Israel and that it would be better to set aside at this juncture any manifestation of this initiative until the time for it would be right.

2. The Opinions of Two Yugoslav Diplomats

While Yugoslavia's official position gave no expression to any change regarding renewal of diplomatic relations with Israel, it is evident that from 1984 onwards other voices became prominent in the Yugoslav press, which was considered relatively liberal in comparison to that familiar to us from the Soviet Bloc. Even though the media did not come out with a decisive call for the renewal of relations with Israel, they did indicate, obliquely as well as directly, Yugoslavia's error in breaking them. I will cite two of the most prominent instances:

The first was a series of three articles on Israel (Palestine) in the 1948–1984 period by Leo Mates in the Yugoslav periodical, *Review of International Affairs*, that appeared in the course of 1984. The author was the former director of President Tito's office and served as Yugoslavia's permanent representative to the UN. With striking objectivity, his articles analysed the history of the Israel-Palestine conflict, and he accused the Palestinians of not being wise enough to establish their own state in the years 1948–67, when the territories of Judea, Samaria and Gaza were held by the Arabs (Jordan). They had failed to do this, he argued, owing to their ambition to create their state on the entire area of the Land of Israel, in which, under their rule, the Jews would live as a national minority. Among other things, Mates pointed out the help given by the USSR in the establishment of Israel and noted that both the United States and the Soviet Union, despite the confrontation between them, had made it unequivocally clear that under no circumstances would they tolerate the annihilation of

Israel. From the declarations of the two powers, the author of the three articles concluded that only they would be capable of imposing peace between Israel and its neighbours. Y. Bar-Yosef, a writer for *Yediot Aharonot* who reviewed Mates' series of articles in the issue of 30 August 1984, indicated that observers in Belgrade interpreted the articles as indirect criticism of Yugoslavia's official policy in the past concerning its decision to sever diplomatic relations with Israel.[19]

Secondly, the last Yugoslav envoy to Israel, Sobajic Vojimir, referred to the reasons for the decision by Yugoslavia to sever its diplomatic relations with Israel and the error of taking that step in an interview for the Yugoslav press, published in Belgrade on 20 February 1985. He stated:

> We believed that chances were on the side of the Arabs, at the end of the 1967 war. All the countries of the East (Eastern Europe), except for Romania, broke diplomatic relations with Israel. We did the same. I am convinced this was an error. Severing relations brought us no benefits. For the simple reason: had we continued to maintain diplomatic relations and our legation in Israel, our influence on the developments in the Middle East would have been much more significant. Moreover, Israel's approach towards Yugoslavia was full of esteem. Israel believed that Yugoslavia as a non-aligned country had influence over the Arab states. Besides this, living in Israel are some 6,000 Yugoslav Jews who arrived there in 1948 and most of them took part in the war of liberation of the Yugoslav peoples against the Nazi occupier.[20]

One may presume that in both instances the Yugoslav Foreign Ministry was aware of the statements by the two diplomats before they were made public. In the first case, the venue was a quasi-official periodical of the Yugoslav Foreign Ministry, and in the second, a senior diplomat of the Yugoslav Foreign Service. From this one may discern the aim: first, of presenting the background of the Israeli-Palestinian conflict in a more objective manner than had been common in Yugoslavia heretofore; second, to moderate the anti-Israeli tone that typified the period of Tito's rule; and third, to prepare the way for political contacts with Israel towards the possibility of the renewal of diplomatic relations. This position was likely to provide Yugoslavia with a certain amount of influence – following the example of Romania – for both parties to the conflict on the path to finding a peaceful solution. On the one hand, Yugoslavia enjoyed more prominent status in the international arena than Romania, since it belonged to the leadership of the non-aligned nations. On the other hand, Romania's standing on the issue of the Arab-Israeli conflict was better, since it maintained diplomatic relations with both sides, a fact that enabled it to act as a mediator between them. Such a role was inaccessible to Yugoslavia, as alluded to by its last envoy in Israel, as a result of the break in relations with one side of the conflict – Israel. From this point we will see that there were more initiatives made on the part of Yugoslavia towards Israel than of Israel towards Yugoslavia.

3. The Discussion between Foreign Minister Shimon Peres and Yugoslav Foreign Minister Raif Dizdarevic

The meeting was held on 30 September 1987 at the UN in New York, at the initiative of the Yugoslav foreign minister, Dizdarevic. This was the first meeting between the foreign minister of Yugoslavia and the foreign minister of Israel after twenty years of severed diplomatic relations. The two ministers happened to be in New York for the opening of the UN General Assembly. Apparently with the aim of breaking the diplomatic ice resulting from twenty years of disengagement from Israel and refraining from meetings and talks with it at the level of foreign ministers, the Yugoslav minister opened his statements by mentioning, first of all, his country's sympathetic stance towards Israel, with Yugoslavia being among the first to recognize Israel's independence; second, he noted the common fate of the Jewish and the Yugoslav people during the Second World War, 'in which 60,000 of the 80,000 Jews of Yugoslavia were murdered by the Nazis. Some 1,500 of them participated in the joint struggle for national liberation.' 'Each of us has', he said, 'a comrade in arms who is Jewish' and that 'whoever wanted to emigrate to Israel – has emigrated'.

The Yugoslav foreign minister explained the reason for not having any meeting to date at the level of foreign ministers as owing to the policy of Israel since the Six Day War. Yet he noted that this did not influence Yugoslavia's basically sympathetic position towards Israel. He mentioned the development of the links between his country and Israel in the areas of commerce, culture, tourism and society, and he added that the 'creation of a positive atmosphere in the Middle East would promote political relations between Israel and Yugoslavia'. (Of note in this context is the opening of an office in Jerusalem by the Yugoslav news agency *Tanjug* in the mid-1980s and publication of interviews with Israeli statesmen in the Yugoslav press by Yugoslav journalists who came to Israel. In both instances, views and opinions from Israel were presented that balanced the picture of the one-sided reporting that was received in Yugoslavia.)

The rationale for initiating the meeting, as defined by the Yugoslav foreign minister, was his country's intention 'to increase in the coming years its involvement in Middle East issues', among other reasons because of its member-ship on the UN Security Council from January 1988. Therefore he wanted to hear directly from Foreign Minister Peres about the political changes that had occurred in Israel regarding the path to the settlement of the Arab-Israeli conflict and what the prevailing differences of opinion on this issue were in Israel. He summarized Yugoslavia's position on this question under the following headings:

1. Convening an international conference was the only way for a settlement of the Arab-Israeli conflict. There

were two preconditions: withdrawal of Israel to the borders on 4 June 1967 and a solution to the Palestinian problem, which was the heart of the conflict. This meant that the PLO should be added to the conference participants, as the legal representative of the Palestinian people.

2. Yugoslavia's position derived in the main from its link to the non-aligned nations.
3. As a Mediterranean country, Yugoslavia had a direct interest in what happened in the Middle East and intended to increase its active involvement in the region.
4. Yugoslavia opposed any aggressive act or annexation. Yet it rejected any attempt to undermine Israel's right to exist and any manifestation of anti-Semitism wherever it might occur.

In his remarks in response, Peres referred to the idea of holding an international conference for the solution of the Arab-Israeli conflict with the five permanent members of the UN Security Council taking part, in the spirit of his speech at the General Assembly. He pointed out that Israel had no reservations concerning the participation of the United States, Britain and France, but that the problems involved the USSR and China. (In his talks with foreign statesmen, Peres usually made it clear to them that the USSR and China in Israel's opinion could not be part of any international conference discussing the solution of the Arab-Israeli conflict, since neither of them had diplomatic relations with Israel. The USSR had broken them, while China had never established them. So, as Israel saw things, they were incapable of being objective participants in an international conference that would involve taking decisions linked to the fate of Israel.)

Regarding the Soviet Union, he said, the problems concerned the nature of the conference, renewal of diplomatic relations with Israel, and the situation of the Jews in the USSR. Peres noted that in his talk with the Soviet foreign minister, Eduard Shevardnadze, within the framework of the UN General Assembly, relative progress had been achieved in all three of these issues. Similarly, he described the differences of opinion within Israel on the issue of an international conference. As to the Palestinian problem, Peres pointed out that self-determination by the Palestinians was not the only solution. The proof was the example of Federal Yugoslavia (although according to the record of the talk, the example of Yugoslavia was not clarified, but the assumption is that the intention was the establishment of a confederation between the Palestinian entity and the Kingdom of Jordan, as then espoused by the leaders of a few parties in Israel).

As for Yugoslavia's link to the Non-Aligned Movement, Peres commented that Tito, Nasser and Nehru were its founding fathers. And now we have a peace treaty with Egypt, with India we have relations, and where is Yugoslavia, he asked. As to Israeli-Yugoslav relations, Peres offered the hope that good relations between the two nations would also be expressed in an improvement in the relations between the two countries, to which the Yugoslav foreign minister replied that progress in this area was the direct result of positive developments for a solution to the Arab-Israeli conflict. Peres responded, saying that 'renewal of diplomatic relations between the two countries is not to be considered a prize or an end in itself. For Israel, this is not an issue of life and death, but we would appreciate it if Yugoslavia would restore the relations that had been broken.'[21]

The discussion between the two concluded with the Yugoslav foreign minister noting that it was important for the dialogue between the representatives of Israel and Yugoslavia to continue and that it would be worthwhile to intensify and strengthen contacts for the purpose of the exchange of opinions, political updates, clarification of positions and political information, and in that context, he proposed that this should be done by means of the two missions to the UN in New York. Foreign Minister Peres, on his part, invited his Yugoslav colleague to visit Israel. This covered the main points of their talk, which perhaps may be described as historic, being the first of its kind after over twenty years.

Even taking the initiative for such a discussion attested to a tactical change in Yugoslavia's approach towards Israel. This was evidenced in the attenuation of the critical tone in its public statements about Israel. The call for the 'right of return' of the Arab refugees (to their homes or their homeland) was not repeated. The demand to impose sanctions on Israel if it did not withdraw to the borders of 4 June 1967 was not heard again, and striking was Yugoslavia's opposition to the Arab proposal for a resolution negating Israel's credentials to the UN. But above all, what was salient in this discussion was Yugoslavia's desire to conduct talks with Israel, prompted by the recognition that its diplomatic severance from Israel had yielded no benefit, either in promoting its status as a mediating factor between parties to the conflict, or in promoting its status in the West. Its connection with the non-aligned nations – as noted by the Yugoslav foreign minister – had placed Yugoslavia in a trap; when aspiring to attain presidency of the movement (at the end of 1988), it apparently thought that renewal of diplomatic relations with Israel would be an obstacle, since most of the non-aligned countries did not have diplomatic relations with Israel. Conversely, there were proven advantages in the renewed relations with Israel by two of the countries in the Soviet Bloc, at the level of Interest Offices, namely Poland and the USSR. Thus, Yugoslavia sought the golden mean, by conducting a political dialogue with Israel, to stress its standing as a committed player in the peace-making process in the Middle East, without this demanding, so it assumed, the necessity to renew diplomatic relations with Israel. Since Yugoslavia was aware of the divided opinion among the Israeli public, and especially among the political parties, over the issue of Israel agreeing to the convening of an international conference for settling the Arab-Israeli conflict – with the Labour Party more in favour than the Likud centre-right party – it was certainly convenient for Yugoslavia to underscore its aim of reinforcing that part of the Israeli public that favoured the idea of holding an international conference and the notion of the Palestinian right to self-determination.

4. Decision by the Foreign Relations Committee of the Yugoslav Parliament Concerning Expanding Relations with Israel

At the end of the discussions that had continued for about two years in the Yugoslav Federal Parliament, at the inspiration of pro-Israeli elements in the Republics of Slovenia and Croatia that were calling for a renewal of diplomatic relations, the Foreign Affairs Committee of the Yugoslav parliament on 1 July 1988 made a decision in which it determined that despite the fact that Israel's foreign policy continued to place a stumbling block in the path towards reinstituting diplomatic relations between the two countries, there was no hindrance preventing Yugoslavia from working for the development of economic, cultural and tourism relations between the two states or from enabling political dialogue with progressive organizations in Israel. In addition, the Foreign Affairs Committee decided to turn to the Yugoslav Interior and Foreign Ministries with a request to simplify the processes for granting entry visas and visitors' visas to Israeli guests.[22] These decisions by the Foreign Affairs Committee of the Yugoslav parliament paved the way for the following:

1. Cancellation of the need for Israeli citizens to receive entry visas to Yugoslavia.
2. Opening of direct flights between Yugoslavia and Israel, through the Slovenian airline, Adria, simultaneously with granting permission for direct flights of the Israeli airline El Al to Yugoslavia. It was in the interests of Yugoslavia to increase the tourist flow from Israel to Yugoslavia, while this was also considered an achievement of some

significance in the area of expanding bilateral relations between the two countries.

3. Intensifying the dialogue between Yugoslav and Israeli statesmen and with representatives of the left-wing parties in Israel – particularly Mapam – what they termed 'progressive circles'.

4. Establishing an Israeli-Yugoslav chamber of commerce in Belgrade and a parallel chamber in Tel Aviv, with the presence of representatives from Yugoslavia.

5. Sending television teams and journalists from Yugoslavia to Israel, who would report even-handedly on political events in Israel and the region, including interviews with the prime minister and his deputy, as well as with other Israeli statesmen.

6. Giving permission to the Yugoslav chief rabbi to participate in Jerusalem in a solidarity conference of world Jewry with Israel.

The decision to expand relations was therefore a compromise between the demand to renew diplomatic relations and opposition to it.

5. Discussion between Foreign Minister Shimon Peres and Yugoslav Foreign Minister Budimir Loncar

The meeting was held in New York on 27 September 1988, when both had come to take part in the opening of the new session of the UN General Assembly. It focused on the problem of the Arab-Israeli conflict and ways to solve it, and on the approach to the PLO from the point of view of each of the sides. Foreign Minister Peres spoke of the tragedy of the Palestinians 'who had not managed to produce responsible leadership from among themselves' and stressed 'the destructive influence of the PLO' on the development of events in the Middle East. While Foreign Minister Lončar talked about 'the need for Israel and the PLO to come closer together', he defined Arafat as a 'moderate, realistic leader', and urged Israel to recognize the right of the Palestinians to self-determination. Peres emphasized the need to conduct direct, open negotiations between the parties to the conflict 'without harassment or coercion' and his belief in a political solution that would be based on Security Council Resolutions 242 and 338. As to Israeli-Yugoslav relations, Peres reiterated what he has said to his colleague's predecessor, a year earlier, concerning Yugoslavia's lack of balance within the framework of the Non-Aligned Movement and that of its three founders (India, Egypt and Yugoslavia): 'Yugoslavia is the only one that does not have diplomatic relations with Israel.' Yet, 'the decision on renewal of diplomatic relations between them', he said, 'is in your hands'. He also noted that 'the lack of purpose in a single, annual meeting'. The Yugoslav minister responded by saying that they (the Yugoslavs) 'were guided by historical and fundamental considerations' and expressed a hope that they would be able to meet again soon.[23]

This talk, like its predecessor, yielded no results concerning the renewal of diplomatic relations between the two countries. Like the previous one, it reflected Yugoslavia's determination, as a member of the leadership of the Non-Aligned Movement, to hold fast to its 'historical and fundamental' position to reinstitute them only after Israel's withdrawal to the borders of 4 June 1967. The positive aspect of the two discussions lay in the fact that Israel was given the opportunity to clarify its approach to the issue of the Arab-Israeli conflict and the means to its resolution, a topic that in Tito's time was considered taboo.

6. Visit by Knesset Member Abba Eban to Yugoslavia

According to the understanding reached between Foreign Minister Peres and Foreign Minister Lončar, when they met at the UN in New York, Knesset Member (MK) Abba Eban paid a visit to Belgrade on 27–29 October 1988, at the end of his visit to Prague. His visits to the two capitals were intended to clarify Israel's policy – and particularly the positions of the Labour Party – concerning the Arab-Israeli conflict and its resolution. On these two visits, Eban was escorted by his parliamentary assistant, Itamar Bartov.[24]

MK Eban held three political discussions in Belgrade: the first, with a member of the 'Socialist Union' (which had held talks even earlier with Mapam activists); the second, with the Defence Committee of the Federal Parliament of Yugoslavia; and the third, with Foreign Minister Lončar. When speaking to each of them, Eban focused on explaining his opinion regarding the need for Israel to end its rule over 1.5 million Palestinians. Israel's definite military superiority would allow it to reach a territorial compromise and to assume the risks involved by demilitarizing the West Bank. Under discussion, he said, was 'a detailed arrangement and not simply leaving the territories'. Yet he mentioned the internal difficulty in Israel of convincing the public to act in this direction. He made it clear that in order to promote the peace process 'there must be a significant change in the Palestinian stance. Maximalism must be abandoned by both sides', the Palestinians must recognize Israel's right to existence and strive for a solution to the conflict on the basis of Security Council Resolutions 242 and 338, as well as relinquish terror.

His discussion with Foreign Minister Lončar, from whom Eban heard the familiar reservations and positions of the Yugoslav leadership on the issue of the Arab-Israeli conflict (unlimited support for the PLO as the sole legal representative of the Palestinian people and Israeli withdrawal to the 4 June 1967 borders, as a condition for the advancement of the peace process), extended to the important role Yugoslavia could play among the non-aligned states in helping to find a solution to the Israel-Arab conflict. This would require 'intensification of the dialogue with Israel' by establishing a permanent framework 'similar to that of the USSR and Poland, an arrangement that would deepen the connection and prevent the current awkwardness in connections under the current situation of relations'.

Foreign Minister Lončar asked not to refer to the circumstances in which diplomatic relations between Yugoslavia and Israel were severed, since 'the background is known to both sides and currently that is a given factual situation'. Conversely, he praised the development of relations 'on the non-diplomatic level' and the fact that media coverage of Israel in Yugoslavia exceeded that of any Arab state. In principle, he said, he was 'for the maintenance of diplomatic relations between all countries, even between countries in a state of war', and he added that 'Yugoslavia has continued all these years to act to attenuate extreme positions against Israel'. He tried to explain that renewal of diplomatic relations between the two countries 'was in opposition to Israel's interests, since Yugoslavia held a position of great influence over the PLO and having official connections to Israel at any level would constitute an obstacle to having Yugoslavia serve as a moderating element accepted by all Arab elements'. He concluded, however, by saying that there should be intensive political dialogue between the two countries and that bilateral relations should be strengthened in the areas of economics, agriculture, commerce and tourism. He even revealed that he had directed the Yugoslav Embassy in Cairo to establish contacts with the Israeli Embassy there, 'thereby founding a comfortable, nearby channel of communication', although he still did not recommend direct relations 'at this stage'.

This was the longest, most in-depth talk conducted by an Israeli statesman and a Yugoslav foreign minister during the period of severed diplomatic relations between the two states. It demonstrated a distinct retreat in Yugoslavia's hostile attitude towards Israel; it also underscored the Yugoslav interest in playing a moderating political role between Israel and the PLO, as well as Yugoslavia's determination to develop closer relations with Israel in the bilateral sphere despite the many economic difficulties in which Yugoslavia found itself – whether as the result of past failures or whether as the result of the aim of moving from a centralized economy to a free market model. Moreover, the conversations conveyed the belief that renewal of diplomatic relations with Israel was liable to cause Yugoslavia more harm in the Arab world and damage its position as head of the non-aligned nations, which would outweigh any benefit that might accrue from reinstitution of diplomatic relations with Israel.

In light of this background the question arises: was the Yugoslav claim – made for the first time to an Israeli statesman – that renewal of diplomatic relations with Israel was liable to weaken its influence over the PLO – indeed the genuine reason, or perhaps an excuse to postpone a decision on renewal of relations? Moreover, if, as argued by Yugoslavia, the PLO had moderated its positions regarding Israel, then there was no longer any need to attenuate it. And if there was a reason to moderate the PLO's policies towards Israel, that would indicate that the PLO had not become more moderate. In addition, the continuation of severed relations with Israel was more likely to reinforce the PLO's extremist attitudes than to weaken its ambition to annihilate the State of Israel, according to the two-stage theory it had held. Thus, it appeared that more than anything Yugoslavia feared for its own position and economic interests in the Arab countries, especially in Libya and Iraq, and among the non-aligned states. Yugoslavia therefore chose to take a middle path: to carry on a dialogue with Israel towards a settlement to the Arab-Israeli conflict coupled with expansion of bilateral contacts with Israel. But, renewal of diplomatic relations, with no change in the Israeli position in the direction that Yugoslavia expected, – by no means! To this one must add the supposition that the Yugoslav leadership felt, at that time, that being chairman of the non-aligned nations gave Yugoslavia the status of a mediating factor in its own right, between the parties involved in the Israel-Arab conflict, without having to pay for that the price of renewal of diplomatic relations with Israel.

7. Yugoslav Foreign Minister Lončar on the PLO and Renewal of Diplomatic Relations with Israel

As part of the interview granted by Foreign Minister Lončar to the Reuters news agency on 30 August 1989, towards the summit meeting of the Non-Aligned Movement in Nicosia, he was asked, 'Yugoslavia has persistently supported the PLO, in the context of the Israel-Arab conflict, in its refusal to renew diplomatic relations with Israel. Do you feel that its mediation in the Middle East dispute would have been more effective, if it had taken a more neutral position and had, at least, re-established relations with Tel Aviv?' He replied:

> Support for the PLO, and for the legitimate demands of a people whose sole and legitimate representative of their own free will is the PLO, that is one thing, and the renewal of diplomatic relations with Israel is another. Possibilities for the latter have never ceased to exist just as for Israel, too, there have always been enough possibilities to leave the occupied territories. A principled stance which becomes a dogma is not a virtue, far from it. However, any relationship must rest at least on some basic principles. Yugoslavia's influence might have been more productive if it had diplomatic relations with Tel Aviv. But, would this of itself have altered substantially Israel's attitude towards the Middle East crisis? If we were so self-assured, we should ourselves come out with proposals to Israel for a change in the order of preferences, one should be realistic in politics. Formally, we do not have inter-state relations, but we do have diversified rapports and communication with Israel. We want to expand this cooperation, not only for the sake of possible support to the peaceful forces on Israel's political scene, but also because of the strong and emotional ties, in particular with the Israelis whose former homeland was Yugoslavia.[25]

Yugoslavia's official position – on both the issue of the

Arab-Israeli conflict and that of relations with Israel – was also expressed during the discussion between Foreign Minister Arens and Foreign Minister Lončar at their meeting on 3 October 1989, which took place during the UN General Assembly. At this meeting the Yugoslav foreign minister stated explicitly that in light of Yugoslavia being the chairman of the non-aligned nations, it could not renew its relations with Israel. This fact, he said, need not prevent the two sides from carrying on a political dialogue. Differences of opinion between the two ministers came to the fore also regarding attitudes towards the PLO, when the Yugoslav foreign minister expressed his disagreement with Israel's view that the PLO was an obstacle to peace. As he saw it, he said, the PLO was a moderate organization, 'and so is the person who heads it'. Moreover, he noted that he did not believe that the political process could advance without the PLO, which was considered a 'major factor' in the Arab world. Foreign Minister Arens disputed this.[26]

It seems that the only issue on which they both agreed was the mutual desire to continue a dialogue on ways to solve the Arab-Israeli conflict; Yugoslavia, out of its interest to demonstrate involvement in promoting the peace process in the Middle East, as chairman of the non-aligned nations, and Israel, out of its interest in presenting to the Yugoslav leadership its opinions on the way to solve the conflict, giving consideration to Yugoslavia's standing among the non-aligned states, including the Arab countries. In addition, Israel had come forward at that time with its own peace plan. Israel certainly hoped that through this dialogue it would be possible to pursuade Yugoslavia to renew diplomatic relations, as had begun to occur with the other East European countries. Although – and the Yugoslav foreign minister clarified this in his talk with Foreign Minister Arens – there was a difference between those states of Eastern Europe which were satellites of the USSR and Yugoslavia as a member of the leadership of the non-aligned nations, most of which did not have diplomatic relations with Israel; moreover those that had severed relations at the time were in no hurry to renew them.

8. Public and Parliamentary Pressure in Yugoslavia for the Renewal of Relations with Israel

Alexander Perlja, the foreign minister of Serbia, the largest among the six republics comprising Federal Yugoslavia, arrived in Israel for a visit, which was defined as private, on 12–17 December 1989. He was assisted by the journalist Raoul Teitelbaum in the organization of his meetings and excursions; Teitelbaum published articles in the Yugoslav paper *Politika*, of which he was the editor.

During Perlja's stay I hosted a luncheon for him by virtue of my role as deputy director general of the Foreign Ministry. We devoted our talk to Yugoslavia's internal issues, and to the possibility of expanding relations between Israel and Yugoslavia, including the operation of direct flights from Israel to Belgrade to be operated by the Yugoslavian company JAT, a competitor of the Slovenian airline, Adria; in this context, Perlja also met with Minister of Transport Moshe Katzav. And naturally, we also discussed the enigma of the lack of diplomatic relations between Yugoslavia and Israel, while such relations were maintained with Egypt.

The minister opened with an evaluative statement according to which Yugoslavia as a state had effectively ceased to exist since Tito's death. He described extensively the Yugoslav government's weakness in contrast to the increased influence of the federal republics that constituted the state, with Serbia being the largest and most important among these. In the current situation, the small federal republics, such as Bosnia, could forbid the Yugoslav government to conduct diplomatic relations with Israel. Likewise, Serbia did want diplomatic relations with Israel and was urging the central government in that direction. It had also been the Republic that had opposed breaking relations with Israel in the first place, despite Tito's opinion. One of the main factors, in his opinion, for the continuation of severed relations between his country and Israel derived from the inability of the weak Yugoslav leadership to deviate from the policy that Tito had delineated towards Israel. At the same time, he stressed that public opinion in Yugoslavia vigorously demanded the renewal of diplomatic relations with Israel. He saw a good opportunity in the (rotational) change in the Yugoslav presidency in spring 1990, when it was anticipated that the person in charge would be the Serbian leader Slobodan Milosevic, and with the influence of Perlja himself, this bold step in the direction of renewal of relations would be taken. In addition, the Serbian foreign minister noted that at the end of November 1989 the Federal Parliament would hold a discussion on the renewal of relations with Israel, and he had no doubt that 'the conclusion of the deliberations would be positive', and that he personally intended to assist in that.[27]

On his return from his visit to Israel, the foreign minister of Serbia held a press conference in Belgrade, on 7 November 1989, which provoked extensive reactions in the Yugoslav media. The main motif in his statements was the absurdity of a lack of diplomatic relations between Yugoslavia and Israel, and the call for their rapid resumption. He reiterated the argument in an enthusiastic article he published about his visit and his talks in the journal *Politika* on 29 November. His words also provoked extensive debate in the parliament. In response to parliamentary questions submitted concerning the authority of the foreign minister of Serbia to make such declarations, Yugoslav Foreign Minister Lončar responded that the time was not yet right for renewal of relations with Israel and that Yugoslavia would do so when significant progress had been discerned in the settlement of the Arab-Israeli conflict.[28] This reply was given by the deputy foreign minister of Yugoslavia, Milivoje Maksic, to the Arab diplomatic mission that had presented itself to him, prior to the parliamentary discussion, to warn him that there would be repercussions to these declarations on the status and role of Yugoslavia among the non-aligned nations and on its relations with Arab countries.[29]

The discussion of the Foreign Affairs Committee in the Yugoslav parliament on the renewal of diplomatic relations with Israel opened on 23 November 1989, with Serbia and Slovenia calling for their rapid reinstitution (its importance is in that two of the republics in conflict between themselves demonstrated a united front on this issue). A year earlier a similar discussion had been held in the parliament and its summation was in the spirit of the statements of response that were heard this time, too, from the Yugoslav foreign minister. Yet the value of the parliamentary discussion was more public than essential, since at that time it did not have the power to change the position of the Yugoslav government. It did, however, have cumulative weight among the Yugoslav public, which did press their government to alter its policy towards Israel, signifying thereby a transitional stage from discussion of this issue in the Yugoslav media to a broader discussion that included statesmen and members of parliament. The government, however, remained in a defensive position in the face of its critics, and in a dilemma regarding itself, without knowing which course to choose: whether renewal of diplomatic relations with Israel was liable to harm its relations with Arab countries and with the non-aligned nations, or whether renewing them would be likely to contribute to the national unity of the republics comprising Yugoslavia and thereby strengthen the central Yugoslav government that has been considerably weakened after Tito's death. This dilemma apparently led to the idea of following a middle-of-the-road path: instead of renewing relations with Israel at the diplomatic level, Yugoslavia would do so at the consular level. By doing so, the Yugoslav government seemingly thought that proceeding along the middle path would enable it to mollify the public and Yugoslav statesmen, on the one hand, while not endangering its relations with Arab countries and its status among the non-aligned states, on the other.

9. Proposals by the Yugoslav Government for the Establishment of Relations with Israel at the Economic-Commerce and Consular Level

Initial contact on the part of Yugoslavia about establishing relations with Israel at the level of mutual chambers of commerce and later at the consular level was made by the Yugoslav MP Miran Jejak during his visit to Israel in January 1990 as a guest of the speaker of the Knesset, Dov Shilansky, after the two had met at an assembly of the Inter-Parliamentary Union held in London. In the Yugoslav parliament, Jejak served as president of the Chamber of Republics and Provinces, a function which placed him among the heads of the parliamentary hierarchy in his country. In my talk with him on 8 January 1990 at the East European Department of the Foreign Ministry in Jerusalem, Jejak pointed out that, in his opinion, the process of renewal of mutual relations had to be carried out cautiously, 'step by step', and that there was a prospect for the opening of reciprocal chambers of commerce in which it would be possible to post a consular official (at an unofficial level). I summarily rejected this suggestion and underscored the importance of renewing mutual relations on an open and conventionally diplomatic level. I reminded him that Tito had played a most important role in causing the break in relations of the East European countries with Israel, with the exception of Romania. Many years had passed since then. Tito had acted in this way owing to his friendship with Nasser, and neither of them was alive. Israel had diplomatic relations with Egypt, but relations with Yugoslavia – which Israel had aided in the most difficult period in its history – were severed. I asked him, what was preventing Yugoslavia today from renewing diplomatic relations with Israel? Indeed, there had never been a confrontation between Israel and Yugoslavia. Moreover, experience had proven that maintaining relations between countries could only strengthen the system of international relations. Jejak at first argued that Yugoslavia had not renewed it diplomatic relations with Israel to date 'because of its extensive commercial ties with Arab countries', and he went on to claim that Israel's agreement to convene an international conference for the settlement of the Arab-Israeli conflict 'could help the renewal of relations'.

I made it clear to him that Israel could not waive its own interests in exchange for normal relations between itself and another country and that, in general, one must differentiate between normalization and development of relations between two states and regional conflicts. As to the guest's question, did Israel have any (pre-)conditions concerning renewal of diplomatic relations with his country? I replied that it was only natural that Yugoslavia, which had broken its diplomatic relations with Israel, would initiate their reinstitution and that I did not see any obstacle on the part of Israel in responding positively to such an initiative by Yugoslavia, if it were proposed, at the embassy level.[30]

On 28 February 1990, Dragoslav Pavic, the Yugoslav ambassador to the UN, met, at his request, with Israel's ambassador to the UN, Johanan Bein. He asked him to transmit a message to the Israeli government stating that the government of Yugoslavia had decided to propose to the government of Israel the establishment of consular and economic representations in Belgrade and Tel Aviv through which political issues would be treated and developed. His government, he said, was aware that a number of East European countries had recently established full diplomatic relations with Israel, but Yugoslavia was not a member of the Warsaw Pact and its consideration for breaking its diplomatic relations with Israel in June 1967 coincided with the position of the non-aligned nations. He concluded by saying that the government of Yugoslavia would appreciate it if the Israel government would understand his government's position and agree to this step, which would lead towards full diplomatic relations. The Yugoslav government considered this an important step, and this decision had been preceded by many discussions among the ministers of the Yugoslav government and had been accepted by consensus. Its aim was to use this stage to move towards full diplomatic relations at the right time.

Ambassador Bein wondered why it was necessary to renew relations in two stages, since they could be reinstituted in the first stage. To which his Yugoslav colleague had no reply. He only reiterated his request for the Israeli government to give serious thought to the topic, to understand the considerations of the Yugoslav government, and accept its proposal.[31] Support for this message can be found in the declaration of the Yugoslav president, Janez Drnovsek, at the end of his official meeting in Cairo on 28 February 1990 (actually on the same day that the ambassadors of Israel and Yugoslavia met at the UN), that his country would establish full diplomatic relations with Israel only if there were progress towards peace in the Middle East. Yet, he said, Yugoslavia was willing to discuss establishing consular relations with Israel, remarking, 'Now we are ready to discuss with Israel a certain format for economic or consular representation, because we do have some economic connections. Many tourists visit each of the countries.' He added that Yugoslavia was interested, of course, in enjoying normal relations with all states, but it still hoped that it would be possible to achieve a certain amount of progress in the efforts towards peace in the Middle East so as to create the conditions that would allow (establishment) of full diplomatic relations with Israel. And he concluded, 'Our orientation is to normalize relations with Israel. We have declared in the past that we hope that progress will soon be discerned in the advancement of finding a solution to the Middle East crisis, so that conditions will come into being for normalization of relations with Israel.'[32]

One may assume that the president of Yugoslavia chose to say these things in public, precisely in an Arab country that had diplomatic relations with Israel, in order to examine the response of the other Arab states in preparing the way towards the renewal of full diplomatic relations with Israel. Likewise, it may be presumed that the Yugoslav government assumed that Israel would agree to its proposal to establish relations with Yugoslavia on a consular level, as it had reconciled itself to doing so with two of the Warsaw Pact countries – the USSR and Poland – as a first stage towards full diplomatic relations between them. At that time, however, Israel's diplomatic relations had been restored with Hungary, Poland and Czechoslovakia and were about to be renewed with Bulgaria. (The USSR was then the only country in which Israel had agreed to post a chargé d'affaires over Israel's interests under the aegis of the Dutch embassy in Moscow, who represented Israel's interests in the USSR, and this stemmed from Israel's interest in enabling the Jewish USSR residents to emigrate to Israel.) As a contribution to a discussion of the leadership of the Foreign Ministry called 'Whether to Answer Positively to the Appeal of the Yugoslav Government to Establish Consular Relations with Israel', I expressed my negative opinion. In a memorandum I sent on 4 March 1990 to Foreign Minister Arens, to Deputy Foreign Minister Benjamin Netanyahu and to General Director of the Foreign Ministry Reuven Merhav, I explained my position as follows:

> There is nothing new in the Yugoslav proposal to estab-
> lish consular relations with Israel, except that in the past
> this proposal was suggested by its emissaries, while this
> time it is official. We summarily rejected the unofficial
> proposal and it seems that this time too we must reject
> it. The Yugoslav government is in a trap. On one side, it
> is under unceasing pressure from public opinion in its
> country – including leaders of the republics of Serbia

and Slovenia – to renew diplomatic relations with Israel, for three main reasons:

A Repairing the historical injustice done to Israel as a result of the breaking of diplomatic relations, as ordered by Tito.
B Yugoslavia lost its ability to play a constructive role in the Middle East by being disconnected from Israel.
C Its connections with Israel might have been able to reinforce its political standing in the international arena and its economic situation in the national arena.

On the other side, it fears that its leadership of the non-aligned nations and its economic ties with Arab countries are liable to suffer damage as a result of the renewal of its diplomatic relations with Israel. Apparently for these reasons, it formulated its proposal to choose a middle path: establishing consular and economic relations so as to release itself from public pressure without endangering its standing in the Arab world or among the non-aligned nations.

If we were to reply positively, we would help it extricate itself from the trap. To be sure, our presence in Belgrade is likely to lead to full diplomatic relations in the course of time. But regarding this intermediate stage, it is difficult to estimate whether it will be short- or long-term. It is reasonable to assume that the Yugoslav authorities will take all the measures necessary to give these relations a straightforward consular nature – even if it was hinted to us that via these relations it would be possible 'to develop political issues'. Moreover, it will consider itself obligated to balance its relations with Arab countries by attacking our policy [...] If we reply in the negative, we will assist Yugoslav public opinion to continue its pressure on the federal government to renew diplomatic relations with us, and perhaps we will also cause it to make its declaration about Israel less hostile than in a period of consular relations.

In conclusion, the establishment of consular relations – in lieu of renewing diplomatic relations – is not a necessity of the moment or an achievement of Israel's foreign policy, and particularly in light of the renewal our diplomatic relations with Hungary, Czechoslovakia, Poland and in the coming month with Bulgaria.[33]

My opinion was accepted.

At the beginning of May 1990, a special envoy of the Yugoslav government visited Israel, Ambassador Milan Zupan. In a discussion with me at the Foreign Ministry in Jerusalem, he noted the importance of his official visit by its being the first of its kind since the break in diplomatic relations between Yugoslavia and Israel 'and as an indication of his government's orientation, namely – the aim of renewing relations with Israel'. He had brought with him a proposal from the Yugoslav foreign minister to establish representations in Belgrade and Tel Aviv (which it was later clarified would have no diplomatic status) that would deal with the development of tourism and economic and commercial ties, and would be an open channel of communication between the two governments, something that would make easier and expedite the renewal of diplomatic relations between the two countries. These representations, he said, were intended to serve as a gradual step, with the final goal being the resumption of full diplomatic relations. This step, he explained, was temporary since his country was serving as chairman of the Non-Aligned Movement and it had obligations that differed from those of other East European countries which had recently renewed their diplomatic relations with Israel.

In response to his remarks, I noted our disappointment with Yugoslavia's decision to sever diplomatic relations with Israel in 1967 – precisely for motives that differed from those of the other East European countries – and our disappointment at the one-sided approach of the non-aligned nations on the issue of the Arab-Israeli conflict, which did not serve the advancement of peace in our regions. I reviewed the development of the renewal of full diplomatic relations of Israel with East European countries, I pointed out that it had been shown that the establishment of Interest Offices between Israel and Poland – as a precursor to the reinstitution of diplomatic relations between them – had taken too long and had led us to the conclusion that it was not worthwhile repeating. Times had changed and it had been shown – as in the case of Spain – that establishment of diplomatic relations with Israel did not harm a country's trade with Arab countries. I stressed our desire to refrain from taking 'gradual steps' towards the full renewal of mutual relations, and I proposed continuing with the political dialogue between the two countries, until Yugoslavia would feel that the conditions were right for the full reinstitution of relations with Israel.

This same tone was reiterated in the discussion between Ambassador Zupan and Deputy Foreign Minister Netanyahu, and with the director general of the Foreign Ministry, Reuven Merhav.[34] During his visit to Israel, Ambassador Zupan met with MK Shimon Peres, chairman of the Alignment Party; with MK Eliahu Ben Elissar, chairman of the Foreign Affairs and Defence Committee; with Reuven Dafni, deputy chairman of the Yad Vashem Directorate, and with members of kibbutz Sha'ar Ha' Amekim.

On 15 May 1990 Foreign Minister Budimir Loncar and Special Envoy Milan Zupan were invited to a meeting of the Foreign Affairs Committee of the Federal Yugoslav Parliament, and Special Envoy Zupan gave a report on his visit to Israel. During the course of the committee's discussion Foreign Minister Loncar noted that 'it is now easier than in 1967 to evaluate that the severance of diplomatic relations with Israel was a mistake. Yet, it would be an even more serious error to justify it today. Differences of opinion cannot justify breaking relations. For when there are diplomatic relations, it is easier to settle them.' Similarly he pointed out that 'no dilemma exists concerning the issue of whether to renew diplomatic relations with Israel, but they intend (the Foreign Ministry and/or the Yugoslav government? – actually, it made no difference) to do so in a reasoned manner and in protection of the Yugoslav and the Israeli interests and the standing of Yugoslavia in the Middle East'.

In his response to Ambassador Zupan's report and to the comments by Foreign Minister Lončar, the committee chairman, Alexander Simovic, said that the Foreign Ministry's approach had undergone a revolutionary change in contrast to the previous discussion held in November 1989 on the issue of the renewal of Yugoslavia's diplomatic relations with Israel. He expressed doubts about the logic in postponing the final step, since at the time of Ambassador Zupan's visit to Israel, Israel had announced that it would not be satisfied with anything less than full resumption of diplomatic relations, and the hesitation of the Yugoslav government enabled the Arab side to impose pressure (on Yugoslavia) despite its also being clear to it that full normalization of relations was unavoidable.[35]

On 17 May 1990, the plenum of the Federal Parliament held a discussion on Yugoslavia's foreign relations. In the course of that session, Foreign Minister Lončar stated that Yugoslavia was striving to attain renewal of diplomatic relations with Israel (without noting any date). The fact that the special envoy of the Yugoslav government had been invited to the Foreign Affairs Committee of the Federal Parliament to report to its members on the results of his mission to Israel, accompanied by the Yugoslav foreign minister, attests to the importance attributed to this mission. Salient in the statements of the foreign minister who expressed himself, for the first time, in favour of the renewal of diplomatic relations with Israel, was the aim to prepare the way towards a decision for their renewal. And it might be that in publication of the statements, there was a double goal: (a) to examine the response of Arab countries and of the non-aligned nations; (b) to respond to pressure by Yugoslav public opinion that called vigorously for the swift renewal of relations with Israel.

This double aim was also given expression in an interview, the first of its kind, that the Yugoslav Foreign Minister Lončar granted to Teddy Preus, a writer for the Israeli newspaper *Davar*, that was given great prominence in the issue of 20 May 1990, in which he said, that 'Israel had announced that it wants diplomatic relations [with Yugoslavia]. We are now examining the international circumstances, considering the scope of our interests and needs, if they demand a turnabout. Israel on its part is acting in a similar manner, and in this spirit we have reached an agreement that neither of the parties will pressure the other in any way and that relations will be implemented when the two sides find the proper time for that.' He added further that 'the day of establishing diplomatic relations [between Yugoslavia and Israel] was approaching and that even now the relations between the two countries were more extensive than between many [world] capitals in which the Yugoslavian flag is flying'.

10. Final Milestones towards the Renewal of Diplomatic Relations with Israel

Despite the call of the chairman of the Foreign Affairs Committee of the Federal Parliament, and despite the announcement by Foreign Minister Lončar in favour of renewing diplomatic relations with Israel, Yugoslavia's considerations and reservations over this issue continued for about a year and a half, from the time they were voiced in public (May 1990) until the exchange of letters by the two foreign ministers on the renewal of diplomatic relations between the two countries (October 1991). Two additional milestones were reached in the political dialogue between the representatives of Yugoslavia and Israel, as we shall see below.

The first was the discussion between Deputy Prime

Minister and Foreign Minister David Levy with the Yugoslav foreign minister during the UN General Assembly in September 1990. In this talk the Yugoslav foreign minister revealed that the decision about renewal of his country's relations with Israel had already been accepted in principle by his government. The only issue remaining was to determine the proper timing with Israel. He proposed inviting Minister Levy for an official visit to Belgrade. He could not promise that during the course of that visit renewal of diplomatic relations between the two states would be declared, but the visit would not weaken the decision to renew relations as soon as possible. If he himself could not attend, perhaps he might send his deputy? Minister Levy thanked him for the invitation and noted that the basis had not been created for a visit, and he added that Israel did not intend to urge its government to renew his country's diplomatic relations with Israel. If and when they made a decision, they would certainly inform him.[36]

This was the third discussion between Yugoslav and Israeli foreign ministers to take place during the UN General Assembly. The innovation, this time, was in the Yugoslav foreign minister's striking admission that a decision in principle had been taken by the Yugoslav government about the renewal of relations with Israel and in his initiative to invite the foreign minister of Israel for a visit to Belgrade, though not officially – a tactic that was quite typical of the caution that the Yugoslav government exercised towards Israel – a caution that can be defined by Lenin's famous saying, 'One step forward, two steps back'. The second milestone was my official invitation to visit Belgrade, by virtue of my role as deputy director general of the Foreign Ministry in charge of the East European Department (after the dissolution of the USSR, the Department I headed became the CIS Department – for the former republics of the USSR – Eastern and Central Europe) and my being the person who was much involved

276

with the process of the renewal of diplomatic relations of Israel with the East European countries (Yugoslavia among them) that had been broken at the end of the Six Day War.

My visit to Belgrade took place on 28–30 May 1991. It was considered a reciprocal visit in exchange for the visit to Israel by the Yugoslav special envoy, Ambassador Zupan. This was the first time that a staff member of Israel's Foreign Ministry had been invited to pay an official visit to the capital of Yugoslavia as a guest of the government. Since this was the first series of talks involving anyone from Israel's Foreign Ministry in Belgrade during the period of severed diplomatic relations between the two countries, and the last in a series of talks that Israeli representatives conducted with representatives of Yugoslavia before the renewal of diplomatic relations, I will cover at length the content of the talks I held with government officials, which were characterized, on the one hand, by a gap between the positions of the two sides, while being remarkable, on the other, for their congenial atmosphere and the desires of the hosts to show a greater degree of hospitality than was normally awarded to a guest at ministerial level. A programme of meetings was prepared for me with Foreign Minister Lončar; with his deputy, Branco Lukovac; with Alexander Simovic, chairman of the Foreign Affairs Committee of the Federal Parliament; and with Ranko Petkovic, chief editor of the monthly *International Relations*, which was distributed in English, French, Spanish, Russian, German and Serbo-Croatian. In addition to those talks, I held others with the head of the Middle East Section in the Yugoslav Foreign Ministry, Dušan Simeonovic, who escorted me to all my political meetings as well as to a meeting with members of the Belgrade Jewish community, to whom I lectured about Israel, also to a discussion with the community leaders, and a talk with the Belgian ambassador to Belgrade, who represented Israel's interests in Yugoslavia during the period of severed diplomatic relations. The talks centred on bilateral issues concerning Israeli-Yugoslav relations and the Arab-Israeli conflict. I presented the peacemaking process in our region against the background of the changes that had taken place in relations between the United States and the USSR and within the Arab world itself. I gave reasoned explanations for our reservations about conducting talks with the PLO and about the UN participating in a peace conference. I stressed the principle of direct negotiations against the backdrop of Arab hostility and the roots of the Arab-Israeli conflict, the proposal agreeable to us, the USSR, the United States, and some of our neighbours for following a two-track route. I went on to describe the temporary solution of 'self-administration' and the willingness of Israel to discuss regional issues (ecology, development of water and energy sources) and our call for the discussion of the limitation of the arms race, while expressing the hope that Iraq's threatening weapons would be destroyed and that the world's arms suppliers would refrain from starting an arms race in the Middle East. As for the bilateral area, I pointed out a number of developments that had remained rather inchoate. And without referring directly to the issue of the renewal of diplomatic relations, I pointed out that our relations would certainly develop in all areas by paying attention to good will, to our traditional relations, and to the potential that existed, if and when they took on an official and normal nature. Until then, I suggested ways to make connections between the two foreign ministries closer in a more direct manner. My talk with Foreign Minister Lončar was most comprehensive. His statements focused on Yugoslav-Israeli relations, the role of Yugoslavia in the leadership of the non-aligned nations, and of course, the Arab-Israeli conflict. Below I cite the essence of the statements he made then, which I felt were the most all-encompassing and candid of those expressed up to that moment.

First, he expressed a desire for full cooperation between

the two foreign ministers; his government had no problem at all concerning renewal of diplomatic relations. The decision on that had already been taken. Yet the proper time had to be determined (these were statements he had made before), and in any event, this would take place very soon. He asked us to believe this and to find the patience to refrain from applying pressure concerning renewal of diplomatic relations. He again proposed that Foreign Minister David Levy pay a visit to Yugoslavia, or alternately, he himself was ready to pay a visit to Israel.

Second, within the Non-Aligned Movement, Yugoslavia had taken a stance for the restraint of extremists, and that was the main role they saw themselves playing in leadership of the movement. In this spirit, Yugoslavia opposed any extreme anti-Israeli resolutions, while the Latin American states that did maintain diplomatic relations with Israel kept quiet. From his remarks one may understand that Yugoslavia played a mollifying, constructive role for the benefit of Israel among the leadership of the non-aligned countries, perhaps owing to the fact that the two countries did not maintain diplomatic relations.

Third, as to the peace process: Yugoslavia supported the initiative of United States Foreign Minister James Baker (referring to the convening of a peace conference in Madrid), and it considered the USSR's approach to be positive. In his estimation, the attitude of the European Union was balanced and constructive. He himself was realistic in his assumption that the United States had the leading role. The PLO, as far as he was concerned, was still a factor among the Palestinians and the significance of the non-aligned nations should not be diminished (he was referring, apparently, to the post-cold war era). There was a strong desire on the part of the PLO, Arab countries, and the non-aligned nations to discuss the Middle East peace process, and the Yugoslav chairman, according to his instruction as foreign minister, had succeeded in removing the proposal from the agenda, for fear lest it have a negative influence. Yugoslavia was interested in the success of the process, as implemented by the US Foreign Minister James Baker. According to his statement, Foreign Minister Loncar was in permanent contact over this issue with the foreign ministers of the USSR and the United States (apparently, through the role of Yugoslavia as chairman of the non-aligned states).

And fourth, he concluded by stating that he was very happy that I had 'finally' agreed to their invitation and would be their guest in Belgrade. He expressed his confidence that there would be a productive continuation to our contacts and his hope for a forthcoming meeting with Foreign Minister Levy in Yugoslavia or in Israel – and if not – then soon at the UN. He stressed again that renewal of diplomatic relations between our two countries was closer than I had assumed.

In light of the minister's statements I asked to clarify:

1. That the renewal of diplomatic relations did not have to be conditional upon any regional or international event.
2. The normal existence of relations between countries was intended to reinforce the international system of relations and not to weaken them.
3. Resumption of relations must serve the interests of both countries and certainly could not be considered as a prize for one of them. I noted that if interest existed, I could not understand why the process should be suspended, for our relations in all areas could not develop in the way the two sides wished without their renewal. I assured him that from our side no pressure had been applied in the past, nor was it being imposed in the present. I quoted to him what I had once said to the USSR ambassador in Bucharest, when we discussed the issue of USSR-Israeli relations, that our two countries had proven that they could honourably exist even without their having diplomatic relations between them, and that it was only a pity that time had been

wasted owing to the break in relations between them. To that the Foreign Minister Lončar remarked that in the Middle East, too, precious time had been wasted without achieving peace. I responded that the example was not apt for the conclusion drawn from it, and that not only had the lengthening of the Arab-Israeli conflict not been caused by us, but that the massive political and military aid that our neighbours had received from the USSR and the East European countries was understood by them as acceptance of – but not agreement with – their aspiration to annihilate us.

I noted that I had not come to make a historical evaluation as to the development of the events in our region, even though it was important that any future discussion be based on fundamental facts, for the purpose of deepening understanding of the Arab-Israeli conflict, which by its nature was long and complicated and could not be solved in a day. I concluded by saying that my visit to Belgrade, as a continuation of the political dialogue that we had begun at the initiative of Yugoslavia, attested to the interest to gain better knowledge of the positions of the two sides and that it was clear to me that a break of twenty-four years could not be bridged in one or two talks. I supported the idea of frequent meetings between us towards diminishing the gap in our positions as much as possible and for laying a foundation for mutual trust within the framework of normal relations.

Deputy Foreign Minister Lukovac said that the Yugoslavs were satisfied by the growing scope of bilateral relations, and by the political contacts between representatives of Israel and Yugoslavia (in New York, Jerusalem and now Belgrade). They asked to continue with them at the levels of Foreign Ministries, foreign ministers, parliaments and government and public institutions. They were ready for exchanges of economic delegations (in response to the proposal by Yaacov Cohen, deputy director general for economic affairs of the Foreign Ministry in Jerusalem, on the subject of lowering taxes). Likewise, they were ready to invite the minister of transport, Moshe Katzav, to the signing of the parties to the aviation agreement (until then the agreement had only been initialled) and to respond to any initiative on our part in the other areas that would ensure the continued development of mutual relations. He reacted happily to my proposals to receive information about Israel and to maintain a direct connection between the two foreign ministries, without having recourse to intermediaries, such as through our UN missions or through our ambassadors in Egypt (as contacts had been conducted hitherto).

Deputy Foreign Minister Lukovac further said that the Yugoslavs were interested in a dialogue with us and wished to know if they would be able to be of assistance within the framework of their relations with Arab countries, the Palestinians and the non-aligned nations. I replied that if they were able to help in bringing Arab countries to the table for direct negotiations towards peace, they would be most welcome. Yet I assumed that their sphere of influence would certainly be limited, even though their efforts would be accompanied by sincere, constructive intentions, since we considered Yugoslavia as a country conducting a one-sided policy on the issue of the Arab-Israeli conflict, beyond our not having diplomatic relations with it.

As to the suggestion of a meeting between our ministers – in Israel or Yugoslavia – (which was reiterated also in the talk with the deputy foreign minister), I expressed my hope that it would be a 'historic meeting', and not just like all its predecessors. The deputy foreign minister concluded the talk by saying that he anticipated the renewal of diplomatic relations between our two countries 'very soon' and the better times that would follow, with links of friendship and prosperity between our two states and our nations.[37]

Even though my visit was reciprocal to that of the special envoy of the Yugoslav Foreign Ministry who had come to Israel a year earlier as our guest, it differed in the scope of talks and their content. The Yugoslav hosts treated my visit as if it were a state visit at the ministerial level. They tried to endow each meeting with a friendly atmosphere and to give us confidence that the renewal of diplomatic relations between the two countries was coming very soon. The media coverage of the visit was prominent and extensive, including a number of interviews arranged for me with the local press. Underscored in the general review was the announcement by Foreign Minister Lončar, namely, that it had been decided to resume relations with Israel soon, but that a date had not yet been determined.

In my report on my impressions of my visit to Belgrade, on my return to Jerusalem, I indicated that the intention of the visit had, apparently, been: (a) to prepare public opinion for the renewal of diplomatic relations with Israel, so that it would not be a drastic shift between their freeze and their actual resumption; (b) to reduce the pressure of local public opinion in favour of a rapid renewal of relations; (c) to acquire our trust; (d) to allude to their relations with the Arab countries and non-aligned nations which might enable them to contribute positively to the peacemaking process in our region.

As for the Yugoslav interest in renewing diplomatic relations with Israel, I noted:

1. In light of the specific significance of the non-aligned countries in the inter-bloc confrontation, as a result of the rapprochement between East and West, Yugoslavia was seeking for itself 'the right to exist' by means of searching for solutions to the focal point of the Arab-Israeli conflict. Its relations with Israel would enable Yugoslavia to negotiate with the parties to the conflict, something from which they had been excluded until now, and to enhance its prestige in the Non-Aligned Movement itself, in the eyes of the great powers and in the international arena.

2. The severe crisis Yugoslavia was suffering internally,

threatened with the danger of the dissolution of the covenant between the republics, on the one hand, and the danger of constant inflation and ongoing economic crises on the other, was forcing it to rely evermore on the United States and Western Europe, and it therefore had to improve its image among them. Yugoslavia needed their good will – for example, by constructing sympathetic public opinion – to receive economic aid and to strengthen the status of its central regime. Yugoslavia had to change its image as a quasi-communist country, modelled on the non-aligned nations, and resumed relations with Israel were likely to enable it to appear more 'fashionable' and as the possessor of a progressive policy.

3. Relations with Israel were likely to be of benefit in improving the economic situation through technological and scientific cooperation in all of its economic systems. The Yugoslav government felt that it might be that the renewal of its diplomatic relations with Israel would also make it eligible for investments by the wealthy the world over, including the Jews among them.

As to Israeli interest in the renewal of diplomatic relations with Yugoslavia, I noted that even if the importance of the non-aligned nations had declined, they still had considerable influence in the UN arena. Resumption of Israel's relations with Yugoslavia were likely to reduce the extent of hostility on their part towards Israel and to signal to the Arab countries that the leadership of the non-aligned nations was abandoning its ideology of ostracizing Israel. In the bilateral sphere, the increase in commercial and economic relations was indeed to be expected, but this goal, even if it were to be attained, would not have the same value as the renewal of diplomatic relations that might be influential in the arenas of the non-aligned nations and the UN.

In conclusion, I noted, that resumption of Israeli-Yugoslav relations at this stage (after they had already been renewed between the former Warsaw Pact countries) seemed to be more of a Yugoslav priority than an Israeli one. Even so, I would recommend that we encourage the Yugoslav goals, in order to complete the circle of normalizing our relations with all the East European countries. That would be decisive proof of the justice of Israel's path. The uniqueness of the Yugoslavia case was that it was doing so despite no radical change having occurred in its regime, while the former Warsaw Pact countries had acted as a result of the changes of the ruling system in their countries. It was important for us to be present in Yugoslavia not only politically, but also for the purpose of conveying knowledge about Israel. When the time came we would have to bridge the great gap of ignorance about Israel, its policy and its history, as a result of years of severed relations. An additional benefit that might derive from this would be the neutralization of the military and other aid that Yugoslavia had given to the PLO. Finally, I pointed out that we must act towards Yugoslavia as a united country, without considering the danger of its dissolution.

As for future actions, I proposed:

1. To encourage the signing of the aviation agreement between the two countries.
2. To arrange a meeting of the foreign ministers, as suggested by the Yugoslav foreign minister, in Belgrade or Jerusalem. But this, as I had voiced to my Yugoslav interlocutors, was on the condition that at this meeting an announcement would be made of the renewal of diplomatic relations. If not, to ensure a meeting between them at the UN General Assembly, this too as proposed by the Yugoslav foreign minister.
3. To invite to Israel the Yugoslav professional diplomatic level dealing with Israel and the Middle East for the purpose of studying the Arab-Israeli conflict at first hand.
4. To encourage a meeting between two economic missions (since we had an economic interest in such a meeting) in the near future.

5. To encourage a visit to Israel by the chairman of the Foreign Affairs Committee of the Yugoslav parliament.
6. To provide the Yugoslav Foreign Ministry with a regular supply of information on Israel and to maintain close contact with it.
7. To encourage visits of delegations of journalists from Yugoslavia to Israel.
8. To act for the benefit of local Jewry, while making a rapid assessment of their potential needs, in case of an urgent need to evacuate them. This proposal was based on the impressions of my talk with the leaders of the Jewish community in Belgrade, which had been passed on to the Jewish Agency and to Nativ – the organization for the encouragement of Jewish emigration from East European states to Israel. In hindsight, it seems to me that the visit constituted an important means for clarifying our position with regard to the Yugoslav leadership, and assisted in paving the way to strengthening our mutual connections towards renewal of diplomatic relations between Israel and Yugoslavia.[38]

RENEWAL OF ISRAELI-YUGOSLAV RELATIONS – CLOSING THE CIRCLE

In its letter of 2 October 1991, the Yugoslav Foreign Ministry informed the Foreign Ministry in Jerusalem about the decision of its government to renew diplomatic relations with Israel at the level of embassies (until the break in relations in 1967, mutual representation had been at the level of legations), and of its readiness to open embassies on a mutual basis. In that letter the Yugoslav Foreign Ministry expressed its hope that renewal of diplomatic relations would create better possibilities for the development of relations between the two countries on all levels.

At the Foreign Ministry in Jerusalem hesitations arose: Was it worthwhile renewing diplomatic relations with a Federal Republic of Yugoslavia that was on the verge of dissolution? I advised to reply in the positive, giving my reasons as follows:

> Although Yugoslavia is mired in a deep internal crisis and, in effect, in a situation of internal conflict, and no one knows whether its territorial integrity will be preserved, it is most important, in my opinion, that our reply to the Yugoslav Foreign Ministry is sent as soon as possible so as to determine an 'accomplished fact', according to which we are renewing our diplomatic relations within its current borders and through the federal government which, at the time, had severed its relations with Israel. This is the only government in Eastern Europe to offer renewal of relations with us while its regime had not changed as a result of social and political upheavals in the region. Outwardly, Yugoslavia continues to act as a unified country, no country in the world has recognized the independence of Slovenia and Croatia, and as such it is related to by the countries of the world (which are interested in its territorial integrity and its stability in the region).[39]

My proposal was accepted.

In a letter of 8 October 1991 the Foreign Ministry of Israel welcomed the decision of the Yugoslav government to renew diplomatic relations with Israel, as soon as possible, and noted that it considered the date of renewal as valid from the day this reply was sent. As to the opening of embassies, each in the other's country, the Foreign Ministry of Israel proposed to remain in contact with the Yugoslav Foreign Ministry. The latter gave wide publication to the reply of Israel's Foreign Ministry, while stressing the fact that the renewal of diplomatic relations was already in force. Theoretically, the government of Yugoslavia had reached a decision in principle to resume diplomatic relations with Israel in May 1991, while the actual timing of this step was determined only at the beginning of October 1991.

This brought to a close the long chapter of the renewal of diplomatic relations between the two countries. Tito's tenacious ambition to play a decisive role between the Eastern and Western Blocs – from a position of strength in the leadership of the non-aligned nations – dissipated not only because of his death (since his heirs in the Yugoslav leadership continued to support this idea), but also because of the decline in importance of the non-aligned nations in the post-cold war period. Yugoslavia invested great effort after Tito in this movement. It may still be shown that, had his successors in the Yugoslav leadership invested the same energy in the internal unification of the republics, perhaps Yugoslavia would not have reached the point of dissolution and bloody wars, led by Slobodan Milosevic, between Serbia and Croatia, between Serbia and Slovenia, and later between Serbia and Bosnia-Herzegovina. (Macedonia seceded from Yugoslavia in a peaceful process.)

From Israel's point of view there is an interesting parallel between the beginning of the dismemberment of the republics of Federal Yugoslavia and the taking of the decision in principle to renew diplomatic relations with Israel, until its practical implementation. The hope, however, that renewal of diplomatic relations between the two countries would bring with it the immediate flourishing of mutual relations, also waned rather quickly. To be sure, a Yugoslav Embassy was inaugurated in Tel Aviv a short time after the reinstitution of diplomatic relations, but the opening of the Israeli Embassy in Belgrade was delayed and trade and economic relations between the two countries were frozen by the UN decision to impose sanctions on Yugoslavia (1992) as a result of Serbia's war in Bosnia-Herzegovina. During the course of that year, Israel recognized the independence of Slovenia, Macedonia and Croatia and was a patron of their candidacy for UN membership, together with Bosnia-Herzegovina. It was not until 1997 that the Embassy of Israel was inaugurated in Belgrade, the capital of Yugoslavia – which was then composed of Serbia and Montenegro – and until relations returned to their status prior to the dissolution process, and then proceeded to further stages of development.

The high point of the new bilateral relations between Yugoslavia and Israel was expressed in the official visit to Israel of the Yugoslav foreign minister, Goran Svilanovic, escorted by the Israeli ambassador to Belgrade, Yoram Shani, in October 2001. This was the first official visit of its kind by a Yugoslav foreign minister to Israel. During that visit the minister also met with Yasser Arafat, and they agreed to raise the Palestinian representative in Belgrade to the level of ambassador. Besides the Yugoslav Embassy – the name of which was changed from 2003 to 'Serbia and Montenegro' – located in Tel Aviv, there are also embassies representing Slovenia, Croatia and Bosnia-Herzegovina now functioning in Israel. Macedonia is represented by its embassy in Athens. With the secession of Montenegro from Serbia and its declaration of independence, in June 2006, and after its acceptance about a month later as a UN member, Israel also established diplomatic relations with Montenegro.

Israel has good relations with all the independent republics of historical Yugoslavia. In addition to the two embassies – in Belgrade, capital of Serbia, and in Zagreb, capital of Croatia (from 2005) – Israel is represented in Slovenia by its embassy in Vienna (from 1992), in Macedonia, by its embassy in Athens (from 1995), and in Bosnia-Herzegovina, by its embassy in Budapest (from 1997).

THE JEWISH POPULATION

The number of Jews on the eve of the dissolution of Yugoslavia in 1991 was estimated at 5,000, about half in Serbia and half in Croatia. Following the disintegration of Yugoslavia, the Federation of Jewish Communities ceased to exist on a federative basis. The community institutions in Belgrade, Zagreb and other places where Jews lived in the former republics of Yugoslavia continue to operate as independent communal entities in the areas of religion, culture and welfare, with the aid of the Joint Distribution Committee.[40] In 2001 the overall number of Jews was estimated at 3,400 people, as follows: Serbia and Montenegro, 1,700; Croatia, 1,300; Macedonia, 1,700; Bosnia-Herzegovina, 300.[41]

The late president of Croatia, Franjo Tudjman, who presented himself as a historian, even before he became the first president of his country, published, in Zagreb in 1989, his book *Wastelands – The Historical Truth*, containing a chapter of crass anti-Semitism, in which he presented the history of the Jewish people in a distorted manner and, among other claims, accused the Jews themselves of causing the Holocaust. According to him, in the Holocaust, some two million Jews died, and not six million, which is the generally accepted estimate. He stated this even though he himself was one of the anti-Nazi fighters in the Second World War.

As a result of the sharp criticism of his anti-Semitic statements voiced against him in Israel and the Jewish world, and in light of Israel's refusal to establish diplomatic relations with his country as long as he held these opinions, an English edition of the book was published in Zagreb that contained none of his anti-Semitic references. Only after he published, in 1997, an apology and asked forgiveness for his insult to the Holocaust victims, only then did Israel institute diplomatic relations with his country.[42] Following Tudjman's death, Stefan Mesich became president of Croatia, and in the course of his visit to Israel during 2001, he sharply criticized his predecessor on account of his nationalistic leadership and anti-Semitic writings.

NOTES

1. 'Tito', *Encyclopaedia Hebraica*, Supplement 2 (Tel Aviv: Sifriat Poalim, 1983), pp.575–7; 'Yugoslavia', *Encyclopaedia Hebraica*, Supplement 3 (Tel Aviv: Sifriat Poalim, 1985), pp.441–2.
2. (a) Protocol of the Fifth Joint Meeting of the Yugoslavian Presidium and the

Executive of the Yugoslavian Communist Party chaired by Tito, 11 June 1967, as a result of the report that he gave on his visit to Moscow and the situation in the Middle East; (b) Protocol of the visit on the occasion of the meeting of the leaders of the East European Communist Bloc countries, which decided (except for Romania) to break diplomatic relations with Israel, which was summarized in a mere three lines; Protocol of the Sixth Meeting of the Executive Federal Council on 13 June 1967 as a result of the announcement by the Yugoslav government on the severance of diplomatic relations with Israel and the delineation of future methods of operation. Absent from this meeting were a number of senior members of the Council, among them the Yugoslav foreign minister, Marko Nikezic (to demonstrate his dissatisfaction with the decision to break relations with Israel). The two sets of Protocols are given in the Appendix; (c) In the talk between Edgar Bronfman, president of the World Jewish Congress, and Israel Singer, executive director of the WJC, with the president of Yugoslavia and the former foreign minister, Lazar Mojsov, in Belgrade on 13 and 14 July 1987, Mojsov had told them (as well as the Hungarian ruler, Janos Kadar) 'that it was precisely Tito who initiated the break in relations' with Israel. The report by Johanan Bein, ambassador of Israel's Mission to the UN, in his telegram of 27 July 1987 to the Foreign Ministry, File Yug 103.1, Israel State Archive (ISA). All documents cited and quoted in this chapter are in this file.

3. Ranko Petkovic, *Subjectivna Istoria Jugoslovenske Diplomatiej 1943–1991* (Belgrade: Sluzebni list SRJ, 1995), pp.48–9. Dr Ranko Petkovic served for many years as chief editor of the Yugoslav weekly, *Review of International Affairs*, widely distributed in several languages, on foreign affairs, economics, law, science and culture.
4. According to the Yugoslav weekly *NIN*, 26 November 1989.
5. Review by Yoav Bar-On of the East European Department (Europe 3) at the Foreign Ministry, 28 February 1982.
6. A.A. Ben Asher, *Foreign Relations 1948–1953* (Tel Aviv: Ayanot, 1957), pp.196–200, p.234 [Hebrew].
7. Ibid.
8. Zvi Loker, in Ya'akov Tsur (ed.), *Tefutzah: Mizrah Eiropa* (Jerusalem: Keter, 1976).
9. According to *Tanjug* (Telegraphic Agency of New Yugoslavia), Alexandria, 17 August 1967, published on 19 August 1967 in the *Yugoslav News Bulletin*, New York.
10. Circular letter 343, 3 September 1967 and circular letter 380, 4 September 1967.
11. Letter by Yosef Govrin from the Israeli Embassy in Buenos Aires, 13 September 1967.
12. Review by Yoav Bar-On, 28 February 1981.
13. Ibid.
14. *Yediot Ahronot*, 23 December 1977.
15. See n.12 above.
16. Memorandum by Yosef Govrin, director of the Europe 3 Department (that is, Eastern Europe), 6 October 1979, and the reaction of the Yugoslav Foreign Ministry's spokesman, according to *Tanjug*, 2 November 1978.
17. On Resolution 3379 of the Thirtieth UN General Assembly of 10 November 1975, which equated Zionism with racism, as well as Resolution 4686 by the Forty-third UN General Assembly of 16 December 1991 that annulled the comparison. See also Ruth Raeli, 'Zionism Racism, UN Resolution 3379', in Moshe Yegar, Yosef Govrin and Oded Aryeh (eds), *The Foreign Ministry, the First 50 Years* (Jerusalem: Keter, 2002) [Hebrew].
18. Protocol of the Yugoslav Federal Executive Council, 13 June 1967 (see Appendix).
19. *Yediot Ahronot*, 30 August 1984, 'The Yugoslavs Soften Their Position Regarding the State of Israel' [Hebrew].
20. Memorandum by Yosef Govrin, 6 September 1985.

21. According to the report by Raphael Gvir, a member of Israel's Mission to the UN, 1 October 1987.
22. Radio Belgrade on 1 June 1988, according to the notes of the BBC from 10 June 1988, memorandum by Anna Azari of the Europe 3 Department, 17 June 1988.
23. Report by Raphael Gvir of Israel's Mission to the UN, 28 September 1987.
24. Report on the visit by KM Abba Eban to Czechoslovakia and Yugoslavia, 23–29 October 1988.
25. Report by the Israeli Ambassador to Nicosia, Aharon Lopez, 31 August 1989.
26. Report by Aharon Yaacov, Israel's Mission to the UN.
27. Notes of Shmuel Meirom, deputy director of the Europe 2 Department, 19 November 1989.
28. Memorandum by Yosef Govrin, deputy director general for Eastern Europe, 26 November 1989.
29. The Yugoslav weekly, *Politika*, 28 September 1989.
30. Notes of Israel Mei-Ami, Department of Eastern European 2, 9 January 1990.
31. Telegram from J. Bein, Israel's Mission to the UN, 28 February 1990.
32. *Haaretz*, 1 March 1990.
33. Memorandum by Y. Govrin, 7 March 1990.
34. Notes of Talia Lador-Fresher, East European Department, 6 May 1990.
35. Report by the Yugoslav press on 16 and 18 May 1990; memorandum by Yosef Govrin, 31 May 1990.
36. Report by Aharon Yaacov, Israel's Mission to the UN, 26 September 1990.
37. Report by Y. Govrin on his impressions of his visit to Belgrade, 9 June 1991.
38. Memorandum by Yosef Govrin, 11 June 1991.
39. Memorandum by Yosef Govrin, 8 October 1991.
40. Ivan Ceresnjes, 'The Hour of Truth of the Post-Yugoslavia Jews', *Gesher*, 140 (Winter 1999) [Hebrew]; Ivan Ceresnjes, *Caught in the Winds of War: Jews in the Former Yugoslavia*, Policy Study 17 (Jerusalem: Institute of World Jewish Congress, 1999).
41. Based on data from the *American Jewish Yearbook* (New York: The American Jewish Committee, 2001), in conjunction with the World Jewish Congress and the Harman Institute of Contemporary Jewry at the Hebrew University of Jerusalem.
42. Ministry of Foreign Affairs, *Annual of Official Documents 1998* (Jerusalem: Israel State Archive, 2000), p.454 [Hebrew].

Epilogue

Having concluded the gradual process of Israel's renewal of diplomatic relations with the East European states, as well as the establishment of diplomatic relations – for the first time – with Albania and with the fifteen Republics of the Former Soviet Union (FSU), a rapid process of a wide-ranging cooperation began, followed by an unprecedented scale of development of mutual relations, in the seven following areas.

BILATERAL RELATIONS

Mutual agreements were signed in the commercial field and – for the first time in the history of Israel's diplomatic relations with the East European states (excluding Romania, which had maintained uninterrupted diplomatic relations) – a series of agreements were also signed in the areas of industrial and technological cooperation, agriculture, banking, aviation, economics, academic research, medicine, education, culture and science, between Israel and the East European states (including Russia and the Former Soviet Republics). The volume of tourism also grew considerably in both directions.

EXCHANGE OF OFFICIAL VISITS

Already in the first stages of the renewal of diplomatic relations, a series of visits were held – and are constantly continuing – of state presidents, prime ministers, presidents of parliaments, ministers of foreign affairs, ministers of economy, trade, tourism, culture and scientific affairs as well as many other personalities, including heads of political parties. These exchanges were the first of their kind, since they had not taken place at all during the Communist era. The first to break the pattern were the president of Czechoslovakia, Vaclav Havel, the president of Poland, Lech Walesa, the foreign minister of Hungary, Giula Horn, and the foreign minister of the Soviet Union, Boris Pankin.

Israel's President Chaim Herzog was the first Israeli president to visit Hungary and Czechoslovakia. He was followed by other Israeli ministers, including Shimon Peres and Moshe Arens, who paid official visits to all capitals of the East European states, including the Soviet Union. The significance of these visits lay not only in the fact that they were the first to be held as reciprocal exchanges, but also because they paved the way for significant achievements in the fast development of mutual relations and cooperation in all practical fields. Later, during the 1990s and by the beginning of the present century, these exchanges were occurring on a daily basis, but without losing their significance.

FREE CONTACTS WITH LOCAL JEWISH COMMUNITIES

Once again, for the first time, Israel, worldwide Jewish organizations, and representatives of Jewish communities scattered across the five continents were able to establish close and free contacts with the local East European Jewish communities, fostering them over a period of time by laying the basis of Jewish school education, teaching of Hebrew, conducting seminars on Israel, the history of the Jewish people (including the history of the local Jewish communities), the Jewish heritage, the contemporary history of the Jewish communities in the world and the history of the Holocaust, as well as encouraging the emigration of local Jews to Israel. All these activities are being conducted with the full consent of the local authorities.

Moreover, some of the East European states have established – also for the first time – special departments at their
universities for the teaching of Jewish studies, as well as
encouraging academic research in this field. At the same
time, departments for the study of the various East
European states were opened at Israel's universities.

SPREADING INFORMATION ABOUT ISRAEL

Israel's embassies throughout the East European states
conducted a large-scale informative and cultural campaign
scale aimed at closing the gap between the distorted, falsified official information that existed during the communist
regime, on one hand, and the provision of correct information that was available, in the post-communist era, on the
other. The gap had been created during the communist
regime – particularly during the severance of the diplomatic relations – with the purpose of serving the official
propaganda and policy of the central authorities towards
Israel, in each of the East European states. As a result of
overcoming the gap, a positive image of Israel emerged in
the local media, in the social, economic and cultural
domains, such as had never existed before. This radical
change became possible not only because of the efforts
made by Israel, but also because these states established
democratic regimes, free from outside pressure, aiming at
serving their own interests. Whilst during the communist
regimes these countries led an acute anti-Israeli policy, in
the post-communist era, however, they all became a
bastion of friendship towards Israel, on the bilateral level as
well as on the international level.

CONDUCTING AN INTENSIVE POLITICAL DIALOGUE
ON ALL LEVELS

Such dialogue started to take place in Jerusalem and in
each of the East European capitals through the exchange of

opinions, assessment of political situations and the analysis of regional and international problems, seeking for ways and means of solving them, in particular addressing the Arab-Israeli conflict, as well as other problems of mutual interest. This interchange became a quite frequent, normal and fruitful phenomenon that characterized the mutual relations between Israel and the respective states, before and after they joined the European Union in the years 2004 and 2007 (Bulgaria, Czech Republic, Estonia, Hungary, Latvia, Lithuania, Poland, Romania, Slovakia and Slovenia) and NATO, in the years 1999, 2004 and 2009 (Albania, Bulgaria, Croatia, Czech Republic, Estonia, Latvia, Lithuania, Poland, Romania, Slovakia and Slovenia). Owing to the USA initiative their acceptance to NATO membership was conditional upon their confrontation with their Nazi past. Consequently, all these states opened their archives, hitherto closed to the general public.

THE JEWISH ASPECT

This also occupied an important place in this dialogue, in view of the need to undertake legal, educational and administrative means to stop anti-Semitic manifestations that began to develop as a by-product of the democratiza-tion process in the Soviet Union (later in Russia and the rest of the Former Soviet Republics) and in the other of the East European states. This process, however, also enabled, as it is known, the rise of the ultra-nationalist movements – including the anti-Semitic parties – and the development of their activities, threatening at times the physical existence of the local Jews. These manifestations – whose roots are to be found in the classical anti-Semitic theories and practice – found specific expression in some of the former republics of the Soviet Union as well as in the other East European states. Their main argument was – and still is – that the Jews were those who raised the communist regimes to power throughout its existence, and are therefore responsible for the communist regime's persecution of national elements among the respective nations, causing, as the slanderers put it, millions of people to be exterminated. The economies of states which had enjoyed prosperity before the advent of communism had deteriorated to the point of near-bankruptcy, and so according to anti-Semitic nationalists, the Jews who raised the communist regimes to power were again guilty. But even after the fall of the discredited regimes, in the view of the anti-Semites, the Jews were once again accused of ruling the influential circles of the social, economic and political leadership.

At the same time, the remaining communist parties were claiming the opposite, that the Jews in the Western world – including Israel – were responsible for the collapse of the communist regimes, because of the anti-communist propaganda they had initiated and conducted throughout the world; thus they were guilty of the collapse of communism. So, there are two extreme movements, each one in opposition to the other – nationalists and communists – that blame the Jews for all the evils that occurred in their home countries.

Another phenomenon, also characteristic of some of the East European states, stems from the nationalist circles which demand rehabilitation for the former fascist leaders who collaborated with the Nazis during the Second World War in murdering Jews, and who were sentenced to death after the war by the communist authorities. They also demand their recognition as 'national heroes'. This occurred most commonly in Romania, Slovakia and to some extent in Hungary. To this, one should add the legislation of the Baltic states that granted rehabilitation to those who were found guilty for 'political' reasons (which is how it was formulated) by the former Soviet regime, and there is a presumption that amongst those who were rehabilitated are a considerable number of collaborators who assisted the Nazis in murdering Jews.

These anti-Semitic manifestations, even if they do not

characterize the general public and the societies of the East European states, and even if their publications are considered to be marginal, still pose the danger of spreading the anti-Semitic poison. The failure of the central authorities in the post-communist era to bring a decisive end to such movements – despite their genuine will and efforts – results in a certain confrontation within the local public as well as an ever-present issue in the political discussions held between the official representatives of Israel and their counterparts in the East European states. Yet, at the same time, one should mention an important and encouraging fact – that there is a growing tendency, particularly among the intellectuals and the younger generation of these states, to become better acquainted with the history of the Jewish people, their contribution to world culture and to that of their own countries, with the history of Zionism, of Israel and of the Holocaust, in Europe in general and in their own countries in particular.

Presidents and governments of the East European states have often condemned anti-Semitism in their public declarations, calling for all possible measures, legal, educational and administrative, against those who promote such ideas. Even the Episcopal Committee of the Polish Church, through the initiative of Cardinal F. Makharski of Krakow, condemned anti-Semitism, in 1991, in a letter that was distributed to churches all over Poland. With these measures the East European leaders made more efforts against the rise of anti-Semitism at the beginning of the 1990s than any of the leaders of Western nations. However, the process of legislation against anti-Semitism has not yet been completed in all the East European states and at the time of writing (2008), we have not been informed of any severe measures yet taken against those who were spreading anti-Semitism. Hence it may seem that the declarations of the leaders of the various East European states condemning anti-Semitism remain, for the moment, on paper. The declarations serve, perhaps, more for external purposes than for internal use. True, there is a great measure of sensitivity on the part of leaders of these states concerning what is being said about them in Israel and in the West, and they seem to well understand that anti-Semitic manifestations in their own states are not exactly the signs of an enlightened regime and do not constitute a respectable 'visiting card' in Israel.

The Jewish communities, large and small, that encountered abuse and disgrace at the hands of previous regimes became assets in the post-communist era. Leaders of the new regimes are taking advantage of their existence with the aim of building relations between themselves and Israel, the USA and the West. Also, Israel, which was defined by the mass propaganda of the communist regimes as a 'warmonger' and a 'servant of American imperialists' is now perceived as an important bridge to the West and as a significant source of cooperation in the advancement of the economy, technology, science, education and culture of their own states.

THE ARAB-ISRAELI CONFLICT

Whereas during the communist era, the East European states, as part of the Soviet Bloc, conducted a fiercely anti-Israeli policy (with the exception of Romania) with respect to the Arab-Israeli conflict – by granting the PLO massive military, economic and political support in its struggle against Israel – a truly drastic change took place from the very beginning of the post-communist era. As the East European states became independent from the Soviet Union and structured themselves more democratically, they also became increasingly friendly towards Israel, distancing themselves from their previously one-sided policies towards the Arab-Israeli conflict. These measures allowed the conflict to be – what it always should have been – a regional dispute free from superpower involvement, in particular that of the Soviet Union. In addition, the

East European states which eventually joined the European Union and NATO also developed a closer cooperation with Israel, as with the Western states. And, although Israeli-Russian relations – particularly after the dismemberment of the Soviet Union – are viewed as being on their best terms, by comparison with the Soviet past, on all practical levels – including attitudes towards the Arab-Israeli conflict – Russia still causes deep concern to Israel, by supplying major weapons, such as anti-tank rockets (Kornet, Metis) and anti-aircraft missiles (MIG 29) to Syria. These rockets, in addition to the RPG 29 anti-tank grenade launcher that Russia supplied to Syria and Iran, have found their way to the terrorist organization Hezbollah in Lebanon, as Israel discovered during the campaign against Hezbollah in the second Israeli-Lebanese War (2006).

Though Russia denied the fact that it supplied the RPG 29 rocket to Hezbollah, Israel was able to claim from direct experience that there was no doubt that Hezbollah had used this weapon during its war with Israel. Another source of deep concern was Russia's promise to provide Iran with SA-300 anti-aircraft missiles and Syria with advanced supersonic P-800 cruise missiles. Israel regards the supply of all these rockets and missiles as a great danger to her security in view of Iran's frequent declarations that Israel should be wiped from the Middle East map, while Syria regards itself as being at war with Israel. Israel invested great effort in order to convince Russia – as did the USA and some of the West European states – that the supply of these long range anti-aircraft missiles to Iran might grossly inflame the present situation in the Middle East in general, and Israel's security in particular. At the time of writing (May 2010) these missiles have not been supplied to Iran nor to Syria.

Another source of deep concern is Russia's assistance to Iran in the construction of a nuclear power plant and reactor in Bushehr while Iran's extremist Muslim regime is striving to produce nuclear bombs. At the same time, Iran constantly declines close cooperation with the International Atomic Energy Agency. By its ambition to develop nuclear weapons Iran is threatening to endanger not only Israel's mere existence, which Iran openly opposes, but also the Western states, due to its constant military and political support given to terrorist movements such as Hamas and Hezbollah. Even if Russia – like the Western powers – opposes Iran's ambitions to produce nuclear weapons, it still constantly strives to play an active role in the Middle East, including the Arab-Israeli conflict, in a rather more constructive way than during the days of the Soviet Union, as a member of the 'Quartet' of powers dealing with Middle East issues (the UN, EU, USA and Russia) and which seeks to resolve the Israel-Palestine conflict by peaceful means and by maintaining frequent strategic talks with Israel. Avoiding the spread of radical Islam in the Middle East seems to be not only in the interest of the USA, Israel and the moderate Arab States, but also clearly in the interest of the European Union and Russia.

To conclude, in this new era, after the re-establishment of diplomatic relations between Israel and the East European states, their mutual relations are mainly characterized by a constant development in the interests of both sides, through close friendship and fruitful cooperation. The East European states are inspired not only by the sharing of a common past with Israel and its citizens but also by a deep appreciation for Israel's achievements during its sixty-two years of independence. These relations, it is to be hoped, will continue to be cultivated by all possible means and on all possible levels. Because if not, who will be able to guarantee that this asset of mutual friendship, appreciation and close cooperation will indeed endure?

Appendix 1:
Protocols Concerning Yugoslavia's Severance of Relations with Israel

Central Committee
Communist Federation of Yugoslavia
Presidium
Reserved No. 01-327/2-67
8 February 1968l, Belgrade

PROTOCOL

From the Fifth Joint Meeting of the Presidium of the General Council of the Communist Federation of Yugoslavia held on 11 June 1967, in Belgrade.

Not participating in the meeting were the following: as part of his function, Koča Popović, and owing to unexpected circumstances, Lidija Šentjurc, Miha Marinko, Iwan Macek, Albert Jakopic, Albert Roman, Stane Kavčič, Franc Popit.

Participating in the meeting was Marko Nikezic, Central Committee member.

From the professional apparatus, the following attended the meeting: Danilo Purić, Milorad Mijović, from the Department of International Relations: Iwan Laća, from the Information Department, Angelika Veljic, from the

302

Secretariat of the Presidum; Verdonka Rajkovic of the Secretariat of the General Council.

Agenda:

1. Report on the trip to Moscow and on the situation in the Middle East.

The meeting was chaired by Comrade Tito

At the meeting the opinion was expressed that the Federal General Council must inform the government of Israel that in the case of its non-withdrawal of its forces from occupied territories, Yugoslavia would sever its diplomatic relations with Israel.

The leadership of the socio-political authorities must take wide-sweeping measures by arranging various lectures, gatherings, and talks, while exploiting the communications media, to inform the general public of the essence of the conflict in the Middle East and to recruit to that end all the existing organizations and institutions for independent activity, so that all this activity will not be limited solely to the framework of the Communist Federation.

In the implementation of all the maximum measures and plans of action, it is not possible to coordinate effectively between the Council, the Popular Front, and the Communist Party and the other socio-political organizations and institutions. Therefore, the Office of the Presidium of the Central Council will deal with the overall coordination of this activity, so that it will be reviewed and concentrated in one place.

This protocol will be disseminated for the knowledge of the members of the Presidium and the General Council along with an invitation to the Sixth Joint Meeting of the Presidium and the General Council.

Since at this meeting no comments were voiced by members of the Presidium and the General Council, this Protocol is approved.

The President of the Communist Federation of Yugoslavia Josip Broz Tito

Signed: J.B. Tito
Stamp of the Presidium

(This document was obtained by courtesy of Israel's ambassador in Belgrade, Yoram Shani.)

Federal Executive Council
Secretariat
Protocol No. 6
13 June 1967
Belgrade

PROTOCOL

From the Sixth Meeting of the Federal Executive Council
[henceforth 'the Council', the official name of the Yugoslav
government] held on 13 June 1967.

The meeting was chaired by Mika Špiljak, Council president.

Participating in the meeting were: Deputies to the
President Kiro Gligorov and Rudi Kolak as well as Council
members Marko Bulc, Zivan Vasilevic, Toma Granfil,
Aleksander Grlickov, Milijan Neoricic, Janez Stanovnik,
Mustafa Sabic, Mijusko Sibalic, Velizar Skerovic, Ali Sukrija,
Secretary of State for Defence Nikola Ljubicic, and Council
Secretary Rajko Gagovic.

Absent were: Council members Franjo Nadj, Hakija
Pozderac, Milivoj Rukavina, Marin Cetinic, and Secretary
of State for Foreign Affairs Marko Nikezic.

In addition to Council members, also participating were:
Foreign Affairs Adviser Lazar Mojsov, Department Director
in the Secretariat for Communications Stevan Miksic, and
head of the Council Office Nisim Konfino.

In accordance with the recommendation of the President,
the following agenda was set:
1. Severance of diplomatic relations with Israel
2. Questions and proposals

Point One:

After clarification the proposal on the severance of diplomatic relations with Israel was accepted, taking into consideration the fact that the government of Israel has ignored the warning contained in the letter from the SFRI [Federal Republic of Yugoslavia] government of 11 June 1967.

Similarly, the Council has agreed to the text of the letter that the State Secretariat must immediately deliver to the Israeli Legation in Belgrade.

As to the severance of diplomatic relations with Israel, the Council has decided to charge the Committee of the Economic Council, together with the State Secretariat for Foreign Affairs and the Secretariat for Foreign Trade, with examination of the complex of relations between our country and Israel, especially regarding the continuation of economic relations, and with the proposal of appropriate measures.

Further to this point on the agenda: The Council has noted (by agreement) the announcement concerning the shipments of medicines and food, which were sent to the Arab countries as first aid.

Point Two:

There were no questions or proposals.
The meeting lasted from 13:15 to 14:40.

(This document was obtained by courtesy of Israel's ambassador in Belgrade, Yoram Shani. Translated by Israel's former ambassador, Zvi Loker.)

Appendix 2
Coming in From the Cold. Reform in Eastern Europe Sparks off Renewed Ties with Israel

POLITICS

Czechoslovakia Signs Up: Foreign Minister Moshe Arens renews diplomatic relations.

Coming In From the Cold

Reform in Eastern Europe Sparks Off Renewed Ties With Israel

BY EHUD BEN NADAV

For Israel, the restoration of diplomatic relations with Hungary, Czechoslovakia, Poland and Bulgaria marked the end of a dark era of more than 20 years, in which the Jewish State had no formal ties with most of Eastern Europe. With the signing ceremony in the Bulgarian capital Sofia last month, only four countries still lack diplomatic relations with Jerusalem: Yugoslavia - never a member of the Warsaw pact - hardline communist Albania, which broke away from the Soviet bloc because it thought Moscow

had gone soft and revisionist, East Germany, and the Soviet Union itself.

It is doubtful whether the change in the attitudes of Budapest, Prague, Warsaw and Sofia would ever have taken place were it not for the democratic reforms sweeping Eastern Europe. In the view of Dr. Yosef Govrin, Foreign Ministry Assistant Director-General with responsibility for Eastern Europe, renewal of relations with Israel was for these countries a practical demonstration of their new-found independence from the Soviet Union. In an exclusive interview with ISRAEL MAGAZINE, Dr. Govrin said Israel's image in these countries is very positive in spite of the

virulent anti-Israel propaganda that was the official line there for so long. In fact they view the Jewish state as a success story worth emulating.

"They see that Israel has made some striking achievements in its 42 years of independence, in spite of being surrounded by enemies and having been forced to fight for its survival several times," Govrin says. "They regard Israel as a very important source for future cooperation in the fields of science, technology, agriculture, and medicine."

Soviets Stalling: The rapidity with which the four former Soviet satellites followed each other in restoring ties with Israel makes the tardiness of the close them down shortly afterwards when the two Germanies unite. But in Yosef Govrin's view this is unimportant. "I do not think unification will happen overnight," he says. "At present East and West Germany are signing agreements on economic union. They have a long way to go before political union is achieved. In the meantime, if Israel and East Germany reach appropriate agreements, and so long as the flags of other countries are flying in East Berlin, I see no reason why the Israeli flag should not fly there too."

In the past East Germany expressed hostility to Israel not only in propaganda, but also by training Arab terrorists. "It is true that they were carrying out orders from Moscow," Govrin admits, "but they did so with alacrity and great efficiency." Asked whether the new democratic government of East Germany had ceased this activity, Govrin replied, "I am inclined to think so."

In fact, all of the former Soviet bloc countries have adopted a more balanced, less anti-Israel Middle East policy since the democratic reforms began to take effect. The Soviet Union no longer supports Syria's ambition to achieve strategic parity with Israel. It has not stopped supplying Syria with state-of-the art weaponry, but Damascus no longer receives every weapon it requests and the Soviets no longer provide long-term credits for arms purchases.

"We would like to see the Soviets go further in restricting the arms race in this region," Yosef Govrin says, "but at least they are urging Syria to seek a negotiated settlement to the conflict, and that is a positive development."

Content in Background: Hungary, Czechoslovakia, Poland and Bulgaria are too preoccupied with their domestic problems, economic and constitutional, to play an active role in Middle

> **Israel's image is very positive in spite of the virulent propaganda. In fact they view the Jewish state as a success story worth emulating.**

East diplomacy. There were raised eyebrows in Jerusalem when the new President of Czechoslovakia, Vaclav Havel, received Yasser Arafat. On the other hand Israel welcomed the statement by the Czechoslovak Foreign Minister Jeri Dienstbier that the conflict must be solved in the Middle East, not in Prague.

"These countries show a tendency to disengage from the Middle East conflict to an extent that we have not seen before," says Yosef Govrin. "Bear in mind that for decades they supported the most extremist forces in the Arab world without reservation. This is no longer the case. I do not expect them to abandon all their positions on the Middle East, for example on the Palestinian issue, but I do believe that the future of our relations with these countries is a bright one." □

Friends Again: Agreement reestablishing Israeli-Hungarian Relations.

to acknowledge responsibility. The existing lies and distortions in East German history text books and other official publications must be corrected as well, Govrin says.

It is possible that Israel and East Germany might establish diplomatic relations and open embassies, only to

Rumania - The Odd Man Out

Rumania was the only Warsaw Pact country which refused to sever relations with Israel in 1967. This was because former ruler Nicolai Ceaucescu was already pursuing an independent foreign policy. During the years of Ceaucescu's dictatorship the Jews of Rumania enjoyed freedom to worship and to maintain communal organizations, and were permitted to emigrate to Israel. Emigration was restricted by quotas, but these were very large, and hundreds of thousands of Rumanian Jews left. The new, democratic regime in Rumania has abolished the quotas and all Rumanians are now free to emigrate. At present there are 19,000 Jews left in Rumania.

Ceaucescu played a key rôle in the early stages of the peace negotiations between Israel and Egypt, acting as an intermediary between Israel's Prime Minister Menachem Begin

and Egypt's President Anwar Sadat. For this he earned enormous prestige in the Western World, and a grudging admiration in the Eastern Bloc. "We pointed out at the time that Ceaucescu had proven that it was possible to maintain full diplomatic relations with Israel without losing influence in the Arab world," Yosef Govrin recalls. "He brought home to the Soviets the fact that they were unable to play a role in the peace process at that time precisely because they had relations with only one side in the conflict.

Israel's diplomatic ties with Rumania have not been affected by the change of regime there. During the fighting between the democratic forces and the notorious *Securitate* secret police, Israel sent medical staff and supplies to Bucharest. Later, Israel-Rumania friendship societies were established in the two countries.

Appendix 2

Soviet Union all the more incongruous. At present the Soviets show no sign of wishing to proceed beyond the present stage of consular missions in Moscow and Tel Aviv. Yosef Govrin admits that he cannot put his finger on their precise motive. "At one time they might have feared reaction in the Arab world, but this is no longer such an important factor. President Gorbachev even went so far as to tell Syrian President Hafez el-Assad that Moscow's lack of diplomatic relations with Israel was 'abnormal.' The competition between the two superpowers for influence in the Arab world is much less intense than it used to be, just as their rivalry in Europe itself and in the global arena is less acute."

There was a time when the USSR refused to restore relations with Israel until a settlement to the Middle East conflict was achieved. More recently Soviet spokesmen have said no such political conditions would be imposed.

"The Soviets have made dramatic changes in their internal regime and in their foreign policy - in the areas of disarmament and rapprochement with the United States, the withdrawal of troops from Eastern Europe and the virtual dismantling of the Warsaw Pact as a military force," Yosef Govrin says. "It is difficult to comprehend why they are unwilling to reconsider their policy in the area of relations with Israel, which is for them a relatively minor aspect of foreign policy. After all, Soviet diplomats have admitted that the severance of relations was a mistake."

In Govrin's view the answer may lie in aspects of Soviet domestic policies which are not always clear to the outside observer. "We are very pleased with the fact that Jews are now permitted to leave the Soviet Union," he concedes. "In fact there is virtually no impediment to their departure, except for the shortage of airline flights out of the Soviet Union." He notes with regret that this shortage persists because the Kremlin has not approved the agreement for direct flights between Moscow and Ben Gurion airport, which was signed last November between the Soviet airline Aeroflot and El Al.

Yugoslavia Hesitates: Yugoslavia, never a Soviet satellite, nevertheless broke off relations with Israel after the Six Day War. This was mainly because of late President Tito's position as head of the so-called Conference of Non-Aligned Nations, which has a built-in anti-Israel majority. (The Conference includes such "non-aligned" countries as Cuba). Last month Yugoslavia sent an envoy of ambassadorial rank on a visit to Israel to discuss the possibility of restoring relations. Yosef Govrin, who conducted the talks, says the Yugoslavs have not yet made up their mind what level of relations they want, nor when.

"Tito severed relations with Israel because of his friendship with Egypt's President at that time, Abdel Nasser. Now Tito and Nasser are both dead, and Israel has had relations with Egypt for more that ten years. It is therefore paradoxical that Belgrade still refuses to change its mind."

Govrin attributes Yugoslavia's hesitation to its desire to retain its leadership of the Non-Aligned bloc. "It seems the time is not yet right." He notes with approval, however, that public opinion in Yugoslavia is increasingly in favor of restoring relations with the Jewish State. "Israel has no quarrel with Yugoslavia and never has had. In fact our two countries have many cultural links, with affection and sometimes nostalgia on their old country. There is no tradition of virulent anti-Semitism in most areas of Yugoslavia, and many Jews fought with the partisans against the Nazi occupation."

Even Albania?: A year ago no one could have dreamed that tiny, isolated Albania, that last bastion of Stalinism outside Ceaucescu's Rumania, might establish relations with Israel. However, democratic reforms are taking place,

even in Tirana, with the passing of the veteran dictator Enver Hoja. "Albania recognized Israel *de jure* in 1949," Govrin recalls, "but our proposals to establish diplomatic relations were not answered." Recently, however, one Albanian writer, taking advantage of the new atmosphere of freedom, had the audacity to declare that his government ought to establish relations with Israel. "It is only a sign," Govrin says, "but it is very encouraging."

East Germany falls into a different category from other Eastern bloc countries in that Israel has never had relations with it nor ever sought them. This is because East Germany never accepted historic responsibility for the Nazi holocaust, as West Germany did. Nor did the East German regime agree to pay compensation to the surviving vic-

Yosef Govrin: Optimistic about future relations with the Eastern Bloc.

tims. This has now changed.

New Government, New Direction: The democratic government of East Germany has acknowledged historic responsibility and agreed in principle to compensate the survivors. This has been endorsed by a resolution of the *Volkskammer*, the East German parliament in Berlin.

Israel maintains that it is not enough

Bibliography

ARCHIVE DOCUMENTS AND MATERIALS

Archive of the Israel Foreign Ministry at the Israel State Archive (ISA), Jerusalem.
Archive of Yad Vashem, The Holocaust Martyrs' and Heroes' Remembrance Authority, Jerusalem.
Divrei Haknesset (Verbatim Record of Knesset Proceedings).

PERIODICALS, DAILIES AND BROADCASTS

Israel: *Haaretz, Davar, Ma'ariv, Yediot Ahronot, Jerusalem Post, Israel Magazine.*
Yugoslavia: *Tanjug, Politika.*
Albania: *Zeri i Popollit.*
Radio Free Europe.

DOCUMENTARY FILM

Schifter, Paul (producer). *A Historical Sketch: Five Decades of Diplomatic Relations between Hungary and the State of Israel,* written and directed by Peter Bokor. Budapest, 1995–1997.

BOOKS AND ARTICLES IN HEBREW

Ben-Asher, A.A. (Pseudonym of Katriel Katz). *Yahasei Hutz 1948–1953* [Foreign Relations 1948–1953]. Tel Aviv: Ayanot, 1957.
Bentzur, Eytan. *Haderekh Lashalom Overet et Madrid* [The

310

Road to Peace goes through Madrid] (Tel Aviv: Sifrei Hemed, Yediot Ahronot, 1997); English edition: *Making Peace: A First-Hand Account of the Arab-Israeli Peace Process* (Westport, CT: Greenwood Publishing, 2001).

Cotic, Meir. *Mishpat Prag, Mishpat ha-Ra'avah ha-Anti-Zioni ha-Rishon ba-Gush ha-Komunisti* [The Prague Trial, The First Public anti-Zionist Trial in the Communist Bloc] (Tel Aviv: Milo, 1964).

Dagan, Avigdor. 'Ha-Mishpat ha-Anti-Zioni ha-Rishon' [The First anti-Zionist Trial], *Gesher*, 114 (Summer 1986), pp.146–9.

Doron, Eliezer. *Be-Tatzpit u-ve-Imut. Mi-Yomano shel Shagrir Israel* [Observing and Confronting. From the Diary of an Israeli Ambassador] (Jerusalem: Keter, 1978).

Eban, Abba. *Pirkei Haim* [Chapters of Life] (Tel Aviv: Sifriat Maariv, 1978).

Eban, Abba. *Diplomatia Hadasha. Yahasim Beinleumi'im ba-Idan ha-Moderni* [The New Diplomacy. International Relations in the Modern Era] (Tel Aviv: Edanim/Yediot Ahronot, 1985).

Gefen, Aba. *Eshnav le-Masakh ha-Barzel* [A Small Window through the Iron Curtain] (Tel Aviv: Sifriat Maariv, 1985).

Gilboa, A. Yehoshua. 'Siyutei Prag, 15 Shana le-Mishpat Slansky' [Prague Nightmares. Fifteen Years since the Slansky Trial], *Gesher*, 2–3, 51–2 (September 1967), pp.65–82.

Gorbachev, Mikhail. S. *Perestroika: Hashiva Hadasha le-Artzi ve-la-Olam* [Perestroika: New Thinking for My Country and the World] (Tel Aviv: Sifriat Maariv, 1988).

Govrin, Yosef. 'Gorbachev, Mikhail Sergeevich', *Encyclopaedia Hebraica*, Supplement 3 (Tel Aviv: Sifriat Poalim, 1995), pp.252–3.

Govrin, Yosef. *Yahasei Yisrael-Brit ha-Mo'atzot mi-Hidusham bi-Shnat 1953 ad Nitukam bi-Shnat 1967* [Israeli-Soviet Relations 1953–1967. From Confrontation to Disruption] (Jerusalem: Magnes Press, Hebrew University of Jerusalem, 1990; English edition: London and Portland, OR: Frank Cass, 1998).

311

Govrin, Yosef. 'Yahasei Israel–Mizrah Europa' [Israeli–East European Relations], in Haim Opaz (ed.), *Yahasei Hahutz shel Israel* [Israel's Foreign Relations] (Jerusalem: Ministry of Foreign Affairs, Ministry of Education and Culture, L. Davies Institute of International Relations, and the Abba Eban Center, Harry Truman Institute for the Advancement of Peace, Hebrew University of Jerusalem, 1999), pp.71–5.

Govrin, Yosef. 'Yahasei Israel–Brit ha-Mo'atzot mi-Kinunam bi-Shnat 1948 ad Peruka shel Brit-ha-Moatzot bi-Shnat 1991' [Israel-Soviet Relations. From their Establishment in 1948 until the Dismemberment of the Soviet Union in 1991], in Moshe Yegar, Yosef Govrin and Arye Oded (eds), *Misrad ha-Hutz 50 ha-Shanim ha-Rishonot* [Ministry of Foreign Affairs: The First Fifty Years] (Jerusalem: Keter, 2002), Vol.1, pp.445–58.

Govrin, Yosef. *Yahasei Israel-Romania be-Shalhei Edan Ceausescu, mi-Rishumav shel Shagrir Israel be-Romania 1985–1989* [Israeli-Romanian Relations at the End of the Ceauşescu Era, as observed by Israel's Ambassador to Romania 1985–1989] (Jerusalem: Magnes Press, Hebrew University of Jerusalem, 1999; English edition: London and Portland, OR: Frank Cass, 2002).

Katz, Katriel. *Shagrir li-Mdinot Mitnakrot: Budapest, Warsha, Moskva* [Ambassador in Estranged Lands: Budapest, Warsaw, Moscow] (Tel Aviv: Sifriat Poalim, 1976).

Keshles, Haim. 'Bulgaria', in Jacob Tsur (ed.), *Hatefutza: Mizrah Europa* [The Diaspora: Eastern Europe] (Jerusalem: Keter, 1976), pp.317–35.

Loker, Zvi. 'Yugoslavia', in Jacob Tsur (ed.), *Hatefutza: Mizrah Europa* [The Diaspora: Eastern Europe] (Jerusalem: Keter, 1976), pp.301–16.

Marton, Yehuda. 'Hungaria', in Jacob Tsur (ed.), *Hatefutza: Mizrah Europa* [The Diaspora: Eastern Europe] (Jerusalem: Keter, 1976), pp. 237–68.

Mendelson, Ezra. 'Polin' [Poland], in Jacob Tsur (ed.), *Hatefutza: Mizrah Europa* [The Diaspora: Eastern Europe] (Jerusalem: Keter, 1976), pp.169–210.

Nir, Baruch (ed.). *Hashmada ve-Hisardut be-Bulgaria ha-Me'uhedet* [Extermination and Survival in United Bulgaria] (Tel Aviv: Tamuz, 2002).

Orenstein, Shimon. *Alilat Prag* [The Prague Plot] (Tel Aviv: Am Hasefer, 1968).

Palzur, Mordechai. 'Polin – Hidush Yahasim' [Poland – Renewal of Relations], in Moshe Yegar, Yosef Govrin and Aryed Oded (eds), *Misrad ha-Hutz 50 ha-Shanim ha-Rishonot* [Ministry of Foreign Affairs: The First Fifty Years] (Jerusalem: Keter, 2002), Vol.1, pp.505–19.

Raeli, Ruth. 'Ziyonut Giz'anut, Hahlatat ha-U'm 3379' [Zionism Racism, UN Resolution 3379], in Moshe Yegar, Yosef Govrin and Aryed Oded (eds), *Misrad ha-Hutz 50 ha-Shanim ha-Rishonot* [Ministry of Foreign Affairs: The First Fifty Years] (Jerusalem: Keter, 2002), pp.871–6.

Rafael, Gideon. *Besod Leumim. Sheloshim Shnot Mediniut Hutz, Mabat mi-Bifnim* [Peace Destination. Three Decades of Israeli Foreign Policy] (Jerusalem: Edanim/Yediot Ahronot, 1981).

Raviv, Moshe. *Be-Misholei ha-Diplomatia ha-Yisra'elit, mi-Ben-Gurion ad Barak* [On the Path of Israeli Diplomacy, from Ben-Gurion to Barak] (Tel Aviv: Misrad Habitachon, 2001); English edition: *Israel at Fifty. Five Decades of Struggle for Peace* (London: Weidenfeld and Nicolson, 1998).

Yahil, Haim. 'Czechoslovakia', in Jacob Tsur (ed.), *Hatefutsa: Mizrah Europa* [The Diaspora: Eastern Europe] (Jerusalem: Keter, 1976), pp.213–35.

Yegar, Moshe. *Czechoslovakia, ha-Ziyonut ve-Yisrael, Gilgulei Yahasim Murkavim* [Czechoslovakia, Zionism and Israel: Shifts and Turns in Complex Relations] (Jerusalem: Hasifria Hazionit, 1997).

Zak, Moshe. *40 Shnot Du-Si'ach im Moskwa* [Israel and the Soviet Union, A Forty-Year Dialogue] (Tel Aviv: Sifriat Maariv, 1988).

BOOKS AND ARTICLES IN ENGLISH AND GERMAN

American Jewish Yearbook (New York: The American Jewish Committee, 2001).

Gjurai, Tonin. 'Albania, Cosovo and Israel: Facts and Misconceptions', *The Israel Journal of Foreign Affairs*, 2, 1 (2008), pp.23–32.

Jewish Communities of the World (Jerusalem: Institute of World Jewish Congress, 1996).

Levin, Arye. *Envoy to Moscow. Memoirs of an Israeli Ambassador 1988–1992* (London: Frank Cass, 1996).

Meining, Stefan. 'Kommunistische Judenpolitik, die DDR, die Juden und Israel' [Communist Jewish Policy of the GDR, Towards Jews and Israel] (Lit. diss., Hamburg: LIT Verlag, 2000).

Timm, Angelika. *Hammer, Zirkel, Davidstern. Das gestoerte Verhaltnis der DDR zu Zionismus und Staat Israel* [The Hammer, Sickle and the Star of David. The Troubled Relationship of the GDR, towards Zionism and the State of Israel] (Bonn: Bouvier Verlag, 1997).

Index

Index

317

Index